With Ballots and Bullets

What happens when partisanship is pushed to its extreme? In *With Ballots & Bullets*, Nathan P. Kalmoe combines historical and political science approaches to provide new insight into the American Civil War and deepen contemporary understandings of mass partisanship. The book reveals the fundamental role of partisanship in shaping the dynamics and legacies of the Civil War, drawing on an original analysis of newspapers and geo-coded data on voting returns and soldier enlistments, as well as retrospective surveys. Kalmoe shows that partisan identities motivated mass violence by *ordinary* citizens, not extremists, when activated by leaders and legitimated by the state. Similar processes also enabled partisans to rationalize staggering war casualties into predetermined vote choices, shaping durable political habits and memory after the war's end. Findings explain much about nineteenth century American politics, but the book also yields lessons for today, revealing the latent capacity of political leaders to mobilize violence.

Nathan P. Kalmoe is Associate Professor of Political Communication at Louisiana State University. He is author of *Neither Liberal nor Conservative: Ideological Innocence in the American Public* (with Donald Kinder) and over a dozen academic articles about public opinion and political communication. His work has been featured in *The New York Times*, *The Washington Post*, *The Atlantic*, and other popular outlets. Kalmoe was recognized with the Phi Kappa Phi Faculty Scholar Award and is proud to be an award-winner teacher (Tiger Athletic Foundation Teaching Award).

With Ballots and Bullets

Partisanship and Violence in the American Civil War

NATHAN P. KALMOE
Louisiana State University

CAMBRIDGE
UNIVERSITY PRESS

CAMBRIDGE
UNIVERSITY PRESS

University Printing House, Cambridge CB2 8BS, United Kingdom

One Liberty Plaza, 20th Floor, New York, NY 10006, USA

477 Williamstown Road, Port Melbourne, VIC 3207, Australia

314–321, 3rd Floor, Plot 3, Splendor Forum, Jasola District Centre,
New Delhi – 110025, India

79 Anson Road, #06–04/06, Singapore 079906

Cambridge University Press is part of the University of Cambridge.

It furthers the University's mission by disseminating knowledge in the pursuit of
education, learning, and research at the highest international levels of excellence.

www.cambridge.org
Information on this title: www.cambridge.org/9781108834933
DOI: 10.1017/9781108870504

First published 2020

A catalogue record for this publication is available from the British Library.

Library of Congress Cataloging-in-Publication Data
NAMES: Kalmoe, Nathan P., author.
TITLE: With ballots and bullets : partisanship and violence in the American Civil War /
Nathan P. Kalmoe, Louisiana State University.
OTHER TITLES: Partisanship and violence in the American Civil War
DESCRIPTION: Cambridge, United Kingdom : Cambridge University Press, 2020. |
Includes bibliographical references and index.
IDENTIFIERS: LCCN 2020000224 (print) | LCCN 2020000225 (ebook) |
ISBN 9781108792585 (Paperback) | ISBN 9781108834933 (Hardback) |
ISBN 9781108870504 (epub)
SUBJECTS: LCSH: United States–Politics and government–1861–1865. | United States–
History–Civil War, 1861–1865–Influence. | United States–History–Civil War, 1861–1865–
Political aspects. | Opposition (Political science)–United States–History–19th century. | Party
affiliation–United States–History–19th century. | Political culture–United States–History–
19th century. | Political participation–United States–History–19th century. | Political
psychology–United States–History–19th century.
CLASSIFICATION: LCC E459 .K345 2020 (print) | LCC E459 (ebook) | DDC 973.7–dc23
LC record available at https://lccn.loc.gov/2020000224
LC ebook record available at https://lccn.loc.gov/2020000225

ISBN 978-1-108-83493-3 Hardback
ISBN 978-1-108-79258-5 Paperback

For my forebears
Ole P. Rocksvold, Corporal
Co. G, 12th Iowa Volunteer Infantry Regiment
Veteran of Donelson, Shiloh, Vicksburg, & Red River Campaign
POW at Shiloh, wounded at Pleasant Hill
Charles Brown, Private
Co. I, 8th Wisconsin Volunteer Infantry Regiment
Veteran of New Madrid, Iuka, Corinth, & Vicksburg
Wounded at Corinth

Our popular government has often been called an experiment. ... It is now for [our people] to demonstrate to the world, that those who can fairly carry an election, can also suppress a rebellion – that ballots are the rightful, and peaceful, successors of bullets; and that when ballots have fairly, and constitutionally, decided, there can be no successful appeal, back to bullets; that there can be no successful appeal, except to ballots themselves, at succeeding elections. Such will be a great lesson of peace; teaching men that what they cannot take by an election, neither can they take it by a war.

President Abraham Lincoln
Message to Congress
July 4, 1861

[N]ow we must exterminate [secession], and not lay down the sword until every traitor shall be put down. This rebellion is against the ballot box, which is more vital to the interests of Americans than treasuries, custom houses, armories or arms. It is necessary that forever it shall be lifted up above all party opposition, and if it requires a million cartridges at the end of the struggle it should come out safe and not require one single musket to defend it.

Rev. Dr. Henry Bellows
Sermon in *New York Herald* (NY-Ind)
April 22, 1861

[W]e hold every man in the North as a tory and a traitor who opposes [Lincoln's Emancipation Proclamation] at this time, and that it will be our duty, if this opposition should continue till our return, to put it down as we have been taught to put it down in Virginia.

Illinois soldier's letter
Printed in *Chicago Tribune* (IL-Rep)
November 4, 1862

It is better that Lincoln die and the nation live and those who thus believe will vote for the unconditional union candidate – George B. McClellan.

Davenport Democrat (IA-Dem)
November 8, 1864

As for all the enemies of our Government and Nationality – wherever they may be found in arms – we will resist them by arms, and relying on our cause and trusting in the God of our fathers, we will fight them down. And to-morrow, in the exercise of the sacred right of free election, against which this Rebellion is an armed and treasonable protest...we will march peacefully to the polls, where, if we find enemies. . . . WE WILL VOTE THEM DOWN.

Boston Journal (MA-Rep)
November 8, 1864

Contents

x   *Contents*

Figures

Tables

Acknowledgments

I voted this morning in a meaningful democratic election, and that's a good place to begin my thanks. This was Louisiana's gubernatorial run-off, which is sure to be a nail-biter. There's no sign the vote will be marred by irregularities.[1] Nonetheless, the once-assured concession by the losing candidate is less than certain, at least on the Republican side. That party has recently undertaken delegitimizing and disempowering efforts in several close governor's elections in other states. I share growing fears of the same in upcoming presidential elections. Those steps and others away from democracy are motivated, in part, by the alignment of racial and religious identities in an increasingly homogenous Republican party, epitomized by white Southerners.[2] That combination has gained explosive potential as demographic shifts erode the social and political power of once-hegemonic social groups.

This book focuses on the combustible intersection of partisanship with social identities and elections in the Civil War era when most white Southerners – then aligned with Democrats – viewed nineteenth century demographic-political shifts as existential threats to their group's control of national government and their absolute right to own other people. The Civil War shows how party leaders can violently mobilize ordinary citizens against democracy, as in the partisan rebellion against the 1860 election. But I dwell most on party divisions in the North where, at times, partisanship undermined the nation's war efforts and even threatened widespread partisan violence. Just as important, though, the book shows that strong partisanship – and even violence – can serve to *defend* democracy against its enemies. These powerful partisan extremes are unmistakable in the behavior of ordinary Civil War–era Americans, beyond anything we've seen studying modern Americans. Taking a historical view tests the bounds of mass partisanship at a time of maximum stress, with implications that reverberate across time. Understanding that past focuses our views of party politics today.

Most Americans can't fathom such radical partisanship, and yet, that radicalism is more familiar now than when I first conceived this project in graduate school a decade ago. It was there at the University of Michigan that my dear friend and fellow political scientist Dan Magleby got me hooked on Civil War history. To justify all that reading, I started thinking about how to merge my growing expertise in modern U.S. public opinion with my personal interest in the violent politics of that historical era. Having just read Faust's *This Republic of Suffering*, the public's electoral reactions to casualties were a natural direction (Chapter 6). But I didn't have the data or time to do it, and I didn't know when I would ever have either.

In the meantime, I wrote my dissertation observing a few surprising routes for aggression's influence in mass politics today, drawing heavily from psychology. Shortly before fielding the main surveys for that project, I watched the final speeches in the U.S. House of Representatives before it passed the Affordable Care Act. Speaker John Boehner screamed "Hell no you can't!" as he charged Democrats with a "disgraceful" conspiracy against "the will of the people" and "the ideals of the nation." The preceding year of vitriol culminating in that moment made me realize our placid scholarship on modern American partisanship was woefully inadequate for understanding the direction in which the country seemed headed, and that inflammatory language by demagogic leaders was probably going to act as an accelerant. That's when I decided to add items about public support for political violence to my surveys.

I was lucky to complete that work with guidance from an extraordinary dissertation committee – Don Kinder, Nancy Burns, Ted Brader, and Nick Valentino – all of whom generously supported my idiosyncratic research with great advice. Working with Don in particular taught me how to chase big ideas that require broader views and methods. We first bonded over a shared appreciation of Talking Heads, and, across nine years, we researched and wrote *Neither Liberal nor Conservative*, on ideological innocence in the mass public.[3] Ted taught me in five political behavior classes – what I hope is still a record – and he has remained an incomparable mentor in the many years since I left Ann Arbor. This book wouldn't exist without the foundation those four mentors built, nor without the support of many other faculty members and friends in the program.[4]

Michigan is also where I fell in with the "7th Michigan Volunteers, Company B" Civil War reenacting group, just in time for sesquicentennial events nationwide. The most interesting parts of reenacting weren't the fake battles – they're the physical elements a little closer to true: sleeping fitfully on the ground, overheating in wool uniforms under summer sun or soaked in rain, shivering through cold nights, the weight of carrying a rifle and equipment, the need for hydration, pitching tents to avoid rain flows along the ground, drill maneuvers, the smell and taste of gunpowder when tearing cartridges with your teeth, and the full methodical process of loading and firing an Enfield muzzle-loading rifle. I enjoyed the camaraderie of camping with Civil War buffs from all backgrounds – auto mechanics, authors, engineers, high school students, retirees, and the unemployed – who each contributed stunningly detailed knowledge of niche Civil War topics. Thanks especially to Tom Emerick and Rob Stone for those memories.[5]

I got to Michigan in the first place when the admissions committee led by Vince Hutchings took a chance on an idealistic undergrad from the University of Wisconsin. I'm still convinced I wouldn't have made it without the mentorship of Wisconsin professors Charles Franklin and Kathy Cramer, who also sparked my love of political behavior research in their classes.[6] Cindy Kam also made several key interventions in my career before, during, and after grad school with her sage advice and generous advocacy.

It was as a post-doc with Kim Gross and Bob Entman at George Washington University that this book really began, even though my projects with them were modern in focus. I worked most closely with Kim and benefited greatly from her incisive collaboration and her generous mentoring. The book became imaginable once historian Tyler Anbinder pointed me to the essential soldier data, and he patiently explained that my initial plans to do several times more than what is now here were far too expansive. It was also at GW that I encountered Costa and Kahn's great book *Heroes & Cowards* utilizing that soldier data.

Dick Dobbins, Will Whalen, and the staff at Alexandria Street Press generously shared the complete American Civil War Research Database with me for this research. Infinite thanks to them because this book is impossible without it. Warren Santner provided extensive data support at GW to get the soldier data into the form I needed, and Jason Anastasopoulos directed me to digitized Census figures that saved tons of time and tedium. I spent several months geo-locating soldiers into their home counties by town name using the ACWRD data and Census returns.

Some of my more technically gifted peers can do much of this with automation now, but I think my bespoke efforts retain some advantages in coding quality and data knowledge. Sean Aday, Steve Livingston, and Will Youmans provided valuable feedback on my early plans too. Thanks to John Sides for publishing the first version of the Atlanta analysis (Chapter 7) on the *Washington Post*'s Monkey Cage blog.

I presented the first results with Wisconsin data at the National Capital American Political Science Association's workshop, where I got great input from Dan Hopkins, Jen Lawless, Jon Ladd, Eric Lawrence, Kevin Collins, and Chris Karpowitz, among others. Sarah Croco, David Smith, and Dan Magleby provided comments on the first conference paper covering all the states, and David directed me to key nineteenth century works including Grimsted's *American Mobbing* and Bensel's nineteenth century voting research. Josh Gubler, Matt Wells, Gary Uzonyi, and Paul Poast gave suggestions from international relations and comparative violence perspectives. I presented early versions of several chapters at conferences for the American Political Science Association, Midwest Political Science Association, and the International Society of Political Psychology. As I finished at GW, I collected all the newspapers available from my sample at the Library of Congress – about half of what I needed.

Next, I was lucky to work two great years as an assistant professor at Monmouth College, a working-class liberal arts college in rural western Illinois. I benefited greatly from wonderful colleagues, students, and friends, especially political science chair Farhat Haq, Steve Buban, Hannah Schell, Robin Johnson, and historian Tom Best, who shared his local Illinois Civil War politics files with me. Library staff Rick Sayre and Beverly McGuire helped order many of the remaining newspaper microfilms from around the country, along with Mary Wilke and staff at the Center for Research Libraries.

Now at Louisiana State University, I feel lucky to work with great colleagues and students and to have resources that fully enable my research agenda. I'm particularly grateful for support and friendship from faculty, staff, and students, including Martin Johnson, Katie Searles, Josh Darr, Nichole Bauer, Mike Henderson, Ray Pingree, Yann Kerevel (climbing partner too!), Steve Bien-Aime, Meghan Sanders, Angie Fleming, Wayne Parent, Belinda Davis, Jim Stoner, and Johanna Dunaway.[7]

LSU is where I wrote in earnest, from scraps of conference papers in a sustained push. From Monmouth on, I felt no research pressure beyond my own ambitions, which meant I could undertake a massive unconventional project like this one, which would otherwise have had to wait until after tenure. Thanks to the Louisiana Board of Regents for the ATLAS grant, which funded an extraordinary academic year to finish writing without teaching responsibilities. That was vital for completing the book. Thanks to Ann Whitmer, Angela Fleming, and Martin Johnson for providing extensive administrative support for the grant.

This was also a time for road trips to collect hard-to-find newspapers at libraries in Iowa City, Madison, St. Louis, Boston, Concord, Worcester, and Cincinnati. My newspaper collection for content analysis was aided by excellent research assistance from librarians and archivists at several institutions: George Washington University (David Killian, Laura Wrubel), the Library of Congress, the Wisconsin Historical Society, the Iowa State Historical Society (Randall Schroeder), the New Hampshire Historical Society (Malia Ebel), the New Hampshire State Library (Rebecca Stockbridge), the St. Louis Public Library, the Cincinnati Public Library, the Boston Public Library, the American Antiquarian Society Library (Andrew Bourque, Thomas Knoles), and the Chronicling America online newspaper archive.

For inspiration and encouragement to investigate political behavior in historical cases with contemporary goals in mind, I thank Adam Berinsky; Maya Sen, Matthew Blackwell, and Avi Acharya; Christina Wolbrecht; Ismail White; and Julia Azari. I also miss the insights of great minds who didn't have the opportunities we've had to pursue this fortunate path. Thanks to equity advocates in academia working to end those biases that continue to cost our fields so much knowledge.

Adam Berinsky, Jon Ladd, and Chuck Myers provided great book publishing advice and encouragement early on. Adam, Yanna Krupnikov and Samara Klar, Shana Gadarian and Bethany Albertson, Spencer Piston, and Ashley Jardina shared their book proposals as helpful guides for putting together my own; Spencer and Ashley gave feedback on my initial proposal, along with Don Kinder. Thanks also for encouragement and feedback from historians Jane Schultz, Joanne Freeman, and Aaron Astor, and from political scientists Shom Mazumder, Michael Weaver, David Bateman, Christopher Parker, Brendan Nyhan, Jessica Preece, and Thomas Zeitzoff around this time.

Rob Mickey gave extraordinary feedback on the book throughout most of the project. Rob also connected me with Richard Bensel, who gave detailed feedback on a chapter and broader framing conversations, and with Theda Skocpol, who generously provided state-level Grand Army of the Republic data. Drew Engelhardt pointed me to contemporary county election data for modern comparisons in Chapter 2. Historian Jonathan Earle provided project advice and connected me with other Civil War scholars at LSU. Dan Magleby coded up the ecological inference robustness tests in R for Chapter 4.

I'm grateful for newspaper coding research assistants: undergrads Nick Callaway, Elias Shammas, and Mark Ghaith at Monmouth College and LSU PhD student Tim Klein. Elias (now a Stony Brook PhD student) and Tim tackled the lion's share of this massive content analysis, and they made important contributions to the development of the news chapters as co-authors. LSU PhD students Martina Santia and Paromita Saha also contributed coding for the county-level GAR and monuments data in Chapter 8.

Near the end of writing, LSU's Manship School supported a book manuscript conference that was absolutely critical for refining a 450-page 12-chapter behemoth. The all-star group included political scientists Christina Wolbrecht, Ismail White, Vin Arceneaux, Katie Searles, and Civil War historian Aaron Sheehan-Dean. Aaron was especially helpful orienting me in the nineteenth century parties literature. Mike Wagner read the whole manuscript and provided incisive comments as well. All are as kind as they are brilliant. The book also benefited from input at Binghamton University, Cornell University, University of North Carolina, Tulane University, University of Virginia, and LSU, where I presented selections.

Thanks also to my splendid friends and collaborators not already mentioned, especially Mirya Holman and Lily Mason. We have much more to say about radicalism and group attitudes in partisanship today, which will be in print soon. Working with Lily in particular has deeply informed my thinking here, particularly regarding implications for the present.

I'm honored to have this work published by Cambridge University Press alongside an amazing collection of new titles, and I appreciate the excellent support from editor Sara Doskow, Cameron Daddis, and the rest of the team in getting these pages out of my mind and into print.

Finally, personal notes: I'm grateful to the men and women who sacrificed to advance the work of democracy, military and citizens in all eras, including my Civil War veteran ancestors to whom this book is dedicated: Ole Rocksvold and Charles Brown, and the women who supported them from the home front – Anne Strandbakken and Bertha Prastkvarn.

I owe great thanks to my family for their lifelong support: my parents David Kalmoe and Sharon Bowen, step-father Max Bowen, my sisters Joy, Anna, Sara, and their families, and my extended family – especially the Fischers, the Smiths, and my in-laws Karen Goodreau, Randy Will, and Alex Will.[8]

Thank you most of all to my best friend and partner in life, Katie Will, for your love, encouragement, and support. I owe this wonderful life to you as we've tag-teamed our way across the country through many adventures. I appreciate you more than I can say in words, and I treasure each new chapter of life with you. *Our Union Forever.*

* * *

Writing this book has been a personal and professional traverse across the country, multiple fields, and a full decade. Throughout, I've been humbled by the acute sense of assembling parts made by innumerable others – particularly in the datasets I fused together, and in all the historical and social scientific research that informed this book. I worked with many wonderful people without whom this book would not exist. Many more who I could not meet contributed even more.

Thousands of soldiers and sailors compiled war records for individual Union combatants, archivists copied them, and states later published those records. Librarians archived nineteenth century newspapers around the country, eventually as digital scans, microfilm, and bound originals, at the Library of Congress, online archives, and hundreds of local libraries. Thousands of poll workers recorded votes, which hundreds of civil servants compiled and transcribed into state records. Thousands of Census-takers likewise worked to create demographic records of America's people in the mid-nineteenth century. Most of these contributors passed from this Earth a century or more ago, but the records they kept on the war and its aftermath keep a portion of their legacies alive, including these pages.

More recently, more than 500 volunteers digitized individual soldier records into the ACWRD, and researchers on the Inter-university Consortium for Political and Social Research's (ICPSR) first data project catalogued all presidential, gubernatorial, and congressional election results from the founding to the present at the county level. Others did the same for town-level election data in a few states.

Thanks to them all and to others I inadvertently missed here. As always, any errors in this assemblage are my own. I hope this work helps us understand contentious partisanship in democratic politics better, and, more importantly, that it may aid our essential and unending work to match the practice of democracy with its promises – something worth fighting for.

Nathan P. Kalmoe
Baton Rouge, LA
November 16, 2019

Preface

Godspeed ...

What excuse do these disunionists give for breaking up the best government that the sun of heaven ever shed its beams upon? They are dissatisfied with the result of a presidential election. Did they never get beaten before? Are we to tolerate the idea that a defeated party in a national election may resort to the sword, when defeated by the popular will?

I understand it to be a fundamental and indispensable principle of constitutional liberty that the voice of the people expressed according to the forms of the constitution must command the implicit obedience of every good citizen.

Sen. Stephen Douglas
Chicago, IL
May 1, 1861

Political parties are the encircling metal bands that hold democratic governance together or the match dropped into that powder keg, exploding democracies apart. Ordinary people look to their party's leaders for help interpreting the bewildering world of politics in good times and bad, and they follow those trusted leaders into metaphorical – and sometimes literal – partisan combat, especially in deeply divided societies when party identities align with major social cleavages. The losing party's leaders determine a country's fate after each election. Their choice is especially consequential when that party held power before voters cast their ballots. In a moment, those leaders decide whether a democracy and its citizens will live or die based on what they say about the legitimacy of the outcome and how their followers should respond.

Never was the consequence of that crux clearer in American politics than during the aftermath of Abraham Lincoln's presidential election in

1860. This book's central focus is partisanship's vital role in organizing the violence and voting that followed. Ordinary partisans were galvanized into contentious political action by their individual social-partisan identities, local partisan cultures, and – above all – party leaders, in what was ultimately a partisan civil war. I make that case with an avalanche of historical evidence that reveals the mass politics of that foundational nineteenth century era, but with implications for partisan extremes in our own time. I begin by illustrating the astonishing range of partisan leadership that comes into view when we compare recent political history with a far more contentious past – an unfamiliar environment that grows alarmingly more recognizable by the day.

* * *

The call came at 11 p.m. EST, flashing across screens nationwide: Barack Obama would be the 44th president of the United States. It was Tuesday, November 4, 2008. The projection replicated within minutes across news outlets worldwide as election analysts poring over statistical voting models informed television networks and websites of their conclusions. The polls had just closed on the West Coast. Media outlets had been withholding projections of the now-certain outcome until the final votes were cast to avoid any undue influence on voters. Now the news flew.

Adhering to tradition, Republican nominee Senator John McCain phoned the new president-elect to offer his concession and congratulations, despite a hard-fought and sometimes nasty campaign. A few minutes later, at 11:15 p.m., in another modern election ritual, McCain walked onto a stage in Phoenix, Arizona, to address his disappointed supporters – those at this venue, and the millions watching at home.

As McCain began, the crowd booed at the mention of Obama's name, which McCain tried to quell. "The American people have spoken, and they have spoken clearly," he said. "I had the honor of calling Senator Barack Obama to congratulate him [*audience boos*] – please – to congratulate him on being elected the next president of the country that we both love." Twice, McCain raised his hands to quiet them. With particular magnanimity, he spoke of his respect and admiration for Obama and the historical significance of electing the first black president in a nation that had enslaved millions of Africans and their descendants for centuries until the Civil War's end.

McCain's partisan audience was visibly upset, even distraught: disappointed at the loss, and perhaps angry that the voters had denied their party's claim to continue holding the presidential office. Some probably worried about Democratic presidential leadership amidst a deepening economic crash. Others probably worried about governance led by a black president, though many in the Phoenix audience applauded McCain's tribute to the broken racial barrier. McCain's words were designed to soothe these angers and fears – at least enough so that they would accept the outcome of a legitimate election. This despite his own intense feelings of loss.

Minutes after McCain finished, television audiences teleported to Chicago's Grant Park, where President-Elect Obama strode to the lectern on an unusually warm November night to give his victory address before a rapturous hometown audience of nearly a quarter-million jubilant, tearful supporters. Notables like Oprah Winfrey and Jesse Jackson stood side by side with ordinary Democrats celebrating in the human sea. "Hello, Chicago," he began.

"If there is anyone out there who still doubts that America is a place where all things are possible, who still wonders if the dream of our founders is alive in our time, who still questions the power of our democracy, tonight is your answer."

* * *

Concession speeches are easy to overlook, coming as they do just after the excitement of election projections and right before the winner's speech. Who wants to hear from the candidate who *won't* be president? Audiences and journalists naturally await the first pronouncements of the president-elect, though those words usually only recap campaign themes and predict a bright American future. Concession speeches can seem an impediment on the way to that triumphant address – a 10-minute delay in McCain's case. Nonetheless, news accounts of each historic night include prominent coverage of the loser's speech, as *New York Times* reporter Adam Nagourney did in the fourth and fifth paragraphs of his front-page story on Obama's victory for Wednesday morning's paper. The speech has some audience appeal with its elements of tragic drama – the personal blow of a political rise that fell just short of a pinnacle seemingly within reach, and the personification of a national party's failure (Corcoran 1994).

Those symbolic words of concession are arguably the more meaningful ones spoken by the candidates on election night. The loser's disheartened followers look to their leader for guidance. The defeated candidate's words nearly always say, 'I submit. I stand down. I accept my opponent's victory and their right to govern within the constraints of the office as the leader of all Americans. And you, my fellow partisans, should too' (Mirer & Bode 2015; Ritter & Howell 2001). It is worth pausing to consider McCain's words in detail:

I pledge to him tonight to do all in my power to *help him lead us* through the many challenges we face. *I urge all Americans who supported me to join me* in not just congratulating him but *offering our next president our goodwill and earnest effort* to find ways to come together ... whatever our differences, we are fellow Americans. It is natural tonight to feel some *disappointment, but tomorrow we must move beyond it and work together* to get our country moving again. *We fought* as hard as we could, and though we fell short, the failure is mine, not yours. ... My heart is filled with nothing but gratitude for the experience and to the American people for *giving me a fair hearing* before deciding that Senator Obama and my old friend Senator Joe Biden should *have the honor of leading us for the next four years. [more boos]* ... I wish Godspeed to the man who was *my former opponent* and *will be my President.* [emphases added]

McCain's speech was a ritualized surrender – something like the end of a war, but also a literal foreclosing of war – with the unique understanding that the contest would begin again in less than four years.[1] The losing party accepts their defeat knowing they will have a fair opportunity to win the next election. The speech serves not just as a formal end to the candidate's own claim on the office, but also as a guide leading supporters toward a similar reconciliation and away from dangerous alternatives (Corcoran 1994; Mirer & Bode 2015; Ritter & Howell 2001).[2]

Other concessions occurred under remarkable circumstances. In 1960, Richard Nixon chose not to challenge his loss to John Kennedy despite rumors of potentially decisive election fraud in Illinois and Texas. Similarly, in 2000, Al Gore conceded to George W. Bush one month after the vote, when the Supreme Court stopped a state-mandated recount of votes in Florida and exhausted Gore's legal options. The recounts were as likely to have elevated Gore to the presidency as Bush, but for adverse rulings by Republican election officials and Republican-nominated justices (Imai & King 2004). "[W]hat remains of partisan rancor must now be put aside," Gore said in his concession (Ritter & Howell 2001). Even with real grievances, both Nixon and Gore chose to end their claims to the office rather than endorsing resistance that would throw democratic government into crisis.[3]

Americans have grown accustomed to this ritual acknowledgment of defeat followed by a peaceful transition of power – democracy's sine qui non. Concession is not inevitable, however, and more than a few partisans have urged their defeated leaders to keep hold of presidential power ever since the first change in party control from John Adams to Thomas Jefferson in 1801. The potential consequences when leaders refuse to concede are dire: national paralysis, dismemberment, assassinations, or even civil war. In this way, concession speeches play a critical role symbolic and functional role in preserving democracy.

***

On a similar November night in 1860, nearly a century and a half before Obama's victory speech in Chicago, *two* Illinois politicians waited for confirmation that one of them would be the next president. Telegraph wires hummed through the late night and on into early morning hours, distributing news of state-by-state electoral tallies nationwide. Those sums grew until the total confirmed what was long expected: Abraham Lincoln – only the second Republican presidential candidate in that party's six years of existence – would be its first nominee to win the presidency. Lincoln and most of his fellow Republicans had been Whigs a decade earlier, and Whigs had won the presidency twice under that banner, but this partisan moment was new and, ultimately, epochal.

Concession speeches on election night were not yet traditional, and none was given, though President-Elect Lincoln received a written message soon after from Democratic nominee and longtime Illinois rival Senator Stephen Douglas: "Partisan feeling must yield to patriotism. I'm with you, Mr. President, and God bless you."[4] The election that year was a four-way race, however, and some were not ready for concession. Ultimately, one-third of the American states would give none.

As I write, the United States has held fifty-eight presidential elections, and we approach another that promises to be among the most contentious. Fifty-seven times, the disgruntled losers ultimately accepted the result, even in twenty-two of twenty-three elections that changed which party controlled the presidency. Once, the losers rejected an election, and the country fractured with extraordinary violence. In the pages that follow, I analyze the political and military impact of ordinary people in that exceptional case, which cleaved substantially along party lines. The results tell us much about the bounds of mass partisanship when leaders push it to extremes, with implications far beyond the Civil War era.

I

An Introduction to Partisan Warfare

While you elect Presidents, we submit, neither breaking nor attempting to break up the Union. If we shall constitutionally elect a President, it will be our duty to see that you submit.

Old John Brown has just been executed for treason against a state. We cannot object, even though he agreed with us in thinking slavery wrong. That cannot excuse violence, bloodshed, and treason. It could avail him nothing that he might think himself right.

So, if constitutionally we elect a President, and therefore you undertake to destroy the Union, it will be our duty to deal with you as old John Brown has been dealt with. We shall try to do our duty. We hope and believe that in no section will a majority so act as to render such extreme measures necessary.

Abraham Lincoln
Leavenworth, KS
Dec. 3, 1859

On October 16, 1859, John Brown and twenty-one followers unilaterally sought to end U.S. slavery by fomenting a rebellion among enslaved people. For years, politicians in Washington and Americans beyond had argued and fought over slavery's westward march into new U.S. territories. White Southerners and their allies had overturned a three-decade compromise limiting slavery's expansion, which also smashed the political parties into pieces. Then the Supreme Court declared an inviolable individual constitutional right to own people that threatened to override each state's right to keep slavery out – the specter of universal slavery in a nation where one of every seven people was enslaved.

Brown had no care for the Constitution, Congress, or the Court, however: he believed God had directed his violent mission to end the supreme injustice. The insurrection began – and ended – at the national arsenal in Harpers Ferry, Virginia, and it was doomed from the start. After overwhelming the few guards, Brown and his band of black and white militants made no effort to alert local enslaved people to join them. The insurgents sat inert as alarm spread and military forces gathered over two days to confront them. Colonel Robert E. Lee commanded the U.S. troops that surrounded Brown and his party and stormed the fire engine house in which they were hunkered down. Brown survived to face charges of treason. News from the trial popularized his fervent, articulate, and unapologetic denunciations of slavery – and a nation condemned by it. Brown's inevitable conviction transformed him into a martyr for the nation's few abolitionists and grew his esteem among less radical anti-slavery groups. At the gallows, he passed a note to a guard: "I, John Brown am now quite certain that the crimes of this guilty land will never be purged away but with blood."

Illinois politician Abraham Lincoln was on a speaking tour in Kansas Territory at the time, and he spoke of Brown's execution. Many Southern Democrats threatened to break up the Union if they did not get their way in the 1860 elections, as they had for years. Party nominees were not yet decided, but many slave-state Democrats considered a Republican president intolerable due to Republican opposition to slavery's expansion and the party's anti-slavery rhetoric. Lincoln publicly disavowed Brown's violence to distance his party and himself from unpopular radicalism. But he also warned *Democrats* not to follow Brown into violent treason if they should lose the next election: "if constitutionally we elect a President, and therefore you undertake to destroy the Union, it will be our duty to deal with you as old John Brown has been dealt with." There, in a few words, Lincoln defined the threat that parties and partisanship pose to democracy – a rash, intrinsic motive among losers to reject legitimate elections, and the will to do so if they think their gambit might work.[1]

Democracy depends on peaceful transfers of power when the ruling party is defeated in fair elections, at which point the threat of violence is highest (Rappoport & Weinberg 2000). Winners legitimized by public support promise to uphold civil liberties and the equitable rule of law, which enables losers to contest future elections for power (Levitsky & Ziblatt 2018). That promotes peaceable acquiescence. In exchange, losers pledge to accept the result and abide by the new government's laws (Anderson et al. 2005). Parties implicitly accept this democratic bargain when they compete for power in elections. Having done so, losers cannot walk away from a loss. All parties enjoy long-term governing benefits when they uphold the bargain. Democracy persists, and that stability serves public interests.[2]

Yet, the contentious nature of political parties militates against the immediate compromise inherent in conceding elections. People are psychologically oriented toward groups (Huddy et al. 2015; Kinder & Kam 2010), and politics is about deciding which groups get what (Lasswell 1936). That fuels conflict between groups in society. Parties organize groups into broader coalitions to win elections, and those groupings become party identities in the minds of supporters. Election campaigns and other competitive moments stoke partisan antagonisms and even hatreds, especially when social and political identities align (Huddy et al. 2015; Mason 2018; Sood & Iyengar 2016). In other words, parties play a key role in fomenting group-based conflict, especially if power is at stake.

What happens when a party loses power, but its leaders refuse to concede? The American Civil War offers a vital case study, when Southern Democrats fomented an armed rebellion, Republicans led a war to suppress it, and Northern Democrats split between national and party loyalties. That made the Civil War partisan in its origins and execution, with parties in government and opposition channeling all that followed. Those dynamic elite-level partisan divides manifested as systematic differences in the military and electoral behavior of ordinary partisans in the public.

These, then, are the book's key questions: How did ordinary Republicans and Democrats in the loyal states respond when called by party leaders to put down a rebellion by electoral opponents and erstwhile allies? How did new party loyalties hold up against the upheaval of monumental events as parties fractured before and during the war? With casualty rates orders of magnitude beyond other American wars, how did voters respond when offered the choice to sustain or extinguish the war at the ballot box – and how did those ghastly dead weigh on postwar votes cast in the decades that followed? What role did partisan leaders and the press play in fortifying partisan loyalties, mobilizing combatants, and persuading voters? Finally, what does that incomparable Civil War violence tell us about acrimonious partisanship today?

Answering these questions required collecting and analyzing massive amounts of historical data on voting and violence from a time before public opinion polling existed. Toward that end, I integrated datasets with over one million individual Union soldier records, decades of county-level election returns, and elite rhetoric from a representative sample of partisan newspapers throughout the war. Together, these tests yield new views of mass partisanship under maximal duress along with historical insights on the most defining era of American democracy.

I find remarkable power and resilience in ordinary mass partisanship in the crucible of civil war, with behaviors motivated by individual party identities, mobilized by party leaders, and reinforced by local social contexts. The results reveal how partisanship fueled violence and what violence did to voters in turn. These findings also suggest potential paths *away* from violence when it would destroy democracy as well as paths *toward* violence when violence is necessary to save it.

A War That Remade America

Naturally, this book illuminates the historical contributions of mass partisanship in a pivotal era. The cliché is that "elections have consequences," but some elections matter more than most. Civil War–era elections were arguably the most important in American history (McPherson 2015). The Civil War – fought to upend or uphold Lincoln's 1860 presidential election and his legitimate national authority – was the most destructive and consequential U.S. conflict. The war ultimately sustained democracy, preserved the Union, achieved John Brown's goal of eradicating U.S. slavery, and established de jure racial equality. All that collectively constituted a national re-founding. Brown's prediction of epic bloodshed also rang true – doubtless, the most righteous and necessary work ever done by U.S. military forces, but at great cost. The changes wrought by war far exceeded even these extraordinary ends: ultimately, the war and its elections fundamentally *transformed* the nation, its people, and our politics in ways we still feel directly today.

The war mobilized citizen-soldiers in huge proportions. From a population of thirty-one million, roughly two million Americans volunteered to defeat the rebellion, while a million fought for its success. The per capita equivalent for that fighting force, just for the Union (U.S.) side, matched World War II and was twelve times larger than current U.S. armed forces.[3] Immigrants contributed one in four U.S. fighters, and nearly 200,000 African Americans enlisted as soldiers or sailors, most formerly enslaved. Many more civilians – men and women, white and black, citizens, immigrants, and enslaved people – made essential contributions to the war efforts, most but not all by choice.

The war slaughtered Americans on a scale unmatched by any conflict before or since. The number of dead in national cataclysms is impossible to calculate exactly, but Civil War estimates find roughly three-quarters of a million deaths, with more U.S. dead than rebel dead, and nearly twice as many lost from disease as from combat (Hacker 2011). About half a million more suffered disabling wounds, and untold numbers suffered other physical and psychological traumas. By comparison, mortality rates among U.S. soldiers and sailors in World War II were a tenth as high; the total Civil War toll approaches eight million when adjusted for U.S. population today. Such unfathomable mass death permanently changed American society and culture (Faust 2008).

The war and its elections changed national politics in revolutionary ways, well beyond its best-known outcomes. War politics launched the U.S. welfare state, land-grant colleges, the first income tax and national paper currency, short-lived slavery reparations, birthright citizenship, and absentee voting. It expanded presidential war powers, furthered westward expansion into indigenous lands, and preserved the first federal wilderness in what became America's National Park System. Constitutional amendments after the war established the legal foundation for two centuries of rights movements for African Americans, women, LGBTQ people, people with disabilities, and immigrants. It is no stretch to say the Civil War reverberates subtly and eclectically today in mixed-race households and same-sex weddings, hikes in Yosemite National Park, and student performances at LSU's annual step show, not to mention ongoing disputes over federal power.[4]

The Civil War's roots also resonate odiously in current fights over racial injustices and their links to partisan politics. Backlash by Southern white supremacists in the 1870s overwhelmed political will in the North, erasing egalitarian gains for a century after Reconstruction was dismantled (Blight 2001; Foner 1988). De facto racial discrimination remains in legal force today despite de jure racial equality, and anti-black racism in modern guise retains its political potency (Acharya et al. 2018; Kinder & Sanders 1996; McRae 2018). The clash for and against racial equality still undergirds the current party system, as it has since the Civil War, with Republicans replacing Democrats as the strongest defenders of lingering white supremacy after the 1960s, causing the white South to realign with Republicans in league with racists nationwide (Tesler 2016; Valentino & Sears 2005). And public displays of Confederate monuments and flags – inextricably tied to treason, slavery, and modern opposition to racial equality – continue to spark racial-partisan violence today.

In these ways and others, politics today descend from the Civil War era. The political science classic *The American Voter* (Campbell et al. 1960) put it this way: "The conflict with the greatest consequences for our political life was fought on American soil. ... By comparison with the impact of the Civil War, the effect of the wars of the twentieth century seems slight indeed" (p. 50). That makes deciphering nineteenth century mass politics critical to making sense of our politics today, and everything in between.

<h3>RECOGNIZING THE POWER OF ORDINARY
MASS PARTISANSHIP</h3>

Victory over the rebellion required the combined force of the loyal public's ballots and bullets in a war of wills. Their political resolve determined the outcome as much as the strength of their arms and leaders. Thus, we cannot explain Civil War–era politics without understanding the collective contributions made by millions of ordinary people. This book's biggest contribution toward that end is this recognition: mass partisanship, guided by local and national leaders, was key to mobilizing and sustaining mass warfare and determining the war's political outcomes in elections.

Politics is about power, and parties seek to impose their group's will on society by winning control of government through elections. Competition for that power can lead to violence, especially when opponents fear they may not have another chance to win. The book's first task is to adopt a more expansive view of what American parties and their followers can do.

Partisan comes from middle-French, with early applications to spears, bodyguards, and irregular military forces. In other words, partisanship has had violent connotations from the start. Enlightenment philosophers and American founders recognized latent dangers in partisanship and hoped to avoid parties altogether. Concerns about violence and illiberalism have been mostly absent in modern American views of parties. Political science here matured in relative partisan calm in the mid-twentieth century, with undue focus on that era, particularly in mass politics. Broadening the partisan concept requires looking beyond modern U.S. politics. I begin by reviewing conventional party views and then recall older political thought and contemporary cross-national research on parties fomenting violence. Those works bring surprising and disquieting party traits into view, alongside the mundane but vital functions parties perform in making democracy work.

The Conventional View

For all the popular complaints about partisanship in the United States, political scientists view parties as essential players in a healthy democracy (e.g. Aldrich 1995; Cohen et al. 2008; Duverger 1963; Schattschneider 1942). Parties contribute to efficient governance by organizing groups into coalitions that pursue interests within and between branches and levels of government. That work builds party reputations, which inform policy- and performance-based choices for voters in the public. Parties coordinate internally to select a candidate to represent the party for each elected office. Elections legitimize party governance with evidence of broad public support, especially when parties mobilize high participation rates. Parties can also reduce resistance and violence among their members in competition and defeat. Toward that last end, historians Michael Holt (1978) and David Potter (1977) argue that the party system helped delay the onset of the Civil War by managing violent centripetal forces. In short, parties do crucial democratic work.

Critics note that American parties produce policy gridlock under divided government, and they reduce the range of choices available to the public. Parties also grab fleeting public attention to persuade audiences unfamiliar with political details by simplifying messages in ways that misinform, that inflame conflict between social groups, and that cast opponents as villains. These dissonant notes should be red flags. Each *positive* partisan byproduct is probably conditional on parties *choosing* to make those goods, rather than finding other means to gain power without them. Those goods seem automatic only in the modern U.S. context in which scholars found them.

At the level of ordinary partisans, we know their individual attachments to party are the most powerful and enduring force in mass political behavior. Party identity practically determines vote choice, issue attitudes, political perceptions and information, and participation motives without changing much over the lifespan (e.g. Achen & Bartels 2016; Berinsky 2009; Campbell et al. 1960; Green et al. 2002). The quiescent era in which American scholars conceptualized partisan identity probably contributed to these potent but largely benign parameters: At best, it informs and guides public views; at worst, it distorts political views and causes some small rancor. In the last half century, U.S. party elites have sorted into consistent ideological camps, prominent social groups have aligned more exclusively within each party, and partisan animosity has grown fierce (e.g. Mason 2018; Poole 2015). Accordingly, public opinion scholars have begun to recognize darker aspects of mass partisanship and inched toward a warier view of its capacities – first partisan dislike, then social avoidance, and now material discrimination, all reinforced by partisan homophily (e.g. Iyengar et al. 2019).[5] But that still falls far short of the mass-partisan extremes that become visible in the Civil War era.

Historical & Cross-National Context

What have we missed about partisanship? Parties are supposed to mitigate violent conflict by channeling it into democratic elections, but group identities like party are inherently contentious and insular, fueling in-group bias, out-group hostility, and even violence when party aligns with other social divides (Mason 2018; Tajfel et al. 1971; Tajfel & Turner 1979; Wilson 2004). Basic democratic moments like campaigns and elections tend to be times of greatest rancor and risk.

Philosophers Machiavelli and Hume wrote with concern about the violence and disorder caused by political factions and proposed ways to defang them (North et al. 2009). American founders James Madison, Alexander Hamilton, and George Washington shared worries about party threats to democracy. That contention is manageable, Madison optimistically wrote in *Federalist #10* and *#43*, but its roots are not eradicable: "The latent causes of faction are thus sown into the nature of man," with violent factions as "the natural offspring of free government." He argued that small democracies fail because governing majorities that share a "common passion or interest . . . sacrifice the weaker party. Hence it is that such democracies have ever been spectacles of turbulence and contention . . . short in their lives as they have been violent in their deaths."

The Framers hoped in vain that *large* democracies with well-designed constitutions might avoid that fate – to "break and control the violence of faction," as Madison wrote, and "form a barrier against domestic faction and insurrection," in Hamilton's description (*Federalist #9*). Of course, both men founded America's first parties with help from others who decried factions.[6] The Civil War would show that violent *minorities* could pose as great a threat as majorities (Dahl 1956). In short, theorists and leaders centuries ago recognized far more danger in parties than we do today.

Likewise, many studies of modern violence around the world indict political parties as key culprits. Many parties mobilize strategic violence by supporters for electoral and political advantage – to gain victories, or to protest and challenge defeats (e.g. Blattman 2009; Bratton 2008; Dunning 2011; Hafner-Burton et al. 2014; Harish & Little 2017; Höglund 2009; LeBas 2006; Powell 1981; Snyder 2000; Wilkinson 2006). Surveys of ordinary voters in some of these places show no perceived conflict between democratic values and violence (Fair et al. 2014). Other scholars find political parties escalating conflicts into civil wars, with partisanship motivating individual participation in that violence (Humphreys and Weinstein 2008). However, with a few key exceptions, most comparative politics work neglects individual motives in partisan violence. In short, both cross-national and cross-temporal views of contentious politics challenge contemporary American observers to rethink assumptions of a bright line dividing electoral politics and violence. Political parties can drive *both* simultaneously (e.g. Kalyvas 2006; Tilly 2003).

My Argument

Given the increasing rancor in modern U.S. partisanship, and with what we know about the power of ordinary party identities, it might be hard to imagine that Americans could be *more polarized* than we are now, nor to conceive a *more potent* role for ordinary partisanship in mass politics. That only reflects the limits of our imagination – a blind spot for a time in America's past when partisan conflicts were indeed greater, and when ordinary partisanship was, in some ways, even more potent.

Beyond what we know, I will argue and show that leaders made ordinary mass partisanship *more enduring* through political turmoil and *more resistant* to tumultuous political events and national conditions, and that ordinary partisanship was *extraordinarily lethal* when party leaders explicitly called their voters to arms. I propose partisan opinion leadership as the main force behind these effects, with party leaders guiding the views and acts of loyal followers who looked for cues from trusted sources (Berinsky 2009; Zaller 1992). Partisan social influence and individual reasoning supported those effects – but party leaders also shaped these social networks and individual considerations. Democratic partisanship guided the rebellion and reduced willingness to defend the nation, even as Republican partisanship fueled democratic resolve to fight in battlefields and at the ballot box. Considering mass partisanship in the Civil War context enables us to recognize these extremes.

A Partisan Civil War

The foundation of this book rests on seeing the Civil War as a fundamentally *partisan* war – in long-term predicates, proximate electoral cause, wartime political and military developments, and aftermath. Most historians recognize the war's partisan-sectional roots, though the strongest party claims are not canonical (e.g. Alexander 1981; Holt 1978; Potter 1977; Silbey 1985). For example, Thomas Alexander (1981) writes, "secession was a step so drastic and so contrary to the fervor of American nationalism that it could never have been made persuasive to a majority of voters [based on self-interest]. Only through the vehicle of the Democratic party was secession possible" (p. 29).

In contrast, historians sharply disagree whether partisanship defined Northern politics *during* the war. Adam I. P. Smith (2006), in *No Party Now*, explicitly denies a major role for partisanship in the war's northern upheaval, crediting war-inspired patriotism and self-serving Republican arguments that civil war proscribed partisan opposition. On the other side, Jennifer Weber's (2006) *Copperheads* and Mark Neely's (2002) *The Union Divided* reveal extraordinary conflict – even low-level violence – among Northern partisans over the war. And Joel Silbey's (1977) *A Respectable Minority* presents some evidence of partisan continuity between wartime elections and prewar voting, indicating plenty of enduring party loyalty.[7] Resolving these historical disputes requires broader and more systematic evidence on voting, rhetoric, and violence.

To say partisanship was fundamental is *not* to say party motives and mobilization were the only force behind the war, nor that other social, political, and economic factors were unimportant. I mean only – but importantly – that partisanship tangled inextricably with other causal elements for elites and the public alike. To take a central example, differences over slavery and its expansion *defined* the party coalitions competing for the presidency in 1860, and nineteenth century parties were the main organizing force in politics, as they are today.[8] Efforts by other groups, like anti-slavery societies, were orders of magnitude smaller than party-led efforts. As Republican Senator Henry Wilson (MA) said bluntly in 1863: "this abhorred and accursed rebellion, born of the fell spirit of slavery, was plotted by Democrats, organized by Democrats, and inaugurated by Democrats." All this makes parties the logical place to look for the most impactful collective action in war politics.[9]

MY APPROACH: FUSING SOCIAL SCIENCE AND HISTORY

Recognizing the *partisan* Civil War provides a fresh way to analyze and understand that conflict, its supreme consequences, and its broader implications for contentious mass politics. The partisan framework unlocks a rich array of historical and social scientific theorizing about political behavior and a suite of methods and evidence for systematically identifying those patterns. These approaches are not wholly new, to be sure, but I combine and apply them in innovative ways. We can only recognize the full power of American partisanship by observing its broad range across history, with a concomitant willingness to step beyond the limits of modern survey research.[10]

I take a pluralistic approach with quantitative analysis supplemented by qualitative evidence, motivated by theories and evidence from a mix of history and social science.[11] Throughout, I try to explain methods and results intuitively for a general audience. Unlike many histories, however, I focus on the public as a whole rather than the stories of individual participants. My primary sources are election returns, soldier records, Census data, and newspapers.[12] Here, I go further than most by merging these datasets to yield new insights. Some of the evidence affirms standard views or supports one perspective over others in scholarly debates. Other evidence and arguments are almost wholly new. It all provides novel ways to see mass partisanship's influence on politics and history.

"Seeing the Elephant" with Representative Evidence

The most serious challenge for any claim about Civil War behavior is epistemological. We need representative evidence to know what the public did with any confidence, as with opinion polls using probability samples today. Unfortunately, quality surveys weren't invented until the 1930s. Without representative methods, we have no way of knowing whether collections of individual views – in surveys, letters, diaries, or recorded behaviors – reflect the balance in the population as a whole. We should be similarly skeptical of claims made by nineteenth century elites, who were as unreliable then as cable news pundits are today, because they had no way to get a faithful snapshot of the national public.[13]

The epistemic challenge is like the proverbial blind men with the elephant, each describing a different body part within reach and disagreeing intensely, even violently, about what the elephant actually "looked" like. Unrepresentative evidence is like inspecting a trunk or toe or tusk.

Richly detailed histories contribute much, just as the elephant's anatomical details matter too. But seeing the *whole* elephant of the Civil War public requires representative evidence. (As it happens, "seeing the elephant" is how Civil War soldiers described the terror of first combat, and the cover image of this book is titled "Jeff [Davis] Sees the Elephant." Published during the war in 1862, it was the first representation of Democratic donkey and Republican elephant together, and, appropriately for my purposes, both are ready to fight.)

Representativeness can come from a random sample of the population or evidence from the whole population, and I use a mix of both.[14] Population data are the only option for partisan voting behavior, which means using vote returns aggregated by locality. Researchers at the Interuniversity Consortium for Political and Social Research have collected election data for House, governor, and president in every election since the founding. I focus on elections between 1848 and 1920, and particularly the 1856–1864 period. Election data are perfect for judging voting patterns across elections from place to place, and they can help tell us whether partisanship influenced other political and military behaviors when merged with other behavioral data, like war participation.

I also leverage population data on Civil War military service, demographic information about counties, veterans' organizations, and Civil War–era newspapers. Historical Data Systems generously provided me with comprehensive Civil War soldier records, digitized from each state's catalogue of their war participants after the war – the American Civil War Research Database. These definitive records symbolically honored each state's war veterans and war dead through an act of naming and served bureaucratic needs to adjudicate war pension claims (Skocpol 1992). The individual soldier records detail their full service – including dates and modes of entry and exit, residence before the war, and notes for disabling wounds or death. I geo-located over one million soldiers from fifteen Union states by county to match election data.[15] I likewise integrate population data from the Census to rule out alternative demographic explanations that correlate with partisanship, and I compile all post locations for the Grand Army of the Republic veterans' group. Election data that separate soldiers' absentee votes from the civilians back home also link partisanship and war service. With mostly aggregate war and voting data, several partisan mechanisms – individual loyalties, local leadership, and social influence – are observationally equivalent in the results. For that reason, I mostly draw conclusions about partisanship as a holistic attribute of *communities*.[16]

Partisan newspapers provide rich details about how party leaders thought about the war and its elections, how they strategically framed content to influence the public, and the views that attentive partisans and open-minded readers might hold. How can we know what the average newspaper reader saw? Rather than accumulating and analyzing the content of *all* newspapers published on a particular day (adjusting for circulation), I drew a roughly representative sample of twenty-four newspapers from six regions in loyal states from a population list – Rowell's 1868 national census of newspapers – accounting for circulation size to analyze what the average reader saw. This approach improves on historical methods that often focus on large, influential papers. I also analyze news content more systematically than most. Multiple coders reviewed seven issues from each paper on dates purposefully chosen for military or election significance, categorizing fifty content attributes on each page. In that co-authored section, we leverage quantitative evidence for precise population inferences, but we also present qualitative analysis and vivid illustration of partisan wartime rhetoric.

Partisanship: Says Whom?

Readers familiar with Civil War history might be skeptical about partisan power from the start. On one hand, many Southern Democrats were open about a rebellion against "black Republican rule." There the case is pretty clear that the partisan election result and all it stood for was the proximate cause of their actions. But my focus is on partisanship in the North, and few Northern leaders said, "We should fight this war *because* we're Republicans" or "... oppose *because* we're Democrats," and few ordinary Union citizens described their actions in explicitly partisan terms. Are those stated motives enough to dismiss the role of partisanship in Northern war politics? No.

Most important, public statements justifying war support or opposition were strategic and not always sincere reflections of reasons. Leaders cast their views in the most positive light, and partisan warfare is not that. In the Civil War, patriotism and principle sounded nobler than partisanship. Beyond that, psychologists find that people are bad at explaining their motives – when asked, we tell more than we know (Nisbett & Wilson 1977). People are motivated to hold flattering images of themselves and their groups (Klar & Krupnikov 2016). Even when our identities are not implicated, we struggle with introspection because much of our decision-making is subconscious (Bargh & Chartrand 1999), including political choice (Lodge & Taber 2013). In fact, pausing to list rationales can lead people to make *less* optimal decisions, because conscious criteria that seem reasonable aren't what make people happy (Wilson et al. 1993). Access to our own mental processes is severely limited, even on big life decisions (which politics isn't for most). To be sure, self-reports tell us much, but they shouldn't be taken as definitive evidence of the motives driving behavior.

How then do we identify motives? We can't know for individuals, but social scientists can make good inferences about *categories* of people, on average. For example, the authors of *The American Voter* were able to identify who a voter would choose two months later slightly *better* than the voter could themselves (Campbell et al. 1960). They managed this feat by asking a handful of questions they thought would matter in the average person's vote choice, then statistically compared those factors with the outcome, along with other considerations to rule out alternative explanations.

Adam Berinsky's (2009) study of U.S. war attitudes from World War II through the Iraq War does something similar, with surveys and experiments. Few people explained their support or opposition as due to party, but partisanship was the overwhelming determining factor in each war for citizens who noticed their party's position. Despite few naming partisanship, the proximate cause for these attitudes was party identity. In other words, partisanship guides war attitudes and perhaps behaviors through the choice of which leaders to follow, even when neither leaders nor followers name partisanship as a rationale. In this book, I compare the military and electoral behavior of millions of people clustered in groups with different combinations of attributes. Statistically comparing those traits tells us much about why ordinary Americans behaved as they did during the Civil War.

Partisanship across Centuries

Other readers might wonder whether the modern political behavior studies I use to frame expectations for Civil War partisanship are applicable in a distant era. Reassuringly, much of the historical research I cite presents remarkably similar views of partisan identity and behavior, with partisan descriptions instantly recognizable to scholars of modern political behavior. Thus, though there is a risk in *assuming* similarity across contexts, evidence from historians – and consistent results throughout the book – validate a largely generalizable view of partisanship across centuries.

We can also find cross-temporal reassurance in modern studies spanning many decades. Partisans today behave much as they did seventy years ago, when political scientists first began systematic individual-level studies with survey methods. Many aspects of partisanship and voting in the twenty-first century are indistinguishable from opinion and behavior in the 1860s and the mid-twentieth century (e.g. Kinder & Kalmoe 2017; Lewis-Beck et al. 2008). In particular, Berinsky's (2009) book shows partisanship driving U.S. war attitudes over seven decades from World War II through the Iraq War.

In each case, similar partisan dynamics hold despite massive gains in educational attainment, major demographic change, enfranchisement of racial and ethnic minorities in the South, the rise of voter-based presidential nominations, the end of the Cold War, the resurgence of partisan news, and the emergence of cable television and the Internet. The list goes on. Despite all this change, partisans behave much the same. Much changed in the eighty years between the 1860s and the 1940s too, but probably not enough to alter the roots of partisan psychology and political contestation. Thus, it is no stretch to expect a general continuity of mass partisan behavior across centuries, including the Civil War era.[17]

Inclusions & Exclusions

In most of the book, I focus on voters in the loyal states, comparing political and military behavior of partisans before, during, and after the war. That makes tests for partisanship especially subtle: any differences reflect diverging behavior between Republicans and *Northern* Democrats in a war fought predominantly against *Southern* Democrats, their erstwhile partisan brethren who split just before the 1860 election – comparing parties ostensibly on the same side.

In its electoral and military focus, this book is primarily a study of men's behavior – white men in particular – despite the vital roles of women and people of color in the war and its politics. Where possible, I expand the narrative beyond limits imposed by my electoral and military data, including representations of women and their wartime activities in the news. Suffrage was mostly limited to adult white men, with some exceptions for men of color in the Northeast,[18] and so tests involving elections are limited by race and sex. Likewise, military action was restricted to white men in the first half of the war, though black freemen and emancipated or escaped freedmen served disproportionately once white politicians removed racial barriers. I empirically study the

contributions of black Americans in news coverage and wartime service
and sacrifice. I also summarize substantial women's war service, including
work as hospital and camp staff in the U.S. Sanitary commission and U.S.
Army nursing corps, for which twenty thousand Union women worked
(Schultz 2004).

LOOKING AHEAD

I organize the book by concepts and methods while also proceeding
chronologically. I summarize research methods, with details tucked away
in the endnotes and the Online Appendix to improve the flow. Comparative politics scholars studying civil wars and political violence will find
Chapter 4 on partisan war service most relevant. Chapter 6 engages the
international relations literature on casualties and war support in democracies. Readers interested in partisan news and media history should look
especially to Chapters 3 and 5. My main audience – readers interested in
mass partisanship and Civil War history – will find gratifying content
throughout.

Chapter 2 begins by describing how prewar partisan politics and
violence led to mass partisan warfare. Next, I detail the theoretical
foundations of mass partisanship under duress, drawing on research from
political science and psychology. Lastly, I show the persistence of partisan
voting patterns across party systems in the North – surprisingly stable
electoral coalitions despite changes in name and issue emphasis. That
continuity provides a solid basis for predicting strong partisanship in
individual identities, leaders, and communities during the war.

Part I of the book identifies partisan differences in news content and
war mobilization. Chapter 3 shows how polarized elites guided partisan
followers on the war and its elections with nationally representative
content analysis from twenty-four newspapers in the loyal states. I find
large partisan gaps in war support, enlistment advocacy, and rhetoric that
rationalized support and direct participation in the war's violence. The
newspapers also show extreme partisan vilification *within* the North,
which helps support my claim that partisanship defined contentious Civil
War politics, beyond the primary partisan violence inaugurated by the
rebellion.

Chapter 4 examines partisan war participation differences using
soldier voting tallies and county-level data on soldier service records
linked with election data to test party differences in local military enlistment, desertion, and death. Soldiers in the field voted for Republicans

more heavily than civilians did back home. Likewise, Republican places contributed a larger share of local men to fight, those men were less likely to desert once in the ranks, and they were more likely to die in service. Democratic places were less willing to shoulder the mortal burdens of war to preserve the Union against the assault by their former partisan brethren. Thus, parties substantially organized the war service of their followers beyond the mobilizing power of government. Changes in partisan enlistment gaps over time follow shifts in partisan news support for war – striking evidence of dynamic leadership. Chapter 4 also finds some local partisan influence on African American enlistment and describes women's war service. In sum, partisanship motivated ordinary Republicans to save the Union through violent action, even as Democratic partisanship impeded the war.

Part II investigates wartime election rhetoric and voting patterns. Chapter 5's newspaper analysis shows how partisan editors and correspondents reinforced and polarized partisan voters with how they framed the war's progress, its racial implications, and electoral implications of the dead. For example, Democratic and Republican papers were equally likely to mention Union casualties, but anti-war Democratic papers framed deaths as senseless losses in a hopeless, misguided cause, while Republican papers framed them as heroic martyrs whose deaths required a redoubled devotion to victory. Democrats explicitly tied the dead to vote choice far more than Republicans did.

Chapter 6 analyzes the impact of casualties on voting throughout the war, starting with the national dead. Statewide elections were staggered throughout the calendar in ways that make those election returns function like tracking polls of partisan support. Contrary to modern war studies, I find Republican vote shares did not deteriorate in response to cumulative casualties or recent casualties, and that stability held in prewar Democratic and Republican bastions. I validate my analytical approach with evidence of highly nationalized and synchronized elections linking party votes for House, governor, and president both before and during the war. However, *local* deaths did move voters on the margins, with disparate impacts based on the balance of local partisanship. Local deaths depressed Republican vote share in prewar Democratic bastions but not in Republican strongholds. Recent deaths were especially potent. The result holds for presidential voting in 1864 and House and governor elections too. It suggests that the combination of partisan identities, local partisan leaders, and local social environments shaped local interpretations of the war – including its unprecedented human costs. Local casualties *did* change the electoral behavior of some voters, while most stood pat. Partisan mechanisms guided who responded and how.

Chapter 7 investigates electoral stability in response to specific wartime events with a brief historical narrative of wartime events along the way. Most Civil War accounts describe a highly volatile public mood, threatening Republican electoral fortunes. Instead, I find vote shares were almost entirely stable despite epic events like the 1864 Atlanta victory. The only national dip in Republican support came in fall 1862, and periodic midterm losses for the president's party may explain it best. Overall, the chapter shows shockingly stable national partisan voting in these wartime elections, even with the conditional shifts based on local deaths. Even as party policy positions and monumental events changed rapidly across the war, voters mostly stuck with their own party.

Part III considers some of the enduring consequences of partisan civil war. Chapter 8 investigates postwar partisanship, first in enduring postwar election effects from local casualties, then in war memorialization, and finally in the partisan dynamics of Union veterans' organizations. I describe the political aftermath of the war and test whether wartime voting patterns – including casualty effects – persisted after the fighting and dying ended. I find the massive scale of wartime death continued to shape local political voting patterns in postwar presidential elections for decades, a first in casualty-opinion studies. The chapter also shows how partisanship predicted which states were first to commemorate their dead on Decoration Day – to document their state's war service in bureaucratic records, and to honor their veterans and the dead with local monuments. Chapter 8 also finds more posts of the Grand Army of the Republic (GAR) veteran's group in prewar Republican places, along with evidence of the GAR's indirect impact on General Ulysses S. Grant's 1868 election, when veterans organized actively to boost Republicans.

I conclude the book by reviewing the main findings and their broader implications for mass partisanship and violence beyond the Civil War era. The essential ingredients for partisan conflict have been present throughout most of American history: strong political identities placed in competition. Yet, the United States has been mostly free from partisan violence over the past half-century despite partisan animosity, electoral discontent, and even some public support for violence. What changed in the Civil War era was how partisanship aligned with other important social identities, how party leaders fueled the crisis, and then how parties explicitly organized legitimated violence via party control of government. Before the war, strong party leaders and organizations promoted but also limited low-level election violence (Grimsted 1998). In contrast, party leaders in the 1860s actively mobilized state-based mass violence, to destroy democracy and to save it.

The country is in an uncomfortably similar position today – racial-religious-partisan alignments, political demonization, rhetoric rejecting fair elections, and even language encouraging violence from prominent leaders, including the president. The central dilemma is this: partisanship poses latent threats even in relatively peaceful democratic societies (Tilly 2003), even as democracy is "unthinkable save in terms of the parties" (Schattschneider 1942, p. xxvii). Healthy parties promote democracy and peace, but our national history also shows just how dangerous U.S. partisanship can be. As it's been since the founding, the struggle remains how to encourage the public goods of parties while staving off their worst impulses.

2

The Roots of Partisan Civil War

Continuity across Political Eras

You inquire where I now stand. That is a disputed point. I think I am a whig; but others say there are no whigs, and that I am an abolitionist. When I was in Washington I voted for the Wilmot Proviso as good as forty times, and I never heard of any one attempting to unwhig me for that. I now do no more than oppose the extension of slavery.

Abraham Lincoln
Springfield, IL
August 24, 1855
Letter to Joshua Speed

And so it came to pass that "the North" and "the South" were at last arrayed against each other under color of diverse political organizations.

National Intelligencer (DC-Ind)
November 8, 1864

Before assessing partisan war divisions, we first need historical context to sensibly investigate and interpret those patterns. We also need a social scientific framework that anticipates how and why party might divide the public. Toward both ends, this chapter traces the historical and political-psychological roots that drove mass partisanship in the Civil War era. I begin with a brief history of the parties, the partisan schisms leading immediately into war, and the war's enormous escalation of prewar violence. Next, I relate what we know about the power of ordinary partisanship, including how leaders and social influencers guide the attitudes and behaviors of partisans. I conclude by answering why partisanship could be so potent in a new party system. I find a surprising level of stability in electoral coalitions across party systems. That establishes a firmer foundation for anticipating powerful mass partisanship.

THE "MISCHIEFS OF FACTION" BEFORE THE WAR

The American founders warned against parties, and they thought the Constitution would minimize partisan dangers. Yet, in hindsight, their hope for party-free politics looks naïve. As soon as expediency demanded, these same party critics organized the nation's first parties. These formed from the contentious factions that argued for and against the Constitution, which was ratified by the barest margins. Federalists backed ratification and retained the label as the Washington administration became the Adams White House. In opposition, anti-Federalists organized as National Republicans, often called Democratic-Republicans. Thomas Jefferson and James Madison rationalized away the evils of their own coordinated election efforts as a countermeasure to the evils of Federalist politicians (North et al. 2009). With their 1800 victory in hand, however, the newly empowered partisans found plentiful reasons to keep their party in place to govern and campaign. The Federalist Party disintegrated after the 1816 election, inaugurating the "Era of Good Feelings." Andrew Jackson established the Democratic Party in 1828 with his election, which remains intact today, even as the organization entirely remade itself over the years. The Whig Party eventually coalesced in opposition in the 1830s, producing the political period known as the Second Party System.[1]

Democrats and Whigs dominated American politics from the 1830s to the early 1850s, each internally divided by the issue of slavery, as the cotton gin suddenly made human bondage extraordinarily profitable. Southerners in both parties increasingly argued that slavery should expand nationwide as a positive good. Northerners in both parties were less acquiescing (even hostile) to expanding slavery as new states joined the nation in accordance with the Missouri Compromise's delineation of slavery's reach. At the same time, pro-slavery forces violently sought new southern lands in which to grow their economic and political slave power, most notably U.S. military action in the Mexican-American War and insurgencies launched elsewhere in the Americas. To hold themselves together, the parties tried to limit the slavery debate that threatened the unity of their coalitions (Potter 1977). As Whigs said in their final 1852 platform, "we deprecate all further agitation of the question thus settled, as dangerous to our peace."[2] Both parties won congressional seats in every region that year.

Alongside the new parties, a small band of activists launched a movement to abolish slavery in the 1830s, with organizational roots in the religious fervor of the Second Great Awakening. Women were particularly effective anti-slavery advocates on speaking circuits and as petition organizers (Carpenter & Moore 2014). While some Americans avoided politics out of religious conviction, others joined new anti-slavery Liberty and Free Soil parties in the 1840s, as the major parties refused to engage the issue (Earle 2004). Anti-slavery parties won some Northern votes and a handful of congressional seats, but they did not seriously challenge the major parties. Even so, their advocacy outraged pro-slavery partisans who suppressed anti-slavery petitions and newspapers nationwide. Northern Whigs led by John Quincy Adams opposed these unconstitutional efforts. Meanwhile, Britain abolished slavery in its colonies in 1833, even as American slavery *grew* for another generation due to American independence. Arkansas, Florida, and Texas subsequently joined the Union as slave states, and the population of enslaved Americans *doubled* from two million to four million men, women, and children between 1830 and 1860.

Political summaries can obscure the people held captive and tortured by white Southerners for decades – how slavery not only denied personal freedom, but also invited widespread murder, rape, and other tyrannies. Among countless outrages, owners stripped enslaved people naked on auction blocks to entice buyers with evidence of few whip scars to prove their obedience, and marriage vows were adulterated to read "'til death or distance do us part" as husbands and wives, children and parents were sold to different owners, never to see each other again.

Whigs lost the presidency in 1852 and their party dissolved over the next two years. Then the Kansas-Nebraska Act of 1854 dismembered the Missouri Compromise by introducing "popular sovereignty" – votes for or against slavery by residents in each territory – to determine the slavery status of those regions, regardless of latitude. The new law roiled the North, contributing to the rapid growth of the new anti-slavery Republican Party, founded that year from the remnants of Whigs, abolitionist third parties, and a smattering of Democrats, beginning the Third Party System.

The 1856 presidential election split the votes of former Whigs and Free Soilers between Republican and Know-Nothing parties, the latter a nativist, anti-Catholic party. Democrat James Buchanan took advantage of the divide to win an Electoral College majority. This was the first national election to split the country cleanly into sectional blocs, North and South.

It would remain so for a century, apart from the interregnum of the war and Reconstruction. The white South remains monolithic today, but reversed by a partisan-racial realignment that began locally in the 1930s and solidified nationally in the 1960s onward (Acharya et al. 2018; Schickler 2016).

The Supreme Court's 1857 *Dred Scott* decision served as another rallying cry for Republican activists. The decision created an individual constitutional right to enslave people that threatened to force its legalization even in states outlawing the practice. In elections through the late 1850s, the Republican Party absorbed Northern Know-Nothing voters and retained them going into the 1860 presidential election. All four Republican contenders for the presidential nomination that year were ex-Whigs with varying levels of anti-slavery commitment (Goodwin 2005). Opposition to slavery's expansion defined Republican Party elites and activists, alongside insistence on maintaining the Union. Those two elements occupied the first three-quarters of the party's 1860 platform, which concluded by endorsing tariffs, western settlement, national infrastructure improvements, and opposing anti-immigrant laws. Even so, Lincoln probably would have lost a general election contested solely over slavery, such was Northern ambivalence on the issue and the generally limited role for policy views in vote choice (Converse 1964).

Democrats held off their own schism over slavery until 1860 – a deferral aided by spoils from presidential victories in an era before the non-partisan civil service. Then they fell apart too. The Northern faction nominated Senator Stephen Douglas on a platform that deferred the territorial slavery decision to the Supreme Court, but even that expansive pro-slavery position was not enough for the Southerners. Southern Democrats nominated their own candidate – Vice President John Breckinridge – on a platform aimed almost exclusively at bolstering and expanding slavery.[3] The Democratic split nearly guaranteed a Republican general election victory, an outcome the secessionists may have sought. Ex-Southern Whigs ran Senator John Bell as nominee for a new Constitutional Union party, standing on a minimalist platform pledging – what else? – national unity under the Constitution.

In the campaign that followed, Douglas foresaw the Republican win and knew it probably meant national disunion. Breaking from the traditional silence of presidential candidates, he hit the campaign trail. Rather than promote his candidacy, he went to the South campaigning for the Union, seeking to avert secession and mitigate the damage caused by his pro-slavery work in the 1850s.

From Partisan Elections to Partisan Warfare

Lincoln won 59 percent of 1860 Electoral College votes despite getting just 40 percent of the popular vote and despite his exclusion from Southern ballots.[4] Lincoln won pluralities in every state that outlawed slavery except New Jersey, all in the North or far West. Douglas won 30 percent of the popular vote but was fourth in Electoral College voting, winning Missouri and New Jersey. Constitutional Unionist John Bell won three states – Tennessee, Virginia, and Kentucky – and 13 percent of the national popular vote. Vice President John Breckinridge placed second in Electoral College votes, winning the eleven remaining slave states and 18 percent of the popular vote. Republicans also won a majority of seats in the House of Representatives, expanding their plurality control from the previous session. The Senate was not yet in Republican hands given slow turnover from staggered terms, and the U.S. Supreme Court remained dominated by pro-slavery Southerners and their allies.

Overall, the result was a tectonic shift in party power, one that many Southern leaders found intolerable. Southerners had dominated all three branches of government based on advantageous Senate representation schemes and national parties willing to nominate Southern presidential candidates to appease them. Now their power was slipping. Rather than accept the result, Southern "Fire-Eaters" chose to subvert federal authority by claiming secession, as they had threatened to do many times before if elections did not go their way. Democratic victories in the two prior presidential contests delayed their efforts. An 1852 secession attempt by South Carolina fizzled when other enslaving states balked, a wariness that had largely evaporated in the Deep South in the intervening eight years.[5]

As Lincoln had said the year before, "if constitutionally we elect a President, and therefore you undertake to destroy the Union, it will be our duty to deal with you as old John Brown has been dealt with." In other words, "death to traitors." Most Northerners shared Lincoln's view of secession as treason, particularly victorious Republicans. But a few slavery opponents saw the South's potential departure as a blessing, purging most slavery from the nation. Elite New Yorker George Templeton Strong wrote, "If disunion becomes an established fact, we have one consolation – the self-amputated members were diseased beyond immediate cure, and their virus will affect our system no longer."[6]

South Carolina moved to secede as soon as the election results were in, and the state claimed unilateral withdrawal from the United States in December 1860, months before Lincoln took office in March. South

Carolina's main complaint was unmistakable: "an increasing hostility on the part of the non-slaveholding States to the institution of slavery." Their declaration indicted Northern states for allegedly shirking their duties under the Fugitive Slave clause of the Constitution, and they said the federal government had been too lax in compelling those states to condemn many local blacks to enslavement when slave-catchers came to the North looking for runaway slaves. In other words, federal power was not strong enough in coercing states to act against their preferences. "States' Rights" was the cry of anti-slavery activists in the 1850s who objected to laws mandating Northern participation in apprehending and extraditing people who had escaped from slavery, and others falsely accused. Put differently, like today, both sides took up the "States' Rights" banner when expedient, covering true motives. After the war, ex–Confederate president (and former U.S. Secretary of War and U.S. Senator) Jefferson Davis claimed slavery had nothing to do with secession. Mississippi, Davis' home state, inconveniently contradicted him in its own secession document: "Our position is thoroughly identified with the institution of slavery – the greatest material interest in the world."

Secession documents assumed the new Republican president would subvert the Constitution, if Southern Democrats waited to find out. The 1860 Republican platform and its standard-bearer pledged to prevent the spread of slavery into new territories, but they grudgingly acknowledged that the Court's interpretation of the Constitution protected slavery in states where it already existed. That federal shield is why abolitionist William Lloyd Garrison called the Constitution "an agreement with Hell." South Carolina was unconvinced of Republican tolerance, insisting Lincoln's "opinions and purposes are hostile to slavery," and that that was enough for them to nullify a presidential election. The list of Northern "encroachments" included merely calling slavery "sinful," restating the common slaver demand that all critical speech be forcibly suppressed. Much anti-slavery rhetoric in the North emphasized how the slave power threatened the political rights of whites, and how the practice of slavery morally degraded slaveholders, as much or more than sympathy for the people enslaved.

Over the next two months, the other Deep South states followed South Carolina out of the Union, each before Lincoln took office: Alabama, Florida, Georgia, Louisiana, Mississippi, and Texas. They declared themselves a new, independent nation – the Confederate States of America. But there, secession stalled. Other slave states voted down secession, adopting a wait-and-see attitude. Tennessee and Virginia put it to a public vote, and both electorates rejected secession.[7]

Each state withdrew its representatives from Congress as it seceded, and they departed with blistering speeches. Every U.S. senator withdrawn by the new Confederacy in 1861 was a Democrat. Three-quarters departing from the House were Democrats; the rest had third-party affiliations. No Republicans. Most took roles in the new rebel government or a generalship in its armies. The Republican majority grew in the House, and Republicans gained control of the Senate – a huge shift from their 2-to-1 disadvantage in the prior Congress. The partisan swing was hugely consequential. Beyond war policy, nation-defining legislation passed in the absence of Democratic resistance: land-grant colleges, western expansion (Homestead Act), a transcontinental railroad with Northern origin, and a new national bank, along with the first national paper currency and first federal income tax.

During the Secession Winter, Southern militias seized U.S. arsenals and forts across the South with virtually no federal resistance. Large numbers of U.S. Army and Navy officers from the South forsook their oaths and joined the rebellion, though other Southern-born officers upheld their pledge of loyalty to the United States. Rebels working in the U.S. War Department shipped large caches of weapons from government stockpiles into Southern hands. Outgoing Democratic President Buchanan insisted secession was unconstitutional, but he refused to act in response to the crisis.

In vain hopes of avoiding war, some contemporaries and even a few modern historians have argued that, having won the election, Republicans should have surrendered to the demands of armed losers. But, as Lincoln explained in his 1861 Independence Day message to Congress:

No compromise, by public servants, could, in this case, be a cure; not that compromises are not often proper, but that no popular government can long survive a marked precedent, that those who carry an election, can only save the government from immediate destruction, by giving up the main point, upon which the people gave the election.

Finally, after four excruciating months waiting, Lincoln took the presidential oath of office. He insisted on retaining possession of U.S. military outposts around the continent – including some forts in the South – but he chose not to attempt reclamation of those forts already surrendered to Confederate militias. One month later, Confederate forces attacked Fort Sumter, one of the U.S. garrisons in Charleston Harbor, South Carolina. The assault on U.S. troops galvanized the North. President Lincoln's response, to call up 75,000 troops to suppress the insurrection, was met with rebellion in four more slave states – Virginia, Tennessee, Arkansas, and North Carolina, each joining the Confederacy. Four more slave states – Missouri, Kentucky, Maryland, and Delaware, plus the slave-holding national capital – hung in limbo, deeply divided between loyalty and treason.

In total, eleven Southern Democratic states chose not to accept valid election results, opting for national dismemberment and civil war instead. Nine of those states gave pluralities to Southern Democrat John Breckinridge, and he nearly tied with Constitutional Unionists in the last two. Within a year, the Kentuckian traded his U.S. Senate seat for a generalship in the rebellion, favoring his political party over national and state loyalties. The Democratic-dominated border slave states cast large votes for Breckinridge as well, but they remained nominally loyal while contributing substantial numbers of men to fight on each side. Only deft (and sometimes heavy-handed) measures by the new Lincoln administration kept them formally in the Union.

President Lincoln and his cabinet feared Northern Democrats would see the war in partisan terms, knowing the war would be lost without some Democratic support. Thus, Lincoln reduced the partisan appearance by placing prominent Democrats in top leadership positions. The move was politically astute but contributed to early U.S. military failures (and needless death) due to the incompetence of political generals. At first, Northerners seemed to rally around the flag against secession, regardless of party. Many Democratic leaders in free states joined Republicans in calling for the rebellion to be suppressed and supporting military mobilization. Despite Lincoln's efforts to downplay party, many Northern Democrats soon characterized the war in starkly partisan terms all the same.

Ultimately, wartime divisions between the partisan factions made the violence that followed a *partisan* civil war, grounded in long-standing party divides over slavery. Secession pitted the Republican-led U.S. government against a rebellion led by Southern Democrats.[8] Northern Democrats had some stake on both sides and quickly split: some patriotically backed Lincoln's war efforts, while most eventually opposed war on their estranged partisan brethren. This key insight motivates all that follows as I trace partisan mass behavior through the war and its elections, responding to polarization between leaders. Each chapter's affirmative evidence reinforces the view of partisan warfare that first comes into focus here.

As Indiana Republican Congressman George Julian made plain in 1863, "Democratic policy not only gave birth to the rebellion,

Democrats, and only Democrats, are in arms against their country. . . . Not only is it true that rebels are Democrats, but so are Rebel sympathizers, whether in the North or South. On the other hand, Loyalty and Republicanism go hand-in-hand throughout the Union, as perfectly as treason and slavery" (quoted in Lawson 2002, p. 65).

Partisan Violence before the War

The Civil War exponentially intensified long-simmering partisan violence that stretched back decades, turning localized party and individual action into national, predominantly state-based killing (Sheehan-Dean 2018). Violence played a major part in partisan contestation, particularly after the Republican Party's exclusive rise in the North made party conflict synonymous with conflict over slavery. From the 1830s onward, Southerners – and many Democrats – sought to muzzle all criticism of slavery by any means, threatening the constitutional liberties of white citizens. Mobs nationwide destroyed printing presses and beat or killed those who dared criticize slavery, beginning with the 1837 murder of abolitionist publisher Elijah Lovejoy in Alton, Illinois. Anti-slavery advocates in the North employed mobs for nobler ends, to free black people legally slated to be sent South into slavery.

Partisan election violence was common, with each party employing "toughs" to intimidate opposing voters in the lopsided precincts they controlled. Although individual fights and collective melees often resulted in serious injury, just a few riots saw fatalities in the 1830s and 1850s, both coinciding with major shifts in the party systems (Grimsted 1998). When violence escalated into lethality, local party leaders moved to curb serious fighting by party members, proving the importance of local partisan leaders and organizations in both encouraging and regulating political violence.

Low-level warfare broke out in Kansas in 1854 and continued for years, resulting in dozens or perhaps hundreds of deaths. Pro-slavery Democrats from Missouri tried to impose slavery on the Kansas territory and its mostly Free Soil residents by crossing the border to vote illegally in Kansas elections. Douglas' "popular sovereignty" brought this about by putting slavery up for a vote in each territory. In one infamous episode in 1856, a pro-slavery militia, complete with cannon, attacked the Free Soil capital of Lawrence and shuttered newspapers there. Anti-slavery militiaman John Brown and others retaliated by hacking five unarmed pro-slavery men to death with broadswords in the middle of the night.

Partisan lawmakers were active combatants in the violence as well. Historian Joanne Freeman (2018) writes of tensions so high that congressmen walked the Capitol chambers armed with pistols and knives. They fought dozens of times, sometimes in mass brawls. The new party-section alignment escalated the violence. Most infamously, Democrat Preston Brooks of South Carolina beat Republican Charles Sumner of Massachusetts nearly to death with a cane in 1856 as Sumner sat trapped at his Senate desk. Brooks continued to bludgeon the unconscious Sumner until his cane broke. Another Democratic congressman, Laurence Keitt, held senators at gunpoint to stop them from coming to Sumner's aid. The North was incensed. Illustrating the close link between violence and elections, one Michigander wrote Sumner to say, "Every blow of the ruffian Brooks gives us ten thousand votes."[9] By contrast, jubilant Southerners applauded Brooks and called for more attacks.

John Brown's 1859 raid on Harpers Ferry is the most famous prewar violence of all, as described in Chapter 1. It confirmed white Southerners' gravest and most enduring fears of slave insurrections plotted in the North. The raid galvanized Southern militias to organize with new intensity, according to historian Ed Bearss (1986). White Southerners feared their human property would slit their throats in the night, as they might justly have done. There was no mass killing of slavers, though, and insurrections were rare, because white retaliation always killed more blacks than it did white enslavers, as in Nat Turner's 1831 rebellion in Virginia.

Even nonviolent party politics had a sharp militaristic edge before the war, featuring warlike trappings, language, and militia organizations. Campaign events featured booming cannons, opponents hung in effigy, and speeches filled with martial metaphors exhorting partisans into "battle array" for "increasing and unrelenting warfare," to "strike straight from the shoulder,–hit *below* the belt as well as above, and kick like thunder,"[10] and to "lay down a withering fire on the enemy." They talked of "fights" and "battles" and "campaigns" led by the party's "standard-bearer." A Democratic newspaper wrote in 1854 that Stephen Douglas "seemed not content to butcher his antagonist [Lincoln] with tomahawk and scalping knife, but he pounded him to pumice with his terrible war club of retort and argument."[11] Violent partisan metaphors continued into the Civil War, rich with new meaning when used alongside descriptions of literal partisan warfare. Violent metaphors still appear in politics today, priming people to think aggressively, even violently, about politics (Kalmoe 2014).

Young men joined partisan paramilitary groups and donned uniforms to march in torch-lit nighttime parades, serving as security forces at party functions and acting as election monitors (Grinspan 2009). They adopted military ranks and practiced drill. It was all very exciting – often the most entertaining event in town – and all of it was pervaded with the threatening air of violence. At times, militia-party organizations provoked actual violence. During an 1860 campaign event in Illinois, Douglas and Lincoln supporters brawled and at least one gun was drawn when Democrats, who had expected to speak alongside Republicans, were denied. The same day, a few miles away, Democrats opened fire on Republicans passing by, wounding one man.[12] In tandem with partisan violence, these party-militia activities often made elections and politics look more like low-level warfare.

After Lincoln's victory and Southern secession, partisan militias enlisted en masse to fight directly in unrestrained warfare. Partisan and military organizational linkages grew even stronger during the war. Union League Clubs were militia-like organizations that fused partisan and national identities in their support of the Lincoln administration, as historian Melinda Lawson (2002) describes in *Patriot Fires* (see Smith 2006, p. 69). Likewise, the U.S. military itself was an important a site for political socialization and persuasion, moving combatants more firmly toward Republican politics (e.g. Frank 1998; Manning 2007; Matsui 2016; McPherson 1997). In sum, the Civil War was a massive escalation of prewar partisan violence, not a wholly new phenomenon.

PARTISAN PSYCHOLOGY IN THE CIVIL WAR

What might ordinary partisanship *do* in the crucible of the Civil War? Here, I briefly introduce modern political-psychological insights and historical symmetries that guide my expectations and interpretations for mass partisanship throughout the book. I first describe the social roots of partisanship, then its endurance, resistance, and lethality, as influenced by individual identity, logistical coordination and persuasive mobilization by party leaders, and the interpersonal and social pressures from local partisan environments. I expect the Civil War context to reveal more expansive partisan power than scholars have recognized once the range of political contexts is broadened, unearthing the psychological micro-foundations of partisanship under maximal duress.

Partisanship Is a Social Identity

Identities define "us" apart from "them" (Huddy 2001; Kinder & Kam 2010; Tilly 2003). Partisan identification is, at root, a social identity – an enduring, emotional attachment to a group with which we belong in which we see ourselves reflected, often strongly felt (e.g. Campbell et al. 1960; Converse & Pierce 1985; Greene 2004; Huddy et al. 2015; Iyengar et al. 2019; Mason 2018; Westwood et al. 2018). Party identities take unrivaled precedence in mass politics because parties are the principal organizers of voting and most other kinds of political action. Parents pass partisanship to their children through socialization, with local and national political environments adding supplemental influences (Campbell et al. 1960; Jennings et al. 2009).

Parties are coalitions of social groups and interests (Aldrich 1995; Cohen et al. 2008). Thus, partisanship often coincides with other important social identities and attitudes toward social groups, creating potent identity fusions (Achen & Bartels 2016; Ahler & Sood 2018; Bauer 2018; Campbell et al. 1960; Dawson 1992; Green et al. 2002; Greene 2004; Gubler & Selway 2012; Huddy et al. 2015; Jardina 2019; Mason 2018; Philpot 2017). By contrast, policy views, values, self-interest, and national conditions matter less for most people – those are often *consequences* of partisanship and related identities, not causes (e.g. Achen & Bartels 2016; Barber & Pope 2019; Bartels 2002; Berinsky 2009; Campbell et al. 1960; Donovan et al. 2019; Freeder et al. 2019; Goren 2005; Hetherington 2001; Kam 2005; Kinder & Kalmoe 2017; Kinder & Kiewiet 1981; Lenz 2012; Levendusky 2009; Margolis 2018; Zaller 1992). [13] Few citizens attend closely to politics, leaving many unable to consider politics beyond party teams.

This modern view of partisanship fits well with historians' descriptions of Civil War–era voters. Thomas Alexander (1981) writes, "The attachment of the individual voter to the party in nineteenth century America was affective, even religious," (p. 14). Jean Baker (1983) gives a socialization-based account of stable partisanship passed down within families. Joel Silbey (1977) argues "[t]he American political culture in the pre-Civil War years was dominated by a strong national party system, clung to tenaciously and with intense loyalty for ideological, social, and symbolic reasons" (p. 225). In 1866, Rebekah Shunk, wife of a Democratic politician, reflected on wartime partisanship: "we felt political bonds to be the strongest on earth, for friendship and religion were trampled in the dust" (p. 10). Historian Mark Neely (2017) concurs.

And Paul Kleppner writes, "[p]arty identification mirrored irreconcilably conflicting values emanating from divergent ethnic and religious subcultures ... parties were not aggregations of individuals professing the same political doctrines but coalitions of social groups sharing similar ethnocultural values" (p. 144). Political scientist Richard Bensel's (2004) study of nineteenth century voting arrives at similar conclusions from congressional testimony. Voters generally did not judge party platforms or swing with events like political weathervanes. Instead, long-term social networks, ethnic identities, and local partisan practices – sometimes coercion – drove votes.[14]

Strong, explicit party identification produces powerful partisan behavior, but explicit identification isn't a necessary condition for robust partisan action. Political scientists Samara Klar and Yanna Krupnikov (2016) find that most Americans who identify as "Independent" and eschew public partisan displays still privately behave like partisans nonetheless (see also Ryan 2017). Likewise, Alan Abramowitz and Steven Webster (2018) find modern Americans are motivated more by *negative partisanship* – dislike of political opponents that outweighs positive attachment to one's own party. That antagonism kept voters loyal to Whigs and Democrats in the 1840s (Holt 1978). After Lincoln's 1860 election, one Missourian wrote, "No matter what sad disaster may follow, I shall regard it as a less grievous affliction than the continuance of [Democrats] in power."[15] Joel Silbey (1977) describes partisan enmity similarly as a key force keeping conservative ex-Whigs and ex-Know-Nothings from voting for Democrats, despite many shared political views. "[W]hy break the anti-Democratic habits of a lifetime?" he writes (p. 176). "It was easier to remain where they always had been, opposed to the Democratic party and everything it stood for." Thus, even nineteenth century Americans with unstated or limited commitments to new party alignments still could behave like stable partisans.

Partisanship Is Enduring

My first expectation for Civil War partisanship is that partisan behavior will endure despite the shock of monumental political events. Partisanship tends to crystallize in young adulthood and grow stronger with time, becoming more central and important to self-concepts (Campbell et al. 1960; Converse 1969; Huddy et al. 2015; Jennings et al. 2009). If partisanship moves at all, competing social identities tend to be the cause – often those involving race and racial attitudes (Acharya et al. 2018; Achen

& Bartels 2016; Carmines & Stimson 1989; Cassese & Holman 2019; Kinder 2003; Kleppner 1979; Kuo et al. 2017; Kuziemko & Washington 2018; Ostfeld 2018; Sides et al. 2018; Tesler 2016; Valentino & Sears 2005). Homophily in social networks reinforces partisanship by over-representing corresponding identities like race and religion. At a larger scale, a community's partisanship persists due to aggregate stability in individuals but also due to reinforcement from local political culture across decades and even centuries (e.g. Acharya et al. 2018; Darmofal & Strickler 2019; Key 1949). Thus, while newly salient political divides may occasionally reorient allegiances (e.g. Miller & Schofield 2003), we should expect more continuity than change for individuals and localities.

Times of great political disruption – like the antebellum and war years – seem ripe for shifts in partisan behavior, especially if those times include the death of a major party and the rise of new ones. Notably, though, many of the most pivotal twentieth century political events did little to disrupt mass partisanship (Campbell et al. 1960; Green et al. 2002; Keith et al. 1986). Many historians regard the Civil War itself as intensely disruptive to partisanship, in ways that negate any partisan behavior during the war. Kleppner (1979) describes "an extraordinary level of partisan fluctuation" (p. 29), and Adam I. P. Smith (2006) writes the war's elections "took place in a climate in which 'old parties' had been discredited. Clearly, in such circumstances, party identities and align-ments were fluid not fixed" (p. 6). Likewise, *The American Voter* (Camp-bell et al. 1960) says, "[p]arty identification is a durable attachment, not readily disturbed by passing events and personalities. But there have been occasions when national crises have shaken prevailing political loyalties" (p. 150).

Even so, I expect enduring Civil War–era partisanship in the North – before the war *across* party systems, and through the war despite its maximal tumult. I test the former expectation with election returns in this chapter and the latter in Chapters 6 and 7 analyzing national events. Stability manifests as strong correlations over time that indicate rank-order continuity and as absolute vote percentages. Affirmative evidence would show partisan endurance under far more stress than modern U.S. scholarship has examined. To be clear, partisan votes are unlikely to equal *current* stratospheric levels of stability. Instead, I expect stability *approaching* those levels despite incomparably disruptive times, and per-haps equaling stability across elections within each party system era. Persistence here would be an extreme form of the public's vote insensitiv-ity to events in modern campaigns (e.g. Erikson & Wlezien 2012;

Sides & Vavreck 2013), and stable vote shares would suggest limited retrospective voting despite cataclysmic national conditions (Achen & Bartels 2016; Fiorina 1981). I also expect that any effects the war may have on voting patterns will persist long after its conclusion, which I test in Chapter 8.

Partisanship Is Resistant

Stability implies a resistance against forces of potential change. Motivated reasoning is the psychological process that makes partisanship resistant to change and causes polarized political responses to political developments. Committed partisans prefer news and conversation from fellow partisans and try to avoid views that conflict with their political loyalties (Arceneaux & Johnson 2013; Chen & Rohla 2018; Lelkes et al. 2017; Levendusky 2013; Lodge & Taber 2013; Pew Research Center 2014; Searles et al. 2018; Stoker 1995; Stroud 2011). If avoidance fails, partisans may counter-argue to protect core beliefs (Achen & Bartels 2016; Bartels 2002; Campbell et al. 1960; Hochschild 2001; Huddy et al. 2018; Jones 2019; Nyhan & Reifler 2010; Rahn 1993). In contrast, partisans accept messages uncritically that affirm prior views. These biases hold specifically for war attitudes too (Althaus & Coe 2011; Berinsky 2009).

Motivated reasoning isn't for everyone, however: many partisans fail to recognize threatening information or lack the desire or capacity to put up much resistance (Groenendyk 2013; Kunda 1990; Lodge & Taber 2013). Partisans are willing, at times, to acknowledge inconvenient facts about politics when confronted with credible corrections, but those acknowledgments often fail to change underlying partisan views, because that information is rarely the cause of those views to begin with (Chong & Druckman 2013; Guess & Coppock 2018; Nyhan et al. 2019; Redlawsk et al. 2010). Most Americans today live and work in politically mixed environments (e.g. Cho et al. 2013; Huckfeldt et al. 2006; Mummolo & Nall 2017; Mutz 2006). Unlike today's small partisan news audiences (Arceneaux & Johnson 2013; Levendusky 2013; Pew Research Center 2014), Civil War news was almost wholly partisan, making partisan selective exposure much easier (Schudson & Tifft 2005). Partisan mass polarization was the result when leaders in each party took opposing views.

Partisan politics is also emotional. Conflict makes people angry, and angry people dig in and lash out. Anger mobilizes action based on political habits, and it makes seeking out or weighing alternatives less likely (Banks 2016; Brader & Valentino 2007; Huddy et al. 2007; Mackie et al. 2000; MacKuen et al. 2010; Miller & Conover 2015; Valentino et al. 2011). Campaigns stoke partisan anger (Smith & Searles 2014; Sood & Iyengar 2016), and anger is often a product of moralized politics, which reduces willingness to compromise (Ryan 2017). The Civil War fueled moralized anger in its strongest forms.

I expect partisanship to find partisan resistance and retrenchment through motivated rationalization and anger in the face of the most extreme national circumstances in American history. Direct and indirect evidence of motivated reasoning would take three forms here. First, enduring partisanship hypothesized above would be consistent evidence, though not direct evidence. Second, elite-level rhetoric could directly show partisan rationalization at work in how leaders framed the war's events for their followers. Third, the potential effects of war dead on support for the Republican administration and Republican candidates should be highly conditional on individual and local partisanship, with party-serving rationalizations driving Democrats and Republicans (and corresponding partisan strongholds) in opposite directions on the strength of their party loyalties and the greater weight of their influence on local swing voters. I test elite-level expectations for motivated resistance in Chapter 5 with news analysis, and mass expectations in Chapters 7 and 8 with local data on the war costs, electoral polarization, and memorialization during and after the war.

Partisanship Is Lethal

My most provocative contention is that ordinary mass partisanship can motivate mass violence under extreme conditions. We need to recognize the latent potential for mass partisan violence rooted in individual partisan identities when mobilized by partisan leaders and communities, especially when legitimized by state institutions. This pushes far past current political behavior theories, which recently acknowledged widespread partisan animosity, avoidance, and discrimination (e.g. Iyengar & Westwood 2015; Iyengar et al. 2019). Violent partisanship fits well with broader psychological roots of intergroup conflict in which competing groups favor their own and lash out aggressively against out-group members (Hewstone et al. 2002; Sherif et al. 1988; Tajfel et al. 1971; Tajfel & Turner 1979; Tooby & Cosmides 2010; Wilson 2004).

The likeliest route to mass partisan violence involves direct advocacy by partisan leaders, which would be an extreme form of opinion leadership described above. Leaders also stoke the anger that serves as emotional fuel for aggression (Anderson & Bushman 2002), and leaders supplement explicit calls for violence with moral disengagement rhetoric that makes violence more palatable through rationalization – vilifying enemies, sanctifying one's own group, minimizing harms, and diffusing or displacing responsibility (Bandura et al. 1996).[16] Moral disengagement does not always mean moral incapacity in a broader sense, however. It can make *righteous* violence more psychologically palatable. New studies on present-day partisan hostility provide evidence of extreme partisanship. They show low to moderate levels of support for partisan violence (10–15 percent) and moral disengagement (10–40 percent) representing tens of millions of Americans, even without widespread calls for violence from party leaders (Cassese 2019; Kalmoe 2015; Kalmoe 2017; Kalmoe & Mason 2018; Pacilli et al. 2016).

We know the twentieth century had plenty of political violence by extremists, including anarchist bombings in the 1920s, radical Left bombings in the 1970s, and radical Right attacks in the 1990s and since, but few of these cleaved along partisan lines (until recently). In contrast, nineteenth century U.S. politics clearly shows the danger for *partisan* violence, often fused with white supremacy – before and after the Civil War, but most maximally in the war itself (Acharya et al. 2018; Fisher 1997; Foner 1988; Graham & Gurr 1979; Grimsted 1998; Potter 1977). In that light, early- and mid-twentieth century white supremacist violence in the South was also partisan violence because it helped to maintain regional one-party rule by Democrats.

Chapter 3 looks for partisan differences in widespread calls to arms and supplemental rationalizations in partisan newspapers and gaps that shifted as the war continued. I expect to find Northern Democrats less keen than Republicans about violence against Southern Democrats, but I also expect to find violent partisan rhetoric targeting *Northern* political opponents as well (Chapter 5). Violent intra-sectional partisanship shows the partisan nature of the war independent of sectional divides. Chapter 4 tests the public's polarized response with local war-enlistment data, anticipating partisan gaps in voluntarism corresponding with party war divides.

Put differently, I argue that conventional partisan opinion leadership not only shaped war attitudes in the Civil War era, but that it extended into violent *action*. Parties are key mobilizers of mass political behavior (e.g. Bensel 2004; Rosenstone & Hansen 1993). I argue here that local partisan leaders and activist networks similarly mobilized military voluntarism in the Civil War, in addition to continued efforts at electoral mobilization in wartime elections. And lest we think partisan beliefs could never motivate people to risk their lives, recent studies find some partisans today forgoing healthcare to maintain consistency with their partisan worldviews (Lerman et al. 2017).

***

To recap, I expect Civil War mass partisanship (1) to be more enduring than we might expect under extraordinary duress, (2) to produce extreme war-related rationalizations strengthening partisan behavior, and (3) to mobilize individual participation in mass violence in line with positions of party leaders and local social environments.

Three Mechanisms of Partisan Influence

Three levels of partisanship worked together to influence its political and military power in the Civil War era, as they do today: individual identities, social influence, and the guidance and organization from local and national party leaders. The last – opinion leadership – is most important. First, partisan identities produce powerful loyalties that guide political preferences and interpretation and mobilize partisan action. Party identity is most potent when it provides an enduring sense of attachment, when strongly felt, and when other identities reinforce it (Hillygus 2005; Huddy 2001; Huddy et al. 2015; Mason 2018; Rosenstone & Hansen 1993). James McPherson (1997) reports 40 percent of individual soldiers linked politics to the Civil War in their personal letters, but I would suggest a *primary* political impetus for war participation was probably limited to a small fraction of politically engaged citizens.

Second, interpersonal contacts substantially influence our political views and actions, especially when they are people we trust politically and in-group members who encourage conformity (Beck et al. 2002; Bond et al. 2012; Connors 2019; Finifter 1974; Gay 2004; Jefferson 2019; Karpowitz & Mendelberg 2014; Klar 2013; Lazarsfeld et al. 1944; Nickerson 2008; Noelle-Neuman 1974; White et al. 2014). Social networks and groups encourage communal consensus not only by sharing and endorsing messages from group leaders, but also by collectively reframing those views in their own fashion (Broockman &

Kalla 2016; Corder & Wolbrecht 2016; Cramer 2016; Druckman et al. 2018; Druckman & Nelson 2003; Klar 2013; Mutz 2006; Sinclair 2012; Walsh 2004).

Richard Bensel's (2004) accounts of nineteenth century voting reveal substantial social and local organizational influence on voting behavior, especially because voters cast their ballots publicly. Social pressures related to war participation were similarly strong, with locally organized military units composed of neighbors and community war meetings that pressured individuals to publicly volunteer with communal expectations. Politicized churches played an influential role in Civil War politics and war mobilization too (Smith 2006, p. 81). That shifts our attention beyond individual reasoning to the ways that local political environments around individuals guided their political attitudes and actions. As with leaders, interpersonal influence probably worked most effectively on fellow-partisans but also nudged neutral and weakly politically opposed neighbors through personal relationships.

Third, and most important, partisans turn to trusted leaders to help them make sense of politics, which would otherwise be incomprehensible for nearly everyone. Most partisans get their political views, interpretations, and reasons from party leaders and news, directly and indirectly (e.g. Barber & Pope 2019; Bartels 2002; Berinsky 2009; Darr & Levendusky 2014; Druckman et al. 2013; Freeder et al. 2019; Hetherington 2001; Kam 2005; Karpowitz et al. 2017; Lenz 2012; Levendusky 2009; Searles et al. 2018; Zaller 1992). Party leaders guide their own partisans most, but local leaders also sway neutral citizens and weakly aligned opponents (e.g. Cain et al. 1987; Campbell & Crowley 2014; Key 1949). People also follow authority figures they trust who make explicit calls to violence (or abstention) paired with rationalizations (e.g. Milgram 1965).[17]

Party leaders and organizations also mobilize citizens into political action (Grimsted 1998; Rosenstone & Hansen 1993; Wilentz 2005), and local partisan leaders facilitate or inhibit action with the institutional opportunities for participation they establish or deny (e.g. Cubbison & White 2016; Walton 1985). It may seem obvious, but people are more likely to participate when asked, and political groups don't always ask (Arceneaux & Nickerson 2009; Gerber & Green 2000; Nickerson 2008). Parties mobilized the lethal politics of the Civil War similarly by activating their political action networks. Local leaders also aided military enlistment through their control of local institutions by staging rallies to enhance leader and peer pressures. Allied partisan groups like the Union

League served similar roles in supporting the war, while Copperhead organizations (anti-war Northern Democrats) sought to undermine it.

To put the three mechanisms differently, Republican strongholds had more Republican citizens who interpreted and followed in party-consistent ways; those places had more Republicans influencing their neighbors; and those voters tended to elect Republican leaders who influenced local attitudes and behaviors through persuasion and opportunities offered. The same held for predominantly Democratic places, of course. Civil War historians frequently cite these partisan mechanisms – individual partisanship, social pressure, and leaders (e.g. McPherson 1997), and so do political scientists in cross-national research on war mobilization elsewhere (e.g. Humphreys & Weinstein 2008). In a few tests, I can distinguish between competing but complementary partisan explanations. In most, however, each mechanism is observationally equivalent in aggregated political behavior. Nonetheless, theorizing distinct causal mechanisms is important foundational work.

To be clear, politics was and is not central to most people's lives. Nineteenth century Americans are renowned for their high political engagement, but they differed in degree rather than kind. For example, roughly 80 percent of eligible white men voted in 1860s presidential elections, whereas the 2016 rate was 60 percent, and voting is a low bar for engagement. More evocatively, one New England farmer's diary entry for Election Day 1864 describes spreading manure in his fields and going to the polls, both equally remarkable to him (Baker 1983). Political events and organizations played larger roles then as forms of entertainment and civic association, but politics still was not a *preoccupation* beyond a small class of partisan activists. Thus, when I say that partisanship drove wartime behaviors, explicit identity-based motives were only strongest for a minority of the public, whereas more subtle partisan leadership and social factors probably played greater roles in guiding behavior for weaker partisans.

Partisan Warfare in Comparative Perspective

Partisan violence remains a rare subject in American politics research due to our disciplinary overemphasis on the more peaceful party politics of the past half-century or so. In contrast, a large scholarly literature examines the correlates of domestic political violence in other countries. Many studies consider "greed and grievance" conditions for violence (e.g. Collier & Hoeffler 2004; Kalyvas 2006), which can include identity-based intergroup conflicts. Around the world, ethnic and party identities and organizations often align in mutual reinforcement to propel conflict, though most scholarship tends to emphasize the predominance of ethnic identity even when ethnic parties organize that violence (e.g. Bar-Tal et al. 2009; Ginges et al. 2007; Halperin et al. 2011; Horowitz 1985; Posner 2004; Skocpol 1979; Urdal 2008; Varshney 2003; Wilkinson 2006). Ethnic, religious, and regional cleavages helped delineate partisan votes and military support in the U.S. Civil War era as well (e.g. Kleppner 1979; Neely 2017; Silbey 1985). For example, Irish-Catholic immigrants were mostly Democrats, and they were responsible for the 1863 draft riots in New York City, attacking Republican officials and murdering over one hundred black residents. Aligned social identities with few crosscutting social interactions likely fueled the U.S. Civil War, as they do in other civil wars (Gubler & Selway 2012).

With or without overlapping identities, political parties sometimes strategically mobilize violence by supporters for electoral and political advantage – to gain victories, or to protest and challenge defeats (Blattman 2009; Bratton 2008; Dunning 2011; Hafner-Burton et al. 2014; Harish & Little 2017; Höglund 2009; LeBas 2006; Powell 1981; Snyder 2000; Wilkinson 2006; but see Collier & Vicente 2014 for pacifying electoral effects). The confluence of partisan voting and violence shows that the two are not as diametrical as we might imagine. In the U.S. case, historically minded scholars have found partisan motives in low-level electoral violence before the Civil War (Grimsted 1998; Potter 1977), in the war itself (Costa & Kahn 2008; Silbey 1985), and in postwar intimidation and score settling during Reconstruction (Fisher 1997; Foner 1988; Graham & Gurr 1979). These ethno-partisan groups transition between paramilitary terrorism and electoral forces, like Jim Crow Democrats and, in Northern Ireland, Sinn Féin. As political scientist Charles Tilly (2003) concludes, large-scale "collective violence and nonviolent politics intersect incessantly" (p. 27).

Most of those works – including those attentive to party-based violence – focus on broad contextual factors that vary little across individuals or over time (e.g. Fearon & Laitin 2003; Iqbal & Zorn 2006). Humphreys and Weinstein (2008) provide a notable exception to that macro-level approach by testing individual-level ethnic and partisan correlates of civil war participation in Sierra Leone, including how these identities encouraged or discouraged participation and shaped susceptibility to elite mobilization. I take a similar approach here. Comparative politics scholars generally recognize the intergroup dangers from partisanship, far more than their American counterparts do. It *can* happen here, and it did, as I will show.

PARTISANSHIP ACROSS PARTY SYSTEMS

One potential weakness in taking modern mass partisanship as my motivating model in the Civil War case is that most wartime voters and combatants were already adults when the Republican Party formed. Standard partisan origins from socialization in childhood and early adulthood cannot easily explain a new Republican identity or the time necessary to develop strong party attachments and habits. Thus, the authors of *The American Voter* (Campbell et al. 1960), who first conceptualized party identification, speculated that the usual stability and potency of party identity might not have applied in the mid-nineteenth century:

At some moments of electoral history the attitude forces on the vote may depart so widely from standing party loyalties that these partisan identifications are altered. ... The crisis leading to the Civil War acted so strongly on prior partisan allegiances that the popular base of one of the existing parties was shattered and the popular support of the other radically transformed while a wholly new party catapulted itself into control of the national government.

(p. 530)

Political scientists and historians emphasize disjunctures that justify distinguishing the Second Party System (Whigs and Democrats) from the Third (Republicans and Democrats). For example, Richard McCormick (1966) argues that each party system "must be viewed as a distinctive entity, differing so fundamentally from one another as to constitute separate models" (p. 6). Paul Kleppner (1979) describes such party shifts as "massive transformations in the shape of the electoral universe" (p. xvii), and Adam I. P. Smith (2006) agrees: "For much of the 1850s the party system had been in flux, and the coming war did nothing to dampen the ubiquitous assumption of politicians that important groups of voters – particularly Whigs and Know-Nothings, were ... up for grabs" (p. 6; see also Holt 1978). Among elites, political scientists Keith Poole and Howard Rosenthal (1997) quantified the extent to which slavery defined national politics at this time: a North-South dimension dominated other considerations in the 1850s Congress for the only time in American history.

How could mass partisanship be powerful under these upended circumstances? One answer, from political scientists Ted Brader and Joshua Tucker (2001, 2008), is that habitual partisan mass voting patterns crystallize in just a few years of party competition, where none had existed before – as they find in post-Soviet Russia. That brief timeframe fits well with Republican emergence before the Civil War.

A second, stronger answer is this: the Republican *electoral coalition* in the North was largely new *in name only*, even as the party's regional strength and its focus on limiting slavery's expansion were new for a major party. The new party succeeded in coalescing anti-Democratic voters there who carried constellations of common identities and relationships with them across party systems, mutually reinforced by individual political identities, local leaders, local political cultures, and social networks. The shared social-partisan history of Whig–Free Soil partisans was probably more critical in reconstituting similar voting coalitions under a new Republican banner than ideological and issue continuity among leaders. The Republican Party was more socially exclusive having shed Southern slave-holding Whigs, and that may have helped crystallize Republican identity too, along with anti-slavery commitments for those activists for whom that issue was paramount (e.g. Carmines & Stimson 1989). On the other side, Democrats North and South called on several decades of habit to ground their identities, views, and practices, dating back to Jackson in 1828 (Baker 1983; Edwards 1997). As historian Adam Smith (2006) writes about Northern parties, "anti-Republican feeling on the Democratic side ran deep, as did opposition to Democrats among former Whigs" (p. 65).

Lincoln's 1855 letter to his friend Joshua Speed, which opened the chapter, personalizes that stability and change. Lincoln's political commitments and even his old self-identification held fast at that point despite changing labels applied to him by others – Whig, abolitionist, later Republican. Lincoln helped found the Illinois Republican Party months after writing that letter, formally forging a Republican identity for himself. My argument here is that roughly the same Northern coalitions – leaders and public alike – carried their identities and political commitments with them from one party to the next. Names and policy emphasis changed, but political networks of Northern voters generally did not. Democrats stood pat, and Whigs and Free Soilers united in opposition as Republicans. A few scholars share my view of coalition stability (e.g. Gerring 1998; Mayhew 2002), but most emphasize discontinuity instead.[18]

Thus, despite major party changes on the national stage, when it comes to *subnational* partisanship in the North, what stands out starkly is startling electoral *stability* across party systems. I make that empirical case next with election returns. Partisan *endurance* then provides the psychological, organizational, and social foundations for extreme polarization during the war.

Second Party System Continuity, 1848–1852

The historical description and examples of leadership continuity are compelling, but we only can verify *mass* partisan persistence by comparing state- and county-level voting patterns from the Whigs' last gasp to Republican triumph a few years later. We first need a baseline for stable voting *within* the Second Party System, from one set of Democrat versus Whig (and Free Soil) votes to the next, with which to compare continuity in elections *across* systems as new parties replaced old ones.

Whigs fielded their last two presidential nominees in 1848 and 1852. Of twenty-two loyal states in 1861, nineteen were around to cast ballots in 1848.[19] Voters closely divided between Whig Zachary Taylor (the victor) and Democrat Lewis Cass. One-tenth went to former president Martin Van Buren, who had been a Democrat, then a Whig, and now the Free Soil nominee. The 1852 election saw Democrat Franklin Pierce beat Whig Winfield Scott and Free Soiler John Hale.

The 1848–1852 Whig county vote share continuity for these Union states is a large correlation of +0.85, where 1.0 is a perfect relationship and zero means none, weighted by population.[20] Free Soil votes were robust at +0.70, and a weaker but durable estimate of +0.66 held for Democrats. The results indicate strong county-level voting continuity from 1848 to 1852, as we would expect within the same party system. Slave states that would remain in the Union during the war stood apart politically before and during the fighting, but estimates here are similar when I exclude them.[21]

Sometimes results look different across levels of analysis. In this case, however, *state*-level comparisons are similar or stronger for Whigs (+0.85), Free Soilers (+0.87), and Democrats (+0.76).[22] These align with Kleppner's (1979) nationwide state-level correlations for the same elections. I found similar patterns for presidential votes between 1844 and 1848, which means this late stage of the Second Party System is not uniquely stable (or unstable). In sum, substantial mass voting continuity prevailed for Whigs, Free Soil, and Democrats in the nineteen Union states, as we would expect. With these benchmarks in mind, I proceed with continuity tests from one party system to the next.

Continuity across Party Systems: Republicans' Emergence & Consolidation

The 1856 election was another a three-party race, but the Know-Nothing (American) Party and Republican Party replaced Whigs and Free Soilers in a new party system dividing Democrats and Republicans along sectional and ethno-cultural lines. Know-Nothing Millard Fillmore earned a fifth of the vote despite winning only Maryland, while Democrat James Buchanan went on to beat his main competitor, Republican John C. Fremont.[23] The four-way election in 1860 was even more complicated, though the limited popularity of John Bell and Breckinridge (Constitutional Union and Southern Democrat) in contiguous free states (excluding the West) simplified the jumble a bit. Most Northern votes split between Illinoisans Abraham Lincoln (Republican) and Stephen Douglas (Northern Democrat).[24] In any case, I examine a variety of party combinations in these years to see which coalitions were stable (or not) over time.

Let's begin from 1848, relating those votes to 1856. Democrats faced off against Whigs and Free Soilers in 1848, and Democrats challenged Republicans and Know-Nothings in 1856. In the nineteen states, Democratic county vote shares show substantial stability at +0.76 overall, and +0.80 excluding slave states.[25] State-level analysis confirms the same stability for Democratic votes (+0.81). That continuity *between* party systems fits comfortably with estimates from *within* the Second Party System. Put inversely, the sum of 1848 Whig–Free Soil votes corresponded well with the sum of 1856 Republican–Know-Nothing votes. Starting from 1852 votes adds California and some counties in the "Northwest" states of Iowa, Wisconsin, and Michigan, but with similar results. Continuity from 1852 to 1856 is similar to the 1848 baseline for county-level Democratic votes (+0.65), and electoral persistence is even stronger for Democrats at the state level (+0.75).

A closer look reaffirms the early anti-slavery basis for the Republican coalition: 1856 Republican votes *only* correlate with 1848 Free Soil votes (+0.68, vs. Whig –0.33) and 1856 Know-Nothing votes *only* correlate with 1848 Whig votes (+0.53, vs. Free Soil –0.35). State-level analysis shows the same for Free-Soilers-turned-Republicans (+0.76), and Whigs-turned-Know-Nothings (+0.53). Results from 1852 are similar.[26] Republican strongholds clearly had their roots in Free Soil bastions. However, the conversion for voters was nowhere near one-to-one. The average Free Soil vote share in free states was a measly 14 percent in 1848, and 6 percent in 1852, compared with 46 percent for 1856 Republicans.

Thus, it is likelier that a core of Free Soil leaders and activists became Republicans and then won over their communities, presumably based on appeals beyond anti-slavery commitments.

Many Whigs who later voted Republican shared some anti-slavery views without endorsing the Free Soil party, but that view was not decisive for most in 1848 and 1852. Indeed, anti-slavery Whig William Seward's support for slave-holding Whig nominee Zachary Taylor over the Free Soil candidate is a testament to the strength of party ties over slavery views, even among leaders. Anti-slavery salience and conviction for ordinary voters may have changed in a few years, but there is not much sign of *prioritized*, long-standing anti-slavery views for most Republican votes. Historian Jonathan Earle (2004) explains this anti-slavery transformation from fringe to mainstream: Free Soilers found popular success with the Republican Party by changing their focus from the evils of slavery to the more popular territorial exclusion. That coalition eventually attracted majority support by combining Free Soilers with Whigs and a modest number of anti-slavery Northern Democrats.[27]

Historically, the *winning* Republican coalition in 1860 was more important than the losing one in 1856, though both inform my estimates for prewar local partisanship in later chapters. How did these patterns map onto the complex electoral environment in 1860? Partisan continuity from the Second Party System into 1860 votes is similar to the 1856 results. Democratic voters remained loyal at county and state levels when Northern and Southern Democratic votes in loyal states are *combined* as a bloc (1848: +0.58 and +0.65, 1852: +0.71 and +0.75). Free Soil votes continued to predict Republican vote shares (1848: +0.54 and +0.65, 1852: +0.53 and +0.67), and Whig votes related slightly to Constitutional Union vote shares (1848: +0.25 and +0.40, 1852: +0.22 and +0.40). Like 1856, the joint force of Whig and Free Soil votes predict the combination of Republican and Constitutional Union votes substantially better than the votes for Republicans alone. Bell found most of his support in slave states, but he managed to win one in seven Massachusetts voters (doubtless due to the favorite-son in the vice president slot). Constitutional Unionists belong within the enduring anti-Democratic coalition.

The party coalitions consolidated in the simpler two-party contests of 1864 and 1868 during and after the war. Strong continuity emerges across the party system divide once again. In the contiguous free states (i.e. no California or Oregon), the sum of Whig and Free Soil votes (i.e. the anti-Democrats) predict Republican votes slightly better than Free Soil alone. In particular, 1852 Whig–Free Soil votes correlate strongly with

1864 Republican votes (County: +0.74, State: +0.86) and with 1868 Republican votes (County: +0.74, State: +0.86). In slight contrast, Free Soil vote shares alone predict Republican votes a bit better than the Free Soil–Whig combination when examining all loyal states. Whig votes alone poorly predict Republican votes in these elections, consistent with Kleppner's (1977) nationwide tests. Table 2.1 shows all the permutations in detail.

All this leads to a startling, robust conclusion: despite the death of two parties, the rise of three new ones, and the oldest party split in two, Northerners largely cast votes as if little had changed. The same broad coalitions continuously coalesced to elect and defeat Democrats. The results show a stunning level of voting continuity across party systems, from Second to Third – a partisan break point that hardly looks like a break at all.[28] These findings are even more impressive given the demographic tumult throughout the country from mass migration and immigration and wartime election disruption, all of which would *attenuate* estimates of local stability. Individual voting continuity was probably higher, but to a degree that is hard to know with any certainty.[29] Strong electoral continuity provides a good rationale for expecting potent partisan behavior in individuals, leaders, and communities. It is easy to see why partisan divisions oriented around these two coalitions were so powerful: old party identities carried through in new party names attached to social-political groups that had driven decades of voting behavior.

Third Party System Continuity, before & during War

As a coda on these continuity tests, readers may already sense that voting *within* the Third Party System was similarly stable, despite the chaos of secession and war. Joel Silbey (1977) presents supporting evidence with high voting correlations in several states ($rs \sim 0.90$) and average vote share shifts of less than 5 percentage points. Paul Kleppner (1979) presents similar conclusions. I provide fuller confirmation here.

Table 2.2 shows continuity among Republican votes and among anti-Democratic coalition votes, 1856 through 1868. The table separates results by contiguous free states and for all loyal states, and it shows separate county- and state-level estimates. Overall, Third Party System continuity equals Second Party System stability and the transition period from Second to Third. The wartime results preview later tests for short-term electoral stability through wartime events. The 1860 to 1864 test

TABLE 2.1 *Consolidating coalitions from Second to Third Party systems*

Contiguous Free States

	1848 Whig + Free Soil	1852 Whig + Free Soil	1848 Whigs	1852 Whigs	1848 Free Soil	1852 Free Soil
1864 Republicans	C: +0.49 S: +0.60	C: +0.74 S: +0.86	C: +0.01 S: +0.13	C: +0.25 S: +0.23	C: +0.48 S: +0.52	C: +0.63 S: +0.74
1868 Republicans	C: +0.44 S: +0.57	C: +0.70 S: +0.79	C: −0.08 S: +0.15	C: +0.22 S: +0.19	C: +0.50 S: +0.48	C: +0.63 S: +0.70

Note: C = County, S = State.

All Loyal States

	1848 Whig + Free Soil	1852 Whig + Free Soil	1848 Whigs	1852 Whigs	1848 Free Soil	1852 Free Soil
1864 Republicans	C: +0.37 S: +0.33	C: +0.52 S: +0.47	C: −0.07 S: −0.21	C: +0.11 S: −0.15	C: +0.41 S: +0.45	C: +0.52 S: +0.55
1868 Republicans	C: +0.35 S: +0.41	C: +0.52 S: +0.50	C: −0.16 S: −0.30	C: +0.07 S: −0.29	C: +0.47 S: +0.60	C: +0.57 S: +0.70

Note: C = County, S = State.

TABLE 2.2 *Partisan stability in the Third Party system*

| | Earlier Election | | | |
| | Contiguous Free States | | All Loyal States | |
Later Election	Republicans Only	Anti-Democratic Coalition	Republicans Only	Anti-Democratic Coalition
1856–1860	C: +0.79	C: +0.77	C: +0.85	C: +0.59
Republicans	S: +0.88	S: +0.80	S: +0.95	S: +0.66
1856–1860	C: +0.72	C: +0.76	C: +0.70	C: +0.76
Republicans	S: +0.82	S: +0.81	S: +0.83	S: +0.84
& Constitutional				
Union				
1856–1864	C: +0.69	C: +0.73	C: +0.51	C: +0.56
Republicans	S: +0.79	S: +0.83	S: +0.48	S: +0.61
1856–1868	C: +0.71	C: +0.73	C: +0.66	C: +0.60
Republicans	S: +0.83	S: +0.83	S: +0.81	S: +0.72
1860–1864	C: +0.82	C: +0.87	C: +0.49	C: +0.67
Republicans	S: +0.80	S: +0.87	S: +0.44	S: +0.54
1860–1868	C: +0.85	C: +0.88	C: +0.71	C: +0.74
Republicans	S: +0.87	S: +0.86	S: +0.81	S: +0.73
1864–1868	C: +0.95	–	C: +0.85	–
Republicans	S: +0.97		S: +0.84	

Note: C = County, S = State.

here shows that, despite all the war wrought, partisan voting was highly consistent in the contiguous free states, though less so in the slave states and Western states, some of which were war zones. That suggests the war was generally *not* a disruptive electoral force in voting patterns.

Partisanship across Centuries

Finally, given my application of modern partisan theories to historical behavior, how does partisan stability compare, then and now? Party continuity for Republicans in postwar years resembles county-level continuity today. The 1864–1868 Republican voting correlation for contiguous free states (+0.95) is nearly identical to county-level continuity in presidential votes between 2000 and 2004 nationwide, +0.94 for Democrats and +0.97 for Republicans. The modern basis for that local stability is durable individual partisanship, with roughly 90 percent of voters choosing the same party across presidential elections and 90 percent of partisans voting loyally.[30] However, that stability could be due to unmeasured local reinforcement by leaders and social networks, as hypothesized here. By comparison, about three-quarters of voters in the mid-twentieth century cast consistent party votes across election cycles. The broader implication is that, despite some variation in durability and strength over time, partisan voting appears to be highly durable across centuries. That continuity provides confidence that individual and local partisan votes serve as reasonable proxies for partisan identification, and that individual partisan stability corresponds with aggregate stability in partisan votes.

CONCLUSIONS

The mid-nineteenth century was the most tumultuous period in American political history. Within a decade, one major party died, another split in two, three new parties were born, and a four-way presidential election culminated in a cataclysmic war that legally ended slavery and enfranchised millions of black citizens. These were seismic national disruptions – they could not have been bigger. We might expect that change to register in the electorate in maximally disruptive ways, with rapid and chaotic shifts in voting and little partisan impetus for mass political action, but that is not what I find. Partisan vote stability is a key condition supporting my argument that partisanship *strongly* motivated elite and mass Civil War political behavior.

This chapter traced the roots of partisan civil war in three ways. I began by outlining the history of party contestation before the war, including the prevalence of low-level racial-partisan violence that then exploded with the war itself. That history also shows that political fault lines for the war aligned almost perfectly with divisions between the party factions. That set the stage for a war that was fundamentally partisan in its origins and execution – the Civil War was partisan warfare. Southern Democrats went into armed rebellion, Northern Democrats split for and against the war to suppress their partisan brethren, and Republicans were all-in on that violent yet essential project defending American democracy and expanding liberty.

Next, I described the modern theoretical framework for ordinary partisanship and its political consequences, which aligns closely with historians' descriptions of mid-nineteenth century partisanship. That context generates predictions about ordinary partisanship under the extreme pressures of the Civil War: (1) partisanship is enduring, (2) partisanship is resistant, and (3) partisanship is violent. The partisan combination of individual identities, opinion leadership and institutional opportunity from leaders, and social pressures from local communities are likely to produce partisan polarization in wartime behavior, to the extent that the parties take diverging positions on the war.

Finally, I considered the case for strong partisanship in a new party system, providing a first test of partisan endurance. Despite the unprecedented upheaval in 1850s partisan politics, the transition from the Second Party System to the Third was marked by surprising levels of partisan stability in Northern elections between Democrats and an anti-Democratic coalition, even approaching levels of stability seen today. Republicans rapidly replaced Whigs as the main challenger to Democratic dominance, but the party's initial roots were deepest in places where the Free Soil Party – a small, predominantly anti-slavery party – had been strongest. Free Soil vote shares were nowhere near the size of Republican vote shares a few years later, however, suggesting that the *organizational* core of Free Soilers formed the base of the Republican Party and not a large voter transition from Whigs. Eventually, the Whig–Free Soil combination in the free states coalesced into the Republican coalition that would win the Civil War and persist thereafter. Snapshots of presidential voting in 1860 before the war also mirror late-war votes in 1864, providing the book's first empirical evidence that the war itself did not dramatically disrupt partisanship and may have solidified it instead. In sum, the party system shift, such as it was, did *not* fundamentally alter electoral alignments in the loyal states. That continuity provides a robust foundation for expecting strong partisan behavior among ordinary citizens.

In sum, the war's stable partisan roots – antebellum party conflict, opinion leadership guiding loyal partisans, and stable prewar electoral coalitions – motivate and guide my search for elite and mass party polarization in war attitudes and behaviors in the chapters that follow.

PART I

MOBILIZING PARTISAN WARFARE

3

The Press Goes to War

Partisan Advocacy & Resistance

with Tim Klein & Elias Shammas

[P]ublic sentiment is everything. With public sentiment, nothing can fail; without it nothing can succeed. Consequently, he who molds public sentiment goes deeper than he who enacts statutes or pronounces decisions. He makes statutes and decisions possible or impossible to be executed.

Abraham Lincoln
First Lincoln-Douglas debate
Ottawa, IL
August 21, 1858

The Civil War divided combatants along party lines drawn in the 1860 presidential election, with Southern Democrats leading the rebellion – including the party's Union-state nominee. But Northern partisans also divided deeply over whether to continue the Union's fight in the last two crucial years of the war. We begin our extended investigation of partisan war polarization in the North by tracking views in the partisan newspapers that predominated at the time. That language plausibly reflected the universe of party leadership cues guiding war support and influencing the public's willingness to join the fight, as argued in Chapter 2 and tested in Chapter 4. Here, we calculate average party differences in war advocacy and reasoning, and we trace shifting war positions over time. We also present extraordinary examples of the extreme language propelling Civil War violence more viscerally than our statistical estimates ever could.

Given the war's partisan origins, we expect to find more war support in Republican papers compared with Democratic papers, along with supplemental news frames justifying that legitimate violence. We present affirmative qualitative and quantitative evidence of that party war polarization from a first-of-its kind representative content analysis of twenty-four newspapers evaluating seven moments during the war. Party polarization was also dynamic, with gaps between party positions opening and closing across the breadth of war. Those patterns generate static and dynamic predictions for partisan military service gaps in the next chapter. Here, we take the first step toward demonstrating the capacity of U.S. party leaders to mobilize mass violence against their electoral opponents in rebellion, or for Democrats to resist that mobilization against former (and future) political allies.

Partisan News in Civil War America

The American press during the Civil War was almost wholly partisan, as it was for much of that century (Dicken-Garcia 1998). Unlike today's hybrid of mostly non-partisan professional journalism supplemented by independent partisan outlets, the nineteenth century partisan press was a fully integrated component of each party's organizational apparatus (Holzer 2014). Journalists and editors were not socialized into dispassionate professionalized norms, and only a handful of newspapers sought out a position of political independence (Schudson & Tifft 2005). The guiding purpose of these newspapers was to advance party goals in the public. Explicit party advocacy appeared alongside news, and editors presented current events through partisan lenses. Editors did this work to advance shared political views, to satisfy patrons who financed their paper, and to gain patronage from government printing contracts when their party won control of government (Holzer 2014). Partisan news was thus a product of sincere editorial views, economic responsiveness to patrons' news preferences, and strategic messaging meant to reinforce, persuade, and mobilize audiences for party gain.[1]

Most towns of any size had multiple newspapers – at least one each for Democrats and Republicans – and papers often attacked rival newspapers and editors as much as they targeted opposing politicians. Partisan readers wanted the latest news interpreted through friendly party filters that affirmed their party identities. They also sought cues on what stands to take on the war's complex policy issues, and what arguments to deploy in the party's defense to persuade wavering friends and neighbors (e.g. Searles et al. 2018). Local partisan elites looked to national politicians and major newspapers for cues on how to frame the news of the day. They often went further by running word-for-word reprints (usually attributed) from like-minded outlets, all of which encouraged *nationalized* partisanship. They also reprinted content from antagonistic papers (and rebel news), either as pure news or to add caustic commentary. Literacy rates were high – near 90 percent for white men (McPherson 1997). Those who could not read heard news secondhand through acquaintances who read or discussed content with them (Holzer 2014; Lazarsfeld et al. 1944). Thus, the party line spread broadly. In partisan news, we can pinpoint party war positions, test for elite-level motivated reasoning, and read the actual language they deployed for their cause.

ANALYZING CIVIL WAR NEWSPAPERS

Assessing news impact on public opinion requires identifying news attributes in proportion to their consumption by the public. A perfect portrait of Civil War newspapers in the North would analyze the full population of newspapers: every word of every title published on every date. Scholars would then condense those raw texts through systematic analysis in a way that retains its full shape. That ideal is impossible, even with automated methods. The texts are too numerous for thousands of titles across 1,500 days of warfare. How, then, do we know if claims about Civil War news content are representative?

One common approach simply cites affirmative examples of whatever attribute the researcher is looking for, wherever they happen to find it. The problem, of course, is that the method provides no information about how *prevalent* the content was, even with many instances. The same in-text evidence could be found for content that is ubiquitous or exceedingly rare. Other studies take a "greatest hits" approach. Major papers with agreed-upon influence make the cut due to circulation size and popularity among influential elites. This probably does reasonably well at capturing the rhetoric circulating among national leaders, and major papers certainly influenced minor papers. But that isn't what the *average* reader saw. Detailed treatments of Civil War–era news, like Holzer's (2014), take a wide-bore "all-of-the-above" approach with content from several dozen newspapers – big and small – from around the country. That picks up trends missed in major papers, especially with the care taken to cover diverse outlets, though we still can't know whether the newspaper selection reflects the shape of all news.

For a more representative selection approach, we apply probability sampling to a population list of Civil War–era newspapers. We briefly summarize selection and coding methods here, with more details in the

Online Appendix and Codebook. We began with Rowell's *American Newspaper Directory*, an 1868 census of newspapers ordered by Congress as a public good, designed in part to inform advertisers, the first of its kind. The directory includes the year the paper began publishing, partisan leanings (if any), and circulation by town and state. From there, we probabilistically selected twenty-four newspapers, four from each of six Union regions, with paper selection weighted by circulation within each region, though we mostly focus on national averages by party (Border, Mid-Atlantic, Upper & Lower Midwest, Upper & Lower New England). A weighted sample reflects the news that publics read better – news content at the reader level to infer effects of partisan language and leadership on public opinion and political-military behavior.

The regional divisions ensure representation for potential geographic differences in partisanship. Weighted sampling ensures selections in each region reflect what citizens *read* there. Widely read titles like the *New York Herald* (65,000) had a proportionally greater chance of selection compared with titles like the *Corning Democrat* (950). We limited the search to general interest newspapers, excluding special interest and non-English presses, and only for papers founded before 1861.

Table 3.1 presents details on the selected newspapers. We have seven Democratic papers, twelve Republican papers, and five independent papers – four of which generally backed Democrats but also supported the war. These papers reflect the range of partisan opinion by sampling method and sample result, and party proportions in each region roughly reflect balances at the polls. Twenty-four newspapers is an admittedly small sample for statistical comparisons, but it is the largest tractable number for a manageable coding effort of our depth. Sensitive measures, large party differences, and repeated measurement across the war help to improve precision. Any party polarization we find must be large and reliable to register, and that makes these tests methodologically conservative.

Like the sampling of news sources, we could extend the logic of representativeness with a random sample of dates during the war. However, a more systematic selection better suits our purposes. We want to know how ordinary people responded to calls for more troops, and how they responded to campaign rhetoric just before voting. In each newspaper and for each year from 1861 through 1864, we collected one date in July, roughly one week after the latest major calls for new enlistments (or the 1863 New York draft riots) and adjacent to many important war events. We also added April 1861, just after the first call for troops to suppress the rebellion. Finally, we gathered dates for the presidential

TABLE 3.1 *Newspapers in the sample*

Region	Name, Place, Frequency, Party, Year Founded, Circulation
Upper Midwest	*Iowa State Register* (Des Moines, IA, wk(d), Rep, 1856, 6.5k)
	Davenport Democrat (Davenport, IA, wk(d), Dem, 1838, (1855), 5–10k)
	Detroit Advertiser & Tribune (Detroit, MI, wk (d), Rep, 1829, 20k)
	La Crosse Democrat (La Crosse, WI, wk(d), Dem, 1860, 10k)
Lower Midwest	*Cincinnati Times* (Cincinnati, OH, wk(d), Rep, 1840, 70k)
	Cincinnati Enquirer (Cincinnati, OH, d, Dem, 1841, 10–20k)
	Chicago Tribune (Chicago, IL, wk, Rep, 1847, 41k)
	Toledo Blade (Toledo, OH, wk, Rep, 1836, 75k)
Border States	*National Intelligencer* (DC, wk(d), Ind, 21k)
	Baltimore Sun (Baltimore, MD, d, Ind, 1837, 10–20k)
	Louisville Journal (Louisville, KY, d, Dem, 1830, 20k)
	Missouri Republican (St. Louis, MO, wk, Dem, 1823, 15k)
Upper New England	*Nashua Gazette & Hillsborough Advertiser* (Nashua, NH, wk, Dem, 1827, <5k)
	Burlington Free Press (Burlington, VT, d, Rep, 1848, <5k)
	Cheshire Republican (Keene, NH, wk, Dem, 1827, <5k)
	Rutland Herald (Rutland, VT, wk/d, Rep, 1792, 2.1k/1k)
Lower New England	*Boston Journal* (Boston, MA, d, Rep, 1837, 28k)
	Berkshire County Eagle (Pittsfield, MA, wk, Rep, 1829, <5k)
	Boston Evening Traveller (Boston, MA, wk, Rep, 1845, 17k)
	Boston Herald (Boston, MA, d, Ind, 1846, 30K)
Mid-Atlantic	*New York Evening Post* (NYC, NY, d, Rep, 1801, 5–10k)
	New York Herald (NYC, NY, wk, Ind, 1835, 65k)
	New York Sun (NYC, NY, d, Ind, 1833, 47k)
	Albany Journal (Albany, NY, wk, Rep, 1831, 20k)

Note: Each newspaper entry lists region, name, location, publication frequency (wk = weekly, d = daily), party, date founded, and circulation size category.

election and midterm elections in each state, either Election Day or the earliest preceding date available. Ultimately, we have two dates per year (except 1863 for most, 1862 for a few). These regular intervals provide broad snapshots of news content throughout the war. Table 3.2 lists the dates and some important surrounding events.

Our method risked picking newspapers and issue dates no longer available a century after their printing – a threat to unbiased inferences. However, we were surprisingly successful at gathering nearly all sampled issues. Of 168 newspaper-dates in the study (7 dates, 24 newspapers),

TABLE 3.2 *Newspaper dates & events*

Date	Events
April 22, 1861	Fort Sumter attacked (4/12), Lincoln calls for 75,000 militia (4/15)
July 29, 1861	Bull Run defeat (7/21), call for 500,000 volunteers (7/22)
July 24, 1862	Seven Days defeat (7/1), Militia Act call for troops (7/17)
Midterm Elections Oct & Nov 1862, Mar 1863, Aug 1863	Fall 1862: 2nd Bull Run defeat, Antietam (9/17) & Corinth (10/4) victories, preliminary Emancipation Proclamation; Mar 1863: Draft authorized (3/3)
July 23, 1863	Gettysburg (7/3) & Vicksburg (7/4) victories, NYC draft riots (7/16), Ft. Wagner (7/18)
July 11, 1864	Unprecedented casualties in Overland campaign (May–June), siege of Petersburg begins (7/9), Congress empowers President to call for troops by discretion (7/4)
Lincoln's Reelection Nov 8, 1864	Atlanta (9/2) & Shenandoah victories (10/19)

only 4 are entirely missing. The completeness is remarkable given that some sampled newspapers were of little note beyond their immediate community. It is a tribute to preservation work by two centuries of local historians and archivists (and to the durability of high-quality newsprint). The result is the most systematically representative analysis of Civil War newspapers in the North, at least for content centered on those key war dates.

Our analytical methods were non-traditional for historical analysis too. We independently coded each page and analyzed every newspaper issue. That preserves representativeness by including all content in the sample.[2] Fifty codes detail coverage of war mobilization, elections, and politics. Categorical coding is inherently reductive, but it enables systematic comparisons. All scholars categorize content at least implicitly – we just do so more consciously and transparently. We supplement our systematic efforts with illustrations of unusually evocative examples.

We compare Democratic and Republican newspaper content with averages for the whole war and on particular dates over time. All our quantitative estimates are essentially average partisan differences in proportions or averaged attribute scores from scales. We parenthetically report statistics (coefficients, standard errors, and p-values) indicating how much Republican papers diverged from Democratic ones when that difference is at least marginally significant (roughly, less than a 10 percent chance a difference of that size is statistical noise). The six regions sampled varied in population and so, to estimate a rough but representative national average, we weight all comparisons by regional population.[3]

Our first results are for news agendas – the topics filling newspaper pages. *Every* newspaper date described the latest developments in the war. The war dominated their pages, though recall we chose these dates for proximity to war events, making war coverage more likely. Average newspapers mentioned the war on 80 percent of their pages, and they devoted nearly 40 percent of their page space to war-related content on the average page. Nearly as many pages mentioned politics (74 percent), but that absorbed half as much space as war news (20 percent).[4] Ads covered remaining column inches, along with crime news, markets, travel schedules, poems and stories, and jokes. News agendas generally did *not* differ by partisanship, perhaps reflecting how the war's salience constrained their editorial discretion (Boydstun et al. 2013). Most specific war news and politics topics that we analyzed appeared steadily over time, but a few that were salient at the outset fell off later, including war goals, blame, and moralized language.

MOBILIZING PARTISAN WAR VIOLENCE

How did Northern party newspapers position themselves for and against the war to crush the rebellion? What war policies did they back, and what persuasive frames did they use? Finally, how did those traits change during the war? We begin with direct support or opposition to the war itself, to enlistment and conscription, and to desertion. Then we assess the complementary rhetoric reinforcing those positions, including moral disengagement, social pressure, costs, and prospects.

Partisan War Support

As a first glimpse, we analyze each individual newspaper's war support over time (see Online Appendix). No Republican paper ever wrote clearly against the war. All the Democratic papers opposed the war by November 1864 elections. The *Nashua Gazette, Cincinnati Enquirer*, and *Cheshire Republican* were most consistently anti-war, across a majority of dates. Four other Democratic papers generally favored the war before turning against it. For more precision, we examine the continuous index of each paper's war support, averaged at the date-level from each page on a five-point scale from explicit support (+1) to explicit opposition (−1). Republican papers were substantially more likely than Democratic papers to

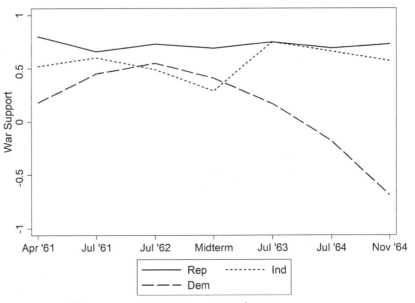

FIGURE 3.1 Newspaper war support over time by party
Note: Average newspaper support over time by party, weighted by regional population.

support the war on average, for the full war (b = 0.60, *s.e.* = 0.11, p < 0.001), and newspaper partisanship explains 65 percent of variance in war support. Independent papers nearly equaled Republican war support, while Democrats were statistically indistinguishable from neutral for the full war average.

Democratic war views dramatically shifted over time, in contrast with Republican pro-war constancy. Figure 3.1 shows average war support by party over time. Democrats sent mixed signals at the start, with some support from free state papers (+0.39) but not slave-state ones (−0.25). Democrats were nearly unanimous war supporters by the midterms but then declined precipitously thereafter. No Democratic papers supported the war near its end – only *independent* papers that endorsed Democrats and backed the war. War views differed significantly between Republican and Democratic papers for all dates except July 1862 and the midterms.[5] Party polarization was small in early 1861, absent in 1862, and then grew into a chasm thereafter.

What did war advocacy sound like? Republicans were especially sanguine about the war early on. To keep the war brief, the *Chicago Tribune*

(IL-R, Apr 1861) demanded "[v]igor, and determination to put down treason at all hazards. ... If necessary, to burn, kill, and destroy, let there be no hesitation. ... To preserve [national institutions] from destruction by a mob in the service of anarchy, is a work worth any sacrifice on the part of the North and the shedding, if necessary, of rivers of blood." But many Democratic papers were equally sanguine.

The *La Crosse Democrat* (WI-D, April 1861) gave early war support in the strongest, purple-est prose. They wrote Wisconsinites were "ready to forget all political differences and but waiting the word to march in unbroken phalanx to the field of battle, there to shed their last drop of blood in defense of honor, and to resent a traitorous and cowardly insult to our national flag. ... [Secessionists] have looked to see the democrats of the Free states aiding them, to whip republicans. In that they have been mistaken." The *Democrat* approvingly quoted a New York politician who "hoped we would strike down in our might and wipe out the whole South from the face of the earth." The paper later became one of the war's most ferocious – even disloyal – critics. There were already hints of that turn in July 1861, when the paper criticized Republican editor Horace Greeley: "Will the people follow these cowards, who are sacrificing the national army for the sake of the sectional party?" The *Cheshire Republican* (NH-D, Apr 1861) was the only free state Democratic war opponent at the outset. The paper wanted Lincoln to convene Congress before striking back: "Hence it is that we can see a chance for negotiations yet, and a settlement of our troubles upon a satisfactory basis."

By 1864, Democrats unified in fierce opposition to the war, and that orientation defined their election campaign. The *Cincinnati Enquirer* (OH-D, Nov 1864) wrote, "If Abraham Lincoln should be reelected there will be interminable and utterly cruel war; war which cannot, and will not, end so long as there is an able-bodied man at the South or at the North. Whereas, if McClellan should be elected, we will have Peace in thirty days after his inauguration – Peace on the old terms of compact – Peace which will leave the negro exactly where this war found him – Peace which will deliver us, white men, from conscription, taxation, and all the other miseries wherewith Lincoln has assured us." Republicans focused on a righteous cause nearly won. For example, the *Boston Journal* (MA-R, Nov 1864) excerpted a campaign speech: "A vote for [Democrat] McClellan would be a vote for slavery when it is nearly abolished – for rebellion, when it is about to expire – for disunion, when the Union has nearly triumphed – a vote for the kingdom of Satan on earth. (Great applause.) A vote for Abraham Lincoln will be a vote for freedom, union and peace."

Representing Party War Views

Newspapers went beyond their own advocacy to tell readers how Democrats and Republicans felt about the war. Given Republican unanimity supporting the war, we coded the presence (1) or absence (0) of that stance on pages mentioning politics, averaged across pages for each date. The Democratic position indicator has three categories: favor (1), mixed (0), and oppose (−1). Figure 3.2 shows how party newspapers represented each parties' views, with claims about the Republican position on the left and claims Democratic views on the right.[6]

Democratic and Republican newspapers sent steady signals of Republican war support, recurring on roughly 40 percent of pages. Both emphasized Republican war support more before the 1864 election, seeking political advantage. In contrast, party papers presented Democratic views *inversely* over the first two years of the war. Democratic papers accurately stated the party's position in line with their arc of war support and opposition in Figure 3.1. In contrast, Republican papers first said Democrats supported the war. Just as Lincoln reduced the appearance of party warfare by recruiting Democratic generals and cabinet members, Republican newspapers tried to minimize partisanship by focusing on pro-war Democrats. The hope was for fulsome war support from united loyal states. The fear was that Democrats might sit out the war, to the ruin of the country. For example, under the headline "Patriotism, not Party," the *Chicago Tribune* (IL-R, April 1861) quoted a Democrat who said, "I did not vote for Abraham Lincoln, but I will sustain him to the last drop of my blood." The paper described "[m]en of all religious creeds and party associations giving in their hearty assent and adherence to the cause of the Government."

For 1862 elections, Democrats claimed to support the war but opposed many specific war measures, leaving an overall impression of a pro-war party. At the same time, Republican papers accused Democrats of being *anti*-war, to the point of disloyalty, for opposing emancipation and other policies. "No-party" rhetoric became a divisive wedge, not the uniting force it had been in 1861. One newspaper decried "aid and comfort [the rebellion] is now receiving from the Democrats of the North, whom the rebels now lovingly call their allies. ... Away with parties now and petty politicians. Let no man compromise his patriotism to furnish a jubilee to traitors" (*Chicago Tribune*, IL-R, Nov 1862). By 1864, all newspapers agreed: Democrats opposed the war. Partisans probably followed their own party's avowed stances, but early war disagreement about Democratic views may have confused unaligned citizens.

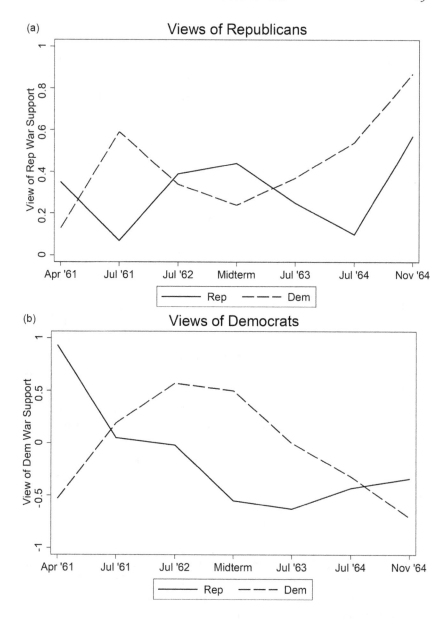

FIGURE 3.2 Representations of party positions over time by party

Enlistment, Desertion, the Draft, & Black Troops

The next chapter tests for partisan polarization in war service, reflecting elite-level polarization. Beyond general war support, we are interested in explicit party calls for military participation or abstention, including white enlistment, enlisting black troops, the draft, and desertion. We measure enlistment support with a five-point scale, like overall war support. Enlistment advocacy naturally corresponds with war views ($r = 0.77$), and so we expect to see similar partisan patterns here. Enlistment news was prominent: 58 percent of pages mentioned enlistment, thus gaining a code for stance. Republican newspapers were significantly likelier to support enlistment than Democratic papers across the war ($b = 0.33$, *s.e.* = 0.10, $p < 0.01$).

The *Chicago Tribune* (IL-R, July 1862) described seven *Tribune* printers enlisting and wrote, "We advise every young man who is intending to enlist to come forward immediately, as in all probability before the week closes the regiment will be full. You will receive a bounty; your family will be cared for, and you yourself, if sick or wounded, treated like a brother. Fill up the ranks." The *Boston Evening Traveller* (MA-R, July 1862) excerpted a speech from a "large and enthusiastic war meeting" in a neighboring town: "It's all very beautiful to talk of the old flag, but why don't you come up and fight for it? (Applause.) It's all very well to talk of human liberty, but why the devil don't you rally to die for it?" The paper also reported "[s]ome miserable traitors at [the Massachusetts town of] Russell having been at work discouraging enlistments." Later in the war, the *Berkshire County Eagle* (MA-R, July 1863) called for more troops: "Let us now witness again the same alacrity, spirit, and earnest patriotism, which distinguished the earlier days of the war . . . the voice of our brothers' blood cries to us from the ground." Among Democrats arrayed against them, the *Chicago Tribune* (IL-R, April 1861) noted Clement Vallandigham's early-war vow that Ohio would send troops "over his dead body." The *Cheshire Republican* (NH-D, July 1862) later urged readers not to enlist due to the war's increasing anti-slavery focus: "Democrats did not engage in this war to carry the emancipation banner."

Polarization patterns for military mobilization mirror war support over time. Figure 3.3 shows support for enlistment, desertion, the draft, and black troops through the war. The first panel presents levels of enlistment support: a small 1861 gap, no 1862 difference, and substantial polarization later. Notably, most Democratic papers never *explicitly* advocated against enlistment, but they did cease to voice support as their war opposition grew. Republicans were strong enlistment advocates throughout.

The most extreme anti-war advocacy short of open rebellion called for soldiers to desert the ranks. For newspapers, that kind of public language could get them temporarily shut down, their editor jailed, or their printing office ransacked by a mob. That made such statements extremely rare, even among the most anti-war editors. In our sample, only four newspaper dates seemed to *favor* desertion. Desertion mentions only appeared on 12 percent of pages. When they did, we measured views in three categories (−1 to +1). Almost all position-taking opposed desertion (−0.40). Republican newspapers were substantially more likely to oppose desertion than Democrats ($b = −0.33$, s.e. $= 0.22$, $p < 0.05$). The second panel in Figure 3.3 shows desertion views by party over time. Republicans were more explicit in opposition, but the gap was largest later in the war as Democrats moved to oppose the war overall.

The Lincoln administration called for a national draft as volunteers dwindled, first from militias and then from the general public. The *Burlington Free Press* (VT-R, July 1863) encouraged cheerful local compliance: "It is gratifying to hear from all quarters that there are those in the community who, when drafted, think it not desirable to pay a commutation fee or procure a substitute . . . those who desire to have the work well done, and so prefer to do it themselves, doubtless do better." Some Republicans saw the draft as a means to raise men among Democratic shirkers. The *Boston Evening Traveller* (MA-R, July 1862) said the draft "will place the burden where it belongs" as "the only proper method of raising more troops in [Democratic] Central and Southern Illinois." And the *Rutland Herald* (VT-R, July 1863) warned Democrats that "to deny its necessity . . . is to incite resistance and bloodshed." Standing opposed, the *Nashua Gazette* (NH-D, March 1863) decried conscription's "naked deformity," and the *La Crosse Democrat* (WI-D, July 1864) predicted disorder: "The Bible speaks of a time when seven women shall lay hold of one man. That unfortunate time will soon be here if Abe Lincoln lays his hands on the half million men he proposes to call out."

When the press mentioned the draft (37 percent of pages), Republican newspapers were far likelier to endorse it than Democratic ones ($b = 0.66$, s.e. $= 0.15$, $p < 0.001$). We coded draft views with a three-point scale (−1 to +1). Average draft support was far below enlistment advocacy for both parties (−0.14 and +0.53). Figure 3.3's third panel shows draft support by party over time. Republican support for the draft rose slowly over time. Democratic papers were initially neutral on the militia draft,

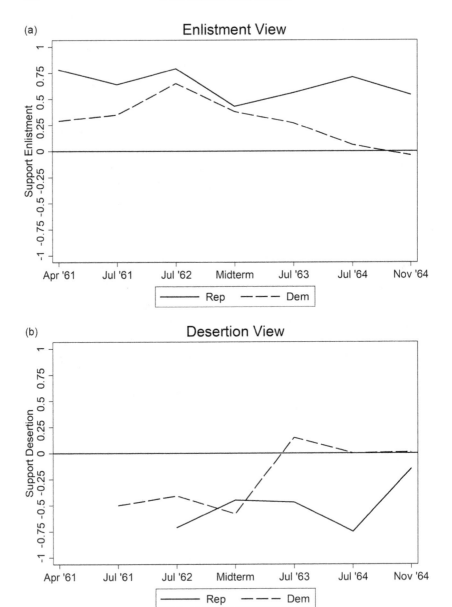

FIGURE 3.3 Support for military personnel over time by party

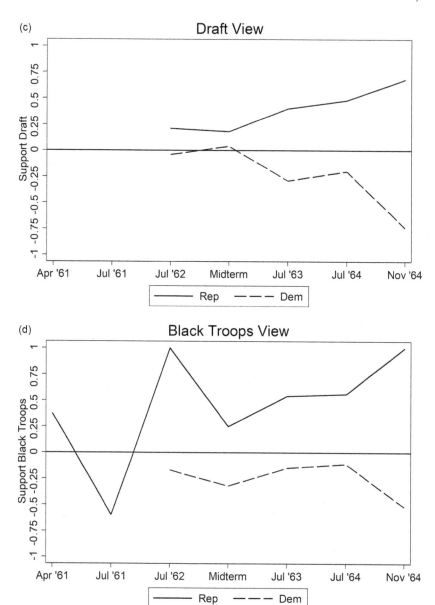

FIGURE 3.3 (*cont.*)

and then moved against federal conscription, much like their trajectory for overall war support.

Finally, Republican newspapers expressed support for black troops through most of the war, while Democratic papers were steady opponents. That isn't surprising since black troops would aid the war effort and undermine the Democratic Party's more virulent white supremacy views at the same time. We measured support for black troops – speculative or realized – with a three-point scale (–1 to +1). News mentioned black troops about a fourth as often as white enlistments (16 percent of pages), due partly to two years of U.S. inaction before finally mustering them. Republican papers supported black enlistment much more than did Democratic papers ($b = 0.78$, *s.e* $.= 0.24$, $p < 0.01$). The last panel in Figure 3.3 shows party support for black enlistment over time.

Early on, the *Toledo Blade* (OH-R, April 1861) noted a local black man who "Wants to be Counted In" despite the law against it. "Upon all occasions, the colored man has proved his loyalty and bravery in this government; and yet, after doing all they could or were permitted to do, their rights have been ignored ... notwithstanding all this, there are hundreds of colored men in the State who would form themselves into Companies, and offer their services to the Government." The *Chicago Tribune* (IL-R, July 1862) likewise lamented, "[t]he black men of the South have stood strong for the Union, and more than a million of them would, most readily and heartily have rushed to the conflict and extinguished the flames, long ere this, had we accepted their services. But no; we have said d—n niggers; this is a white man's war, and we don't want any interference of niggers in our concerns. ... we now see how foolish and weak we have been." The *Rutland Herald* (VT-R, July 1862) wrote of western soldiers realizing the "imperative to use every means in our power, slavery or no slavery, to crush out this rebellion. That every negro to be found should be used as much as we should use a gun or a case of ammunition captured of the enemy." The *Herald* also sought cross-party support by quoting a Democratic general: "I would say to them 'Serve me and aid me in lightening the burdens of my soldiers, and I will make you free' ... while I am reluctant to arm the negroes, for all my prejudices are against that, yet, if necessary to put down this great Treason, I would not hesitate to make them fight against the traitors."

In sum, direct advocacy for *filling the ranks* in the press followed the same dynamic pattern of partisan polarization as overall war support, setting the stage for asymmetric partisan war *participation* in Chapter 4 and war interpretations in later chapters.

Social Pressure

Beyond direct social pressure, citizens respond to what political scientist Diana Mutz (1998) calls *impersonal influence* – the effects of learning information about public opinion. Partisan newspapers frequently invoked local and national public opinion when making their cases for or against the war (56 percent of pages). We coded public directional support on a three-point scale (−1 to +1). Republican news naturally reported more public war support than Democratic news (b = 0.81, *s.e.* = 0.25, $p < 0.01$), nearly always reporting a favorable public compared with mixed public views in Democratic papers. Papers were more likely to represent a supportive public at the war's beginning than by its end, on average, due entirely to shifts in Democratic efforts to show a public more opposed. The *La Crosse Democrat* (WI-D) represents that change well. In April 1861, the initially pro-war *Democrat* praised a local rally reflecting "the generous outpouring of practical sympathy and good will for the national and holy cause, and for the families of those who offer their lives to their country." The *Democrat* later opposed the war, and in July 1864, described a disillusioned public: "When church members ... refuse to go to the front on communion day it is a sure sign they are tired of their faith. And when a people fail to respond to calls for volunteers to fill the army it is a sign that they are tired of war."

We categorized references to (relatively) local military activity if they involved citizens or troops raised in the same state, coded with simple indicators (0, 1). These might provide examples of local war support in action. Republican newspapers described local enlistment efforts more often (b = 0.17, *s.e.* = 0.09, $p < 0.10$) and printed more letters from local military units (b = 0.11, *s.e.* = 0.06, $p < 0.10$). The *Berkshire County Eagle* (MA-R, July 1862) said a local father with three enlisted sons represented a town "willing to give her best blood and her hardest earned dollars for 'Union and Liberty,'" and the *Rutland Herald* (VT-R, July 1862) exulted "Glory to the Green Mountain State! Vermont sends the First Regiment of the 300,000. .... Vermont leads the van with her hardy sons." We found no partisan differences in mentions of local black troops recruited or serving in the field, and we found no party differences in mentions of local deserters.

Appeals to duty with identity-based obligations were another way to leverage social pressure. Duty to country was the most common *primary* appeal by far, as when the *Toledo Blade* (OH-R, April 1861) described a "duty as patriots to wage war." Patriotic duty appeared on 26 percent of pages mentioning enlistment, on average. Republican papers were more likely than Democratic ones to cite duty to country (b = 0.09, *s.e.* = 0.05, p < 0.10). Local duty was next most at 5 percent. Duty to God, family or as a man, were negligible.[7] Some calls combined many kinds of obligation, like this one: "it became the duty of every sensible Christian-minded man in the community to do his duty in defence of the national flag" (*New York Herald*, NY-I, April 1861). The *Louisville Journal* (KY-D, Aug 1863) also fused duties: "To have 'been to the wars' is a life-long honor, increasing with advancing years, while to have died in defence of your country will be the boast and the glory of your children's children."

Moral Disengagement

Pro-war newspapers deployed moral disengagement language to mobilize support for violence and participation in it – various forms of vilification and other rationalizations to make killing feel more ethically acceptable. War opponents, by contrast, described the violence as immoral, making it harder for people to support violence against the rebellion in good conscience. Nearly half of the pages with war news represented the United States as morally right. Republican papers were far likelier to do so than Democrats (b = 0.26, *s.e.* = 0.10, p < 0.05). The *Chicago Tribune* (IL-R, Apr 1861) lauded the "splendid proof that the North is an unit for the just and holy war." Later, the *Boston Journal* (MA-R, Nov 1864) asserted "[t]he armies of the United States are 'ministers of good and not of evil.' ... They can be a terror to evil doers only, and those who fear them are accused by their own consciences."

Republican papers began the war more likely to vilify enemies, but Democrats' rhetoric aimed at Republicans surpassed them by the end. A third of war pages framed the rebels as evil. Republican papers did so twice as often as Democrats (b = 0.22, *s.e.* = 0.08, p < 0.05). In July 1863, the *New York Evening Post* (NY-R, July 1863) reported, "a record of inhuman cruelties" against loyal citizens in Tennessee under the headline "Innocent men hanged – children shot and women tortured to death." Carrying the same text, the *Albany Journal* (NY-R) opined, "The wretches who perpetrated the outrages named are not fit for hanging. Some new and exquisite torture should be invented for their especial benefit." The *La Crosse Democrat* (WI-D, July 1861) explicitly argued that rebel wickedness justified violence during its war-supporting days: "the evil which we failed to dispel by reason, must be put down by force."

Dehumanizing rebels made violence against them more agreeable, and 13 percent of pages mentioning the war did just that. Republican papers were slightly more likely to do so (b = 0.08, *s.e.* = 0.05, p = 0.10). Thus, the *Cincinnati Times* (OH-R, July 1861) cast the war as "a contest between civilization and a species of barbarity that has long shown itself in the South." The *Rutland Herald* (VT-R, July 1863) linked dehumanization and violence (and warned of Northern Democratic plots): "To stop the draft is to stop the war and surrender to the rebellion; and the government is asked to do this when it has got its foot fairly on the neck of the monster, and our victorious armies are everywhere crushing out its life. The forlorn hope of the southern traitors is a northern insurrection on their behalf."

War supporters argued secession was treason (42 percent of pages). For example, the pro-war *Missouri Republican* (MO-D, July 1861) damned a local rebel general for invading the state. "We trust and believe that his unholy and devilish purposes will be thwarted, and he be driven from the soil he has so wickedly betrayed. ... His is a double treason. He has not only levied war upon the Government of the United States, but also upon the sovereignty as well as the security and peace of his own State." Republican papers were not more likely than Democratic papers to assert secession was treason overall, given that most of those statements came early in the war when both parties generally supported the war. Few defended secession (2 percent), but those few were Democrats (b = −0.03, *s.e.* = 0.02, p < 0.10).

Laudable war goals imbued the war with justice. We coded the primary war goal on each page. Restoring the Union was most common (34 percent of war pages), with no partisan differences. The rhetorical preeminence of saving the Union fits historian Gary Gallagher's (2011) argument that unionism was a broader galvanizing factor than anti-slavery. Few papers cited defending democracy as the *primary* war goal, at least not in those terms. Nonetheless, they spoke often of "anarchy" and the need to maintain our system of government, all fused with the Union. In a more explicit example, the *National Intelligencer* (DC-I, July 1861) quoted a senator: "It is plainly a contest whether the people should rule or not. ... The whole course of the South was a system of usurpation, in disregard to popular will."

Ending slavery appeared as a goal on 4 percent of the pages, endorsed or otherwise. Early on, the pro-war, pro-slavery *Missouri Republican* (MO-D, July 1861) anticipated, "the declarations ... of the Anti-Slavery party, will disclose a purpose to make this war, what the bulk of the

Anti-Slavery men desire it to be, a war against slavery." The *Burlington Free Press* (VT-R, July 1862) disagreed: "it is not a war against slavery, though slavery is warring against the Union." Nevertheless, anti-slavery goals appeared in Republican papers too, mixed with others. The *Rutland Herald* (VT-R, July 1862) quoted a local soldier's letter in which right-eousness rationalizes extreme violence:

We can never end this war... till we make common cause with the negro, arm him, ... and by a combination of terror and extermination, destroy the race of slaveholders on this continent. I know this will be a terrible course – bloody and horrible. But by what sort of cataclysm can any one expect the two hundred years of torture and wrong ... to be closed? ... I look to see those fair Southern homes ... sink amid blood and fire. ... To the hands of the North have been committed the sword and flame of avenging justice. With knife and cautery must we pursue this cancer to all its ramifications, unmindful of the writhing and groans of the victim. Our National Life and the hopes of the ages are tied to the thoroughness of our work.

Casualties as Costs, Winning as a Reward

Lastly, we consider costs and benefits of war: casualties and the odds of victory. We might expect war opponents to focus heavily on casualties and war supporters to avoid them. Surprisingly, though, that is not what we find. Democratic papers were no likelier than Republicans to mention casualties. That points us to the importance of how parties *framed* those casualties – senseless losses or heroic martyrs – which we take up in Chapter 5.

The psychological rewards of winning and the costs of losing add more considerations in the war calculus. We might expect anti-war partisans to claim the war's prospects for success were dim and the reverse for the war's proponents. That's what we find with our three-point war progress measure (−1 to +1). Republicans were much more positive about the war's progress on average than were Democrats ($b = 0.34$, *s.e.* = 0.10, $p <$ 0.01). Democratic papers often sounded similar during their pro-war period, however: "The tide of war has just turned, victory has crowned our army in the lower Mississippi. The great river is open, and now its commerce will flow as free as its waters, to the gulf, and all of us will feel the tranquilizing and invigorating effect of the great achievement" (*Missouri Republican*, MO-D, July 1863). The *Rutland Herald* (VT-R, July 1863) concurred, claiming "terrible and irretrievable blows which have just been inflicted upon the rebellion." Party gaps in war prospects were largest in 1864, which we detail in Chapter 5. Of course, *too much* progress might make potential recruits imagine no need for their own sacrifice. The *Boston Evening Traveller* (MA-R, July 1862) reported, "The people had settled down under the conviction that there were men enough in the field, if properly handled, to crush out the rebellion, and it will require some effort to arouse them up to the enlisting point."

CONCLUSIONS

The Civil War partisan press advocated war positions and complementary frames that advanced their military and electoral goals. Republicans strongly and consistently backed the Republican administration in its war to subdue the partisan rebellion. Democrats, by contrast, shifted from tepid war support to virulent opposition. Here, we showed how those conflicts played out in the polarized messages of partisan newspapers, with anticipated consequences for mobilizing or inhibiting mass war participation among ordinary partisans, as the next chapter shows. These texts begin to show the potential role of partisan messages motivating deadly work in the nation's most epic crisis – the language leaders marshalled to drive public attitudes and behaviors in the war.

For evidence, we presented a first-of-its-kind representative survey of twenty-four Civil War newspapers from loyal states. We found large partisan differences in explicit support for the war and its military mobilization efforts, along with argumentative frames and evidence deployed to support those positions. The war began with small war position gaps between the parties. Those narrowed through 1862 with rising Democratic support for war, coupled with opposition to specific Republican war policies including emancipation. After midterm elections, Democrats shifted dramatically into war opposition, generating huge advocacy and framing gaps between the parties by the end of the war.[8] Party newspapers supplemented their direct advocacy with news frames reinforcing their broader outlooks, including reports leveraging social pressures, moral disengagement, casualties, and prospects for victory. Republicans and Democrats differed in these argumentative elements overall, and over time, to the degree the parties endorsed or opposed the war at each moment.

Other historical scholarship shows this partisan advocacy and rhetoric in newspapers and from other elites found its mark – the same language we found in these newspapers appears throughout the letters and diaries of ordinary people, both the righteous and the vitriolic (e.g. Jimerson 1988; McPherson 1997; Weber 2006). Ordinary people adopted the same high-minded language (and low) to express themselves and explain their actions. In other words, the war language of partisan press and ordinary people aligned.

In sum, both party presses sent clear signals on their war positions and rationales, meant to explain themselves and influence war attitudes and military participation of their partisan audiences. Here, we found intense party polarization in war messages overall, though polarization waxed and waned over time. Did polarized calls to arms produce partisan disparities in rates of military service and sacrifice? And did partisan fighting differences follow the changing contours of party polarization over time? The next chapter weighs the evidence of partisan war participation.

4

Filling the Ranks

Partisan Opinion Leadership in Violent Action

There are but two parties now, Traitors & Patriots. And I want hereafter to
be ranked with the latter, and I trust, the stronger party.

Ulysses S. Grant
Letter to his father
Galena, IL
April 21, 1861

Party and party organization rose above country, or duty [during the war].
In fact, party was a substitute for country.

Gideon Welles[1]
Secretary of the Navy, 1861–1869

Why do people volunteer to fight in a war? Why do they leave family and
friends at home to participate in the killing and dying of terrifying battles
and the tedious drudgery of camp life and labor? More telling, perhaps,
what *keeps* them in the ranks once they learn what they've gotten themselves into, continuing to fight in the face of horrifying death, wounds,
disease, and general suffering? [2] The answers vary, of course, but many
common motives recur across eras and circumstances (e.g. Kalyvas 2001).
In this chapter, I look for and find partisan asymmetries in war participation among ordinary Americans, consistent with the static and dynamic
partisan polarization patterns found among partisan elites in Chapter 3.

Mid-nineteenth century Americans were leery of a standing national
army, as they had been since the time of the American Revolution. They
feared tyranny might follow. This posed major problems for the U.S.
government as it faced imminent destruction in the spring of 1861. The

U.S. Regular Army had just 16,000 troops – most stationed remotely in the far West – to quell a seceding population of nine million, all told (Newell 2014). Officers from the South deepened the crisis by resigning in droves – more than one in five of all U.S. military officers forsook their sworn oaths by joining the rebellion (Dudley 1981). State militias initially filled the gaps, but these inexperienced soldiers hardly performed better than new recruits did, and the demand for soldiers quickly surpassed what militias could provide.

The war ultimately mobilized more than two million loyal Americans to crush the rebellion, nine in ten of whom volunteered for the fight. By 1865, it was the largest fighting force in the world (Kreidberg & Henry 1955). One-tenth of the Northern population went to war – roughly half of all military-age males. Ten percent of U.S. forces were African Americans, half of whom were freedmen from states in rebellion. Tens of thousands of women took official roles as well, as nurses, laundresses, cooks, and other service positions. Hundreds of thousands more Americans made informal contributions on the home front, in the nation's capital, and alongside Union armies in the field.

In this chapter, I investigate how partisanship polarized Union military participation in enlistment, desertion, and disparate casualties. I also test contingencies beyond overall voluntarism patterns: Did partisanship's mobilizing influence change as war politics shifted across four tumultuous years? Were Republican leaders and communities more effective than Democrats in mobilizing local African American volunteers? Finally, what can we say about the politics motivating women's war participation? I begin with a focus on white soldiers and sailors, employing tests across several levels of political and military data to produce the most thorough evidence possible. I continue by examining black combatants and women's voluntarism, including participation challenges for both groups arising from their grossly disadvantaged social positions. Ultimately, I conclude that partisan polarization driven by party leaders played an essential role in determining who filled the ranks and who neglected the fight.

LINKING BALLOTS & BULLETS

A broad range of motives compelled individual Americans to volunteer for military service in the Civil War or led them to reject their government's call. Historians endorse Lincoln's assessment of various reasons for joining and then staying in the fight: patriotism, partisanship and ideology, ambition, personal courage, adventurism, employment, and convenience (Costa & Kahn 2008; McPherson 1997). Historian Adam Smith (2006) writes, "enlisted men were deemed to be taking part in a political as well as patriotic undertaking" (p. 95) – a view shared by many soldiers and sailors (Frank 1998; Manning 2007; Matsui 2016; McPherson 1997; White 2014). I focus on *partisan* influences – a more concrete and plausible approach than "ideology" typically cited in many histories.[3]

In an era of extreme party polarization, Republican leaders not only asked Democrats to *support* the war, they also asked them to *die* in support of a U.S. government led by Republicans in a war against their political allies of thirty years, even as many Democratic leaders expressed doubts. Under those circumstances, it would be surprising if Democrats served in equal numbers. Chapter 2 theorized partisan mechanisms driven by individual identity, leadership, and social influence. Chapter 3 showed how Democratic and Republican leaders polarized over war participation and supporting rationales, similar to partisan elites in other American wars (Berinsky 2009; Iyengar & Simon 1993; Zaller 1992). Local partisanship would have been especially important for military units populated locally – soldiers volunteered and served together with their neighbors.

Here, I expect greater rates of war participation from Republicans than Democrats, and larger shares of local military-age males enlisting from strong Republican places than from the bastions of Northern Democrats. Once in service, Republicans and people from Republican places would be less likely to desert, especially given local pressures at home and in the ranks. Predominantly Republican units might even take on more of the hardest fighting, which could produce partisan asymmetries in casualties. Of course, shifts in party war polarization over time would have affected the size of these war participation gaps, especially for enlistment. I begin with white enlistment, with desertion and death later on. I conclude examining black military service and women's voluntarism.

We have some evidence of political forces shaping Civil War enlistment already. Economists Dora Costa and Matthew Kahn (2008) analyzed Massachusetts soldiers at the town level using the American Civil War Research Database (ACWRD). They found towns voting more for Lincoln in 1860 contributed more recruits, with a one standard deviation increase in Lincoln votes yielding thirteen more men, a 4.4 percent gain over the mean. Together, elections and economics accounted for a third of variation in town enlistment in their tests. Historian James McPherson (1997) arrives at similar conclusions from different methods. He analyzes letters and wartime diaries from a thousand soldiers chosen for representativeness through quota-like methods among those enlisting early in the war, to learn why they fought. Like Costa and Kahn, McPherson finds politics among several factors motivating enlistment in the Union army, including patriotic fervor, personal and social pressures to exhibit masculine virtues of duty and honor, and anti-slavery views in religious and political forms. Other historians conclude the same from Union soldier writings (Frank 1998; Manning 2007; Matsui 2016; White 2014).

Historian Mark Neely (2017) disagrees, arguing that war mobilization was largely non-partisan, and that Democrats did not hinder the war effort. He focuses on a lack of explicit partisan mentions in war mobilization, presuming Republicans would openly call for partisan warfare rather than a more lofty call for national defense. Adam Smith (2006) focuses similarly on the explicit rhetoric of non-partisanship as evidence of limited party motives, accepting strategically deployed Republican claims of "no party now" and Republican-dominated Unionist organizations as sincere partisan disavowals.

Systematically identifying the partisanship of ordinary people is far more difficult than doing the same for partisan elites, let alone analyzing whether those commitments motivated choices to fight or abstain. To test how individual and local partisanship shaped war participation, I'd ideally have records of individual partisan votes (better yet: self-identification) in 1860 for all combatants and all military-eligible noncombatants from the same communities. Unfortunately, no one recorded that data back then – at least not known or accessible – and so we need alternatives. I leverage three primary data sources with complementary strengths and weaknesses: (1) state-level absentee votes soldiers cast during the war compared with non-combatants back home, (2) state-level aggregates of war service and deaths, and (3) county-level aggregates of voluntarism, desertion, and death.

Ballots from a Cartridge Box

White soldiers' votes provide the most direct evidence we have on partisanship and war participation for individuals sorted into combatant and civilian groups. With up to a million voters away at war at any given time, most soldiers and sailors lost their vote for much of the war, sometimes exceeding 10 percent of a state's electorate (Benton 1915). Both parties were keenly aware of the electoral power in missing soldier votes, and they maneuvered for advantage based on the strong belief that soldiers would vote disproportionately for Republicans. Newspapers noticed the same. On Election Day in 1862, the *Detroit Advertiser & Tribune* (MI-R) calculated the year-to-year decline in Pennsylvania congressional vote totals from absent soldiers as three Republicans for every Democrat, concluding "[t]hat shows who are fighting the battles of the nation." Democrats in every state resisted efforts to enable absentee soldier voting, while Republicans pushed for the allowances.

Three heavily Republican midwestern states (plus a reconstituted Missouri government) began absentee voting in time for the fall 1862 elections. Eleven more states eventually made absentee voting allowances for the 1864 elections, while seven never made provisions for absentee ballots from soldiers.[4] When and where states disenfranchised their soldiers, the Lincoln administration furloughed Republican-leaning military units so they could vote at home in close elections. As a bonus, the presence of soldiers served to rally and persuade (and occasionally intimidate) local civilians to vote for Republicans too.

In the eleven states tallying soldiers' votes separately, an average of 78 percent of soldiers chose Lincoln over McClellan in 1864 – remarkably close to the Detroit newspaper's 1862 Michigan estimate. By comparison, 53 percent of voters chose Lincoln in those same states, excluding military ballots, producing a 25-point gap. The soldier-home difference showed a similar 20-point gap when excluding slave states and the far West (79 percent vs. 59 percent). Put differently, individual soldiers were about 1.4 times more likely to choose Lincoln than voters back home. Table 4.1 shows the difference was consistent across nearly all the loyal states that tabulated soldier votes separately. Only Kentucky and Vermont were low and high outliers, respectively.

These results provide strong, direct links between individual Republican partisanship and war participation. Partisan voluntarism differences may have been even larger, given that home votes included Republican men *too old* to fight mixed with young Democrats who *chose not* to fight. On the other hand, non-Republican soldiers may have felt pressure to conform to their predominantly Republican peers, inflating Republican votes among Democrats and independents in the ranks (see Bensel 2004; Frank 1998; Matsui 2016; White 2014). However, the fact that those potential pressures would be pro-Republican is itself evidence of disproportionate Republican men in ranks.

The bigger limitation is that most of these votes come from the end of the war, and we cannot rule out the possibility that war experiences changed some soldiers' views, the reverse of my argument. James McPherson (1997)

TABLE 4.1 *1864 absentee soldier votes by state*

State	1864 Total State Vote (% Lincoln)	1864 Civilian Vote (% Lincoln)	1864 Soldier Vote (% Lincoln)	Difference: Soldiers – Civilian (% Lincoln)	State Vote Cast by Soldiers (%)
IA	63	59	90	+31	14
WI	56	54	82	+28	8
OH	56	53	81	+28	11
MI	55	53	78	+25	7
KY	30	30	30	0	4
ME	59	58	85	+27	5
CA	59	58	92	+34	3
VT	76	–	83	+7 (from state total)	– (Few counted)
PA	52	51	68	+17	7
RI	62	62	85	+23	1
NH	53	52	75	+23	4

Source: Benton (1915) on soldier votes, Burnham (1955) on total state votes. Civilian vote calculated.

and other historians find some anecdotal evidence of political change over time in soldiers' letters and diaries.[5] Young adults are especially susceptible to political influence, and so military-age males would respond more to war experiences and social pressures than older voters.

As a strong counterpoint, however, *early-war* soldier votes were cast in similar Republican disproportion too. For example, Pennsylvania soldiers who had not yet left the state were allowed to vote in 1861, and they cast 78 percent of their ballots for Republicans, and 88 percent of a much smaller in-state force cast Republican votes in 1862 (Benton 1915, p. 203). Likewise, the 1862 absentee soldier votes in Iowa and Wisconsin showed large Republican majorities around 80 percent, soldier votes in 1863 were closer to 85 percent, and their 1864 presidential votes were around 90 percent. Those small increases could be war effects, or they could also signal fewer Democratic volunteers as that party's leaders moved against the war. In any case, the shifts are not large and do not disrupt the overall impression of large Republican majorities among soldiers from the start, beyond those back home.

In sum, soldier votes provide the clearest systematic evidence of individual-level partisanship linked to war participation. Election returns from eleven of twenty-two Union states show large vote gaps between soldiers and civilians, indicating greater Republican war participation throughout the war.

State-Level War Participation

State-level data provide a second test for partisan asymmetries in military service. State data aggregate local and individual mechanisms, and they lack the individual-level sorting of party and combatant status that made soldier data ideal. I draw state-level tabulations from Frederick Dyer's (1908) authoritative *Compendium of the War of the Rebellion*. The data conflate volunteers and draftees, which weakens tests for partisan mechanisms among the 90 percent of volunteers. I assess white troops here and black troops below.[6] The 1860 Census gives state counts of military-age males. I calculate state rates of war participation for white men between eighteen and forty-five years old as the denominator (military-eligible for enlisting).[7] State electoral data are from Walter Dean Burnham's (1955) *Presidential Ballots, 1836–1892*.

War participation was broad. States averaged 53 percent of their white military-age males in the army (weighted by population). State contributions varied. Illinois, Indiana, and Ohio contributed the most, with close to 70 percent of eligible men at war. Oregon and California gave least, around 10 percent. Union enslaving states fell between the two groups, near 40 percent.

What of partisan war service? Figure 4.1 shows white Army service against Lincoln's 1860 vote share. States voting less for Lincoln in 1860 clearly contributed a smaller share of white combatants, as expected. The simple linear relationship is positive and strong for Union states ($r = 0.55$). Every ten-point gain in Lincoln vote share corresponds with a 4 percent gain in fighting rates. The figure plots a flexible fit line (weighted) to show the rise and then slight fall in service rates with Lincoln's votes, consistent with linear estimates. However, excluding slave states and the West Coast shifts the voting-enlistment relationship in the sixteen free contiguous states to null, even negative. In other words, the state-level relationship can't disentangle partisanship from state type. The result supports my expectation that Republican places contributed more men, with that caveat.

White County-Level Voluntarism

I turn next to county-level enlistment data. Those cover wide partisan ranges *within* each state to rule out state-level confounds in the tests above. These

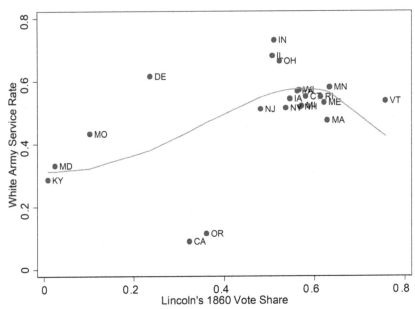

FIGURE 4.1 Total proportion of white combatants & Lincoln's 1860 vote share by state

measures focus specifically on voluntarism rather than total participation, and they include enough cases to allow statistical controls for competing explanations correlated with local partisanship. County-level data also reflect the hypothesized local partisan mechanisms better than state-level tests. Costa and Kahn (2008) conducted enlistment tests on Massachusetts soldiers at the town level from the American Civil War Research Database (ACWRD). I pursue a similar strategy for county votes on a national scale.

The ACWRD's unique individual-level soldier data gives service details for all soldiers from state-by-state Adjutant General Reports compiled during and after the war.[8] Fifteen of the twenty-two loyal states in 1860 have sufficient data for these tests – prewar residence or enlistment place for most of the state's combatants – covering the Northeast, Midwest, an enslaving state, and the West Coast.[9] For compatibility with county-level election data, I geo-located over one million Union soldiers and sailors from the fifteen states into home counties with the 1870 Census publication, which included 1850 and 1860 returns, manually matching tens of thousands of Census town names with soldier residences and enlistment places. That located 86 percent of white soldiers, 75 percent of black soldiers, and 99 percent of sailors from these states.[10] I aggregated war experiences into county-level counts of voluntarism, desertion, and casualties for each year of the war and for its entirety, transformed into proportions based on military-age males and total *serving*, as appropriate. Individual enlistment, draft, and death details include dates, enabling tests at different points in the war.

I measure local partisanship with county election data collected by the Inter-university Consortium for Political and Social Research (ICPSR 1999). For a more sensitive measure of prewar partisanship than 1860 Lincoln votes alone, I created an index averaging Republican vote share for president, House, and governor between 1856 and 1860, all highly correlated in strong prewar partisan voting patterns (Cronbach's α = 0.86; see Chapter 6 for more details). Finally, I include statistical controls for county population, immigrant proportion, and wealth per capita from the 1860 Census since each related to voting (McPherson 1997) and voluntarism (Costa & Kahn 2008). To better estimate behavior for the average *voter* rather than county, I weight all models by voting-age white males (age twenty and up in 1860). All this yields full data on 724 counties in 15 Union states.

What role did local partisanship play in filling the Union ranks? I start by testing total partisan mobilization among white men during the war. Table 4.2 presents three ordinary least squares (OLS) models predicting

TABLE 4.2 *County prewar partisanship & white voluntarism*

	Total White Volunteers 1861–1865 (MAM)		
	All States	**All but KY**	**Free Contiguous**
Republican Votes (1856–1860 prop.)	0.27*	0.31*	0.14*
	(0.05)	(0.05)	(0.06)
Total Population (1860 in 50k)	0.014*	0.015*	0.010*
	(0.001)	(0.001)	(0.002)
Immigrants (1860 prop.)	−0.13*	−0.12^	−0.03
	(0.06)	(0.07)	(0.07)
Wealth per Capita (1860)	−0.01	−0.03	−0.02
	(0.03)	(0.03)	(0.03)
Constant	0.22*	0.21*	0.28*
	(0.03)	(0.04)	(0.04)
R^2	0.13	0.17	0.06
N	724	615	572

Note: Table entries are unstandardized ordinary least squares (OLS) regression coefficients with robust standard errors in parentheses. Weighted by white voting-age male population. MAM = military-age males.
* $p < 0.05$, ^ $p < 0.10$, two-sided t-test.

enlistment rates for the full war for all fifteen states, for all but slave state Kentucky, and for free contiguous states (dropping California as well). These variations help to show the robustness of evidence across wide state variations in partisanship and politics generally.

All three models affirm that Republican counties supplied a larger share of white military-age males as volunteers to the war effort, all else equal. The strong, persistent relationship among the free contiguous states in particular reduces any remaining concerns from state-level tests that differences might reflect state-level differences other than partisanship.[11] A 20-point rise in Republican vote share (roughly one standard deviation) corresponds with a 3–6 percentage point rise in local white enlistment rates, depending on which estimate is operative. Nationally, that difference translates into 62,000–136,000 additional troops.

The results are robust in several other ways. First, partisan estimates are larger and stronger when limited to the nine states with over 90 percent of their soldiers geo-coded.[12] That partisan estimate is twice the size of the free-contiguous result ($b = 0.30$, $s.e. = 0.10$), which is remarkable given that all nine states are from that larger group of thirteen. Second, separate models for each individual free contiguous state generally show similar positive relationships between Republican votes and white voluntarism. Third, partisan results are essentially unmoved when I add denominational church capacities per capita to the models, ruling out local religious identities as an alternative explanation in place of partisanship.[13] Fourth, ecological inference estimates show white enlistment rates nine points higher for Republicans than for Democrats, yielding a fighting force that was 59 percent Republican (among soldiers who voted). Southern Democratic voters were eight points *less* likely to enlist than other voter categories.[14] In sum, the full-war county-level tests are consistent with soldier votes and state-level data: individual Republican voters and Republican places collectively were more likely to fight for the Union.

Dynamic White Voluntarism over Time

Political scientist Adam Berinsky's (2009) World War II–era tests show public war opinion moving dynamically as party elites shifted from consensus to polarization and back again, with attentive partisans closely following their leaders. Chapter 3's news analysis found a small partisan gap in war support in 1861, no clear gap in 1862, a gap again in 1863, and then a chasm in 1864. Enlistment advocacy followed a similar pattern in partisan news. The opinion leadership model therefore leads us to

TABLE 4.3 *County prewar partisanship & white voluntarism – free contiguous states*

	Portion of White Military-Age Males			
	1861 Volunteers	1862 Volunteers	1863 Volunteers	1864 Volunteers
Republican Votes (1856–1860 prop.)	0.44* (0.22)	0.25 (0.22)	0.48 (0.34)	0.65* (0.25)

Note: Table entries are standardized OLS regression coefficients with standard errors in parentheses. Same controls applied. 1861 excludes 3-month volunteers.
* $p < 0.05$, two-sided t-test.

expect war voluntarism gaps in 1864 and perhaps 1861 and 1863, but little or no partisan differences in 1862 when the Democratic war position was least distinct from Republicans.

As expected, white enlistment rates closely followed shifts in partisan news war positions. Table 4.3 presents the same OLS models of enlistment by year, focusing on the free contiguous states. For better comparability of partisan change over time, I standardize the voluntarism measure by the average voluntarism rate in each year. The results strikingly fit opinion-leadership predictions.[15]

Figure 4.2 directly shows the high congruence between party war polarization – the gap between Republican and Democratic newspapers (see Figure 3.1) – and partisan gaps in war voluntarism over time (Table 4.3). Both have the same J-pattern: a small gap in 1861, an 1862 nadir, a rebound in 1863, and wartime peaks in 1864. The close resemblance between the extent of party war polarization expressed by party leaders and local partisan enlistment gaps is remarkable.

In sum, local partisan variation predicted rates of local white enlistment patterns – but only at times when Democratic leaders supported the war less than Republicans did. That result is a striking affirmation of predictions from the party opinion-leadership model. The dynamic consistency also helps to rule out static alternative explanations for the average partisan relationship across the war that might arise from other local factors or from incomplete data, for example.

WHITE PARTISAN DESERTION

Volunteering was just the first step. What kept soldiers in the ranks once the discrepancy between imagined war and its reality became clear? Many

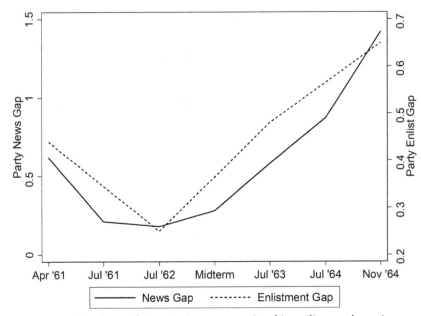

FIGURE 4.2 Partisan polarization in war news & white military voluntarism over time
Note: Party news gap calculated as the difference in party newspaper estimates in Figure 3.1.

of the same considerations influenced a soldier's choice to remain rather than desert. Staying meant risking death in battle or by disease, so desertion could be safer than service. Desertion also carried risks to life – the official penalty was execution – but deserters were more likely to escape than be caught, and few soldiers caught were put to death (Costa & Kahn 2008). Civil War soldiers served in locally organized units, so most men serving with them were neighbors, adding social rewards and punishments.[16] Despite war hardships and conscription, less than 10 percent of soldiers deserted (Costa & Kahn 2008).

The costs of desertion back home were apparently lower for soldiers from predominantly Democratic counties, where the war was less popular. With individual-level data from a random sample of U.S. military units, Costa and Kahn (2008) find that desertion rates were significantly higher for soldiers from Democratic counties. Soldiers from counties with 20 percent Republican vote in 1860 deserted at a rate of 11 percent, whereas soldiers from counties voting for Republicans at 60 percent deserted at a rate of about 9 percent. Desertion rates were also lower among men who were farmers, older, from large cities, single, native-born, literate, in heterogeneous military units, and had more money.

McPherson (1997) finds soldier letters motivating continued participation – even after the horrors of war were apparent – in terms of religious belief, unit cohesion, support from home, discipline and trust in commanders, the appeal of honor, and fear of social shaming or even execution. He says political ideology and issues, patriotism, and commitments to democracy helped glue the armies together even as the churn of war decimated their ranks, with political sentiments "leaping" off the pages of soldiers' letters. These provided a primary motivation for *fighting* once enlisted, "to shoot as they had voted" (p. 92). Some 49 percent of Union officers and 36 percent of enlisted men tied politics to the war in their writing. Emancipation grew from minority to majority support in the ranks as the war progressed, supplementing the desire to preserve the Union (pp. 118, 123). Many soldiers hated Peace Democrats ("Copperheads"), whom they saw as traitors slyly aiding the enemy.

Even after accounting for partisan enlistment patterns, partisanship might shape the likelihood of leaving the ranks through desertion. I measure desertion rates as a fraction *among those serving*, which controls for the partisan selection effect identified above. Were white soldiers from Republican places less likely to desert? Yes. Table 4.4 shows significantly lower desertion rates for white soldiers from Republican

TABLE 4.4 *Prewar partisanship & white desertion rates*

	Total White Desertion 1861–1865 (Prop. of Serving)		
	All States	All but KY	Free Contiguous
Republican Votes	−0.11*	−0.12*	−0.11*
(1856–1860 prop.)	(0.02)	(0.02)	(0.02)
Total Population (1860	0.005*	0.005*	0.006*
in 50k)	(0.001)	(0.001)	(0.001)
Immigrants (1860 prop.)	0.09*	0.08*	0.08*
	(0.03)	(0.02)	(0.02)
Wealth per Capita	0.07*	0.08*	0.08*
(1860)	(0.01)	(0.01)	(0.01)
Constant	0.05*	0.05*	0.04*
	(0.01)	(0.01)	(0.01)
R^2	0.38	0.52	0.62
N	696	604	567

Note: Table entries are ordinary least squares (OLS) regression coefficients with robust standard errors in parentheses, weighted by 1860 voting-age males.
* $p < 0.05$, two-sided t-test.

counties, and those estimates are consistent across the three models of varying state inclusion. A gain of 20 points in prewar Republican vote share corresponded with a desertion rate 2.2 percentage points lower among white troops. This is an enormous drop relative to the 8.4 percent mean in these 15 states. That rate equaled about 50,000 more men serving from total combatants. The tests are compelling because they show partisan war participation differences that extend *beyond* selection effects for voluntarism, revealing even deeper direct and indirect party influence sustaining U.S. military forces. Soldiers from places with more population, immigrants, and wealth per capita were also more likely to desert.

How did local partisanship relate to desertion over time? Soldiers from Republican places deserted at significantly lower rates in every year of the war. The size of the unstandardized partisan gap is similar for the first and second halves of the war ($b = -0.08$ and $b = -0.07$, respectively). Standardizing the gap as a proportion of average desertion rates each year, the gap is largest in 1861 and declines annually thereafter. Therefore, desertion did not follow the same dynamic opinion leadership paths over time as those for civilians considering military service.

PARTISANSHIP IN DEATH

Desertion was not the only form of avoiding the fight. One remarkable dynamic of the war was the large number of short-term shirkers, who "skedaddled" during or just before a battle, returning to their unit afterward one by one or sometimes as nearly whole units. Before battles, many Civil War soldiers feigned illness or injury to avoid combat, and as each battle commenced, many fled outright, were overwilling to help lightly injured comrades to the rear, or found a minor scrape to justify their own departure (McPherson 1997). Others sought "bomb-proof" service away from combat. For some, it was habitual; other times even the most stalwart veteran might simply break in the chaos and run away. Such was the terror of battle and the uncertainty of human psychology. Few of these temporary escapes counted as desertion. A pattern of short-term shirking might improve a soldier's odds of escaping death in combat, and politics may have been one motive.

Beyond individual soldier choices, there might be other explanations relating partisanship and war deaths. Military commanders put more faith in military units that proved their war commitment – often from Republican communities – and leaders assigned those units to do the hardest fighting. A single unit that failed to hold the line could doom the whole army, given Civil War–era battle tactics.[17] Thus, military commanders may have been reluctant to send troops from anti-war Democratic areas into the most critical combat situations. Both mechanisms – personal motives and politically informed decisions by commanders – suggest that the human costs of combat may have been borne more heavily by soldiers from Republican communities.

Disease – the most common cause of Civil War death at over 60 percent – might relate less to partisanship. Men who had little exposure to germs suddenly faced contact with thousands of other men from around the country in frequently dirty camps and hospitals, sometimes encamped near malarial swamps. Disease deaths may have been less avoidable than combat. It could strike anyone in camp. Germs and polluted waters did not distinguish by party. Of course, soldiers who shirked by feigning illness found themselves with those who were actually sick, increasing odds of contracting a lethal illness. However, soldiers who sought "bomb-proof" roles would likely have had more sanitary conditions. Thus, expectations for disease deaths are more muddled.

McPherson (1997) lists political belief – broadly conceived – as a combat motivation, a force sustaining participation not just at times of quiet but also in the maelstrom of battle. He argues the enormous casualty rates of the war could only be borne with some fortification from belief in the cause. McPherson quotes an Illinois cavalryman, who said "the *best*, and *truest*, and *bravest* of the nation" were most likely to die in battle (p. 116). It would be no surprise to find more war deaths in Republican areas because they sent their men to fight at greater rates, putting a larger share of their men at risk. But shirking dynamics would produce differences in partisan mortality rate *among troops serving*, even after accounting for those who fled by desertion. This, too, would show partisan influence beyond initial selection into service.

State Deaths

Did the war's mortal burdens fall along party lines? First, I examine how state partisanship related to deaths in combat among those serving. I divide total dead by the total of white troops serving from the state based on Dyer's (1908) statistics. Figure 4.3 shows the comparison.

The casualty results are strikingly similar to enlistment rates – more in Republican states – even though the denominator is those serving, not military-age males. The relationship is stronger for all states ($r = 0.46$)

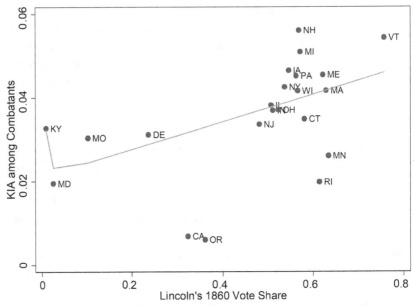

FIGURE 4.3 Combat deaths of white soldiers & Lincoln's 1860 vote share
by state

than when limited to free contiguous states ($r = 0.19$). Only the estimate
for all states is statistically significant. In contrast, state partisanship fails
predict the rate of non-combat deaths for either grouping of states
($r = 0.11$, $r = 0.06$, respectively). That highlights a unique link between
partisanship and combat, and it suggests systematic partisan differences
at another stage of war service and sacrifice. To my knowledge, this is the
first quantitative evidence of partisan asymmetries in Civil War combat
deaths, though it aligns well with qualitative historical evidence.

County-Level White Soldier Mortality

County-level data affirm the state-level relationship between partisanship
and death with better resolution. Table 4.5 presents OLS models predicting white soldier deaths in combat (or mortal wounds), disablement,
disease deaths, and total death rates, all divided by those serving. These
results are for all fifteen states, but models excluding California and
Kentucky – or limited to states with virtually all soldiers located (and
done so by residence rather than enlistment place) – produce very similar
results. As predicted, the proportion of soldiers disabled by wounds or

TABLE 4.5 *Prewar partisanship & white soldiers' deaths (prop. serving in military)*

	Killed in Action 1861–1865 (Mil.)	Wounded Out 1861–1865 (Mil.)	Died of Disease 1861–1865 (Mil.)	Total Dead 1861–1865 (Mil.)
Republican Votes (1856–1860 prop.)	0.03* (0.01)	0.21* (0.09)	0.08* (0.01)	0.11* (0.01)
Total Population (1860 in 50k)	0.001* (0.0003)	0.005* (0.001)	0.00 (0.00)	0.001* (0.0004)
Immigrants (1860 prop.)	−0.02* (0.01)	−0.12 (0.09)	−0.01 (0.01)	−0.04* (0.02)
Wealth per Capita (1860)	−0.002 (0.004)	0.06 (0.04)	−0.03* (0.01)	−0.03* (0.01)
Constant	0.03* (0.01)	−0.01 (0.04)	0.04* (0.01)	0.07* (0.01)
R^2	0.05	0.02	0.16	0.16
N	696	696	696	696

Note: Table entries are OLS regression coefficients with robust standard errors in parentheses, weighted by 1860 voting-age males.
* $p < 0.05$, two-sided t-test.

killed in action was significantly higher for soldiers from Republican areas than in Democratic places. A 20 point gain in Republican vote share meant an increase in combat mortality of 0.6 percent above an average of 4.6 percent in these states. With 140,000 Union troops killed in battle for the whole war, this difference added 840 more combat deaths among troops from Republican places, which would surpass all U.S. combat deaths in the 1863 Chattanooga Campaign.

What about the second prediction, that local prewar partisanship might shape disease deaths less? A first glance shows a similar positive relationship between Republican votes and disease deaths among those serving. A 20 percent increase in prewar Republican vote share increases soldier mortality rate substantially by 1.6 percent above an average 4.7 percent rate in these data. Given the ways in which partisans could reduce the risk of disease deaths as well as combat, this test cannot function as a placebo test in the ways that we might wish. Overall, then, we see that soldiers from Republican places suffered disproportionate casualty rates in all forms, not just in combat.

* * *

In sum, I find substantial and largely consistent evidence of individual and local disparities in several forms of white Civil War service and sacrifice across a broad range of data and methods. Next, I consider the effects of local white partisanship on the war service of African Americans and women.

MOBILIZING WAR SERVICE AMONG DISENFRANCHISED AMERICANS

Hundreds of thousands of black men risked their lives in the ranks to save the Union and destroy slavery, and tens of thousands of women worked in essential service roles that enabled victory, in what historian Elizabeth Robertson calls an "'army' of their own" (p. 2).[18] Hundreds of thousands more women and people of color made less formal but still vital contributions to the war effort. What personal and contextual factors motivated black men to enlist in the U.S. military, and what motives compelled women to volunteer for life-threatening service roles far from home? In particular, did their personal politics and the politics of the communities around them galvanize their voluntarism similar to white men? Despite vastly different social positions and circumstances, I still expect local partisanship to mobilize black men into military service and women into national service. I describe each group's essential work, their motives, and the evidence for politics in turn.

"Bullets in His Pocket": African American Service & Sacrifice

Once let the black man get upon his person the brass letter, U.S., let him get an eagle on his button, and a musket on his shoulder and bullets in his pocket, there is no power on earth that can deny that he has earned the right to citizenship.

Frederick Douglass
April 6, 1863

And then, there will be some black men who can remember that, with silent tongue, and clenched teeth, and steady eye, and well-poised bayonet, they have helped mankind on to this consummation; while, I fear, there will be some white ones, unable to forget that, with malignant heart and deceitful speech, they have strove to hinder it.

President Abraham Lincoln[19]
August 26, 1863

Free blacks from the North and former enslaved people from loyal and rebel states formed 10 percent of U.S. military forces, nearly 200,000 men all told. One in three died saving the Union and ending slavery. Black war participation was a major factor in military victory for the United States, which makes understanding their motives especially important. What drove these men to fight?

Of 4.5 million African Americans living in the United States at the start of the war, 4 million were enslaved in the South, including those held captive in loyal Border States. The United States and the Confederacy each recognized the military value of skilled and manual black labor, enslaved and free, but prejudice and politics delayed U.S. mobilization of black combatants and prevented it entirely in the Confederacy. The rebellion's use of slave labor for war gains was prodigious enough to provide legal justification for Lincoln's Emancipation Proclamation to free slaves in actively rebellious places.

Concerns over the precarious loyalty of Union slave states initially thwarted any thought of Southern freedmen or Northern free blacks serving as soldiers. Meanwhile, African Americans – Frederick Douglass most prominent among them – lobbied Congress and the president to enlist African Americans as combatants, and white allies did the same. Thousands of free black men were eager to volunteer, along with freedmen emancipated by advancing U.S. armies (or who freed themselves). Lincoln collectively called them "the great available and yet unavailed-of force for restoring the Union."

The 1863 Emancipation Proclamation and subsequent acts of Congress provided the legal framework for African American enlistment in the U.S. armed forces. Forty-five percent of black troops came from loyal states. Local Republican officials and anti-slavery groups tried to spur enlistment in these new units, but African American enlistment did not take off until Frederick Douglass and other black leaders took charge of promoting black war participation.[20] Their opinion leadership was essential in resolving the ambivalence many African Americans felt about striking blows against slaveholders to preserve a Union that had enslaved them for centuries (Parker 2010). Ultimately, a startling 78 percent of age-eligible black men from free states enlisted in the war (Costa & Kahn 2008).

The U.S. War Department began wider recruitment in the nominally loyal Border States. There they mostly mustered enslaved people who fought in exchange for emancipation. The U.S. government paid their enslavers for the loss of property. Kentucky alone provided nearly one-third of U.S. black troops who came from loyal states. A majority of black soldiers were from rebel states, virtually all freedmen. All told, three-quarters of black servicemen joined straight from slavery (Costa & Kahn 2008). Federal efforts created regiments organized as United States Colored Troops (USCT), totaling nearly 200,000 soldiers and sailors. White commissioned officers commanded these units, and black enlisted men served as sergeants (non-commissioned officers). White leaders finally permitted black men to serve as low-ranking line officers in 1865, and about seven thousand did so.

White military leaders disproportionately assigned USCT regiments to guard and fatigue duty due to prejudices among commanders who doubted their ability to fight, and black troops received lower pay than white troops until 1864. Nonetheless, black soldiers fought valiantly in dozens of battles, including the 54th Massachusetts Infantry Regiment, which was decimated at Fort Wagner and immortalized in the 1989 film *Glory*. Other prominent battles featuring African American troops included Port Hudson and Milliken's Bend in Louisiana, and The Crater near Petersburg, Virginia. Sixteen black men earned the Medal of Honor for valor.[21] Their heroic actions under fire helped change the minds of many white comrades and other Americans who heard of their brave service.

Confederate President Jefferson Davis decreed that his forces would execute captured black soldiers as slave insurrectionists. Confederate General Nathan Bedford Forrest – who founded the Ku Klux Klan terrorist group after the war – was among rebel officers who did so, butchering hundreds of captured black soldiers at Fort Pillow, Tennessee. Rebels sold other black POWs into slavery. President Lincoln vowed he would retaliate in kind against an equal number of white rebel prisoners for the execution or enslavement of black soldiers. The presence of black troops among U.S. prisoners of war ended prisoner exchanges for the second half of the war, as rebels refused to recognize black troops as combatants. Nearly 40,000 black soldiers and sailors died in the war, a substantially higher mortality rate than for white U.S. combatants (Costa & Kahn 2008).

Military Motives among African Americans

African American soldiers enlisted to establish and maintain their own freedom outside of slavery, to free others including family members, and to achieve political equality through citizenship, the last consistent with patriotic black military service throughout American history (Parker 2010). Soldier-historian George Washington Williams (1887/2012), author of the first history of black war service, said black troops were "proud of the generous invitation to aid in destroying slavery and in preserving the Union," that those who had been enslaved "were eager to establish their freedom and vindicate their manhood" (pp. 79, 99). More personally, an enlisted father promised his enslaved daughter that his regiment would arrive soon to free her: "I will have you if it cost me my life." And, in a letter to the matriarch who owned his daughter, he wrote, "The longer you keep my child from me, the longer you will burn in hell, and the quicker you will get there."[22] Wartime discrimination against black troops reduced their willingness to fight, as did worries that the United States would not respond harshly enough to rebel depravities against them (Berlin et al. 1998).

Black men in free states faced fewer existential pressures compared to men in slave states, but their disadvantaged social status continued to shape the appeal of their options. Modern studies of black political behavior emphasize the importance of group interests, social pressures, and group opinion leaders in political action (e.g. Dawson 1992; Gay 2004; Jefferson 2019; Lee 2002; White et al. 2014), which fits military voluntarism in the 1860s. Appeals to racial group interests resonate differently in black and white public opinion – messages that are more explicit exert stronger effects on black attitudes (White 2007). Extrapolations from these works suggest black Civil War leaders and communities probably played an extensive role in military enlistment decisions of black men.

Leaders seeking African American enlistment in the war held public meetings in churches and other public venues, leveraging opinion leadership and social ties (Williams 1887/2012). When a white official asked a black reverend the best means to recruit newly free black men into the Army, he replied, "The ministers would talk to them, and the young men would enlist."[23] Even so, some recruiting posters featured quotes from exclusively white leaders, touting "protection, pay, and a call to military duty" and reminders of Lincoln's decree to free three million enslaved people.[24]

The Influence of Local White Partisanship

To the extent black Americans felt the pull of partisanship, nearly all would have sided with Republicans, even as Republican temerity on fighting slavery continued to disappoint. Soldier-historian Williams (1887/2012), for instance, was active in Republican politics after the war, but Northern whites had denied most black men voting rights before the war, and so they could not express their party preference at the polls. Nonetheless, the social and institutional context of local partisanship likely played a role for motivating African American war mobilization as well.

Here, I focus on whether local prewar partisan environments (reflecting white male votes) corresponded with African American war service. Even though local voting tallies cannot tell us about black partisanship, white Republican leaders shaped local public opinion, organized recruitment drives, and solicited volunteers in Republican places. Likewise, social pressure in pro-war Republican areas might have mobilized enlistment, though segregation rooted in prejudice still would have limited interaction between white partisans and their black neighbors. Conversely, the threat of violence from white Democrats may have been demobilizing for black residents in those areas, though perhaps it could *motivate* local blacks to enlist, to get away from local racial hostility and danger. I expect the sum of these local pressures produced greater black enlistment rates in Republican places. Those pressures would be weaker once soldiers were in the ranks, however, given that their immediate comrades would not reflect the balance of partisan voters from back home, unlike for white troops.

White Partisanship in Black War Service

I begin again with state-level enlistment from Dyer's (1908) tallies and Census data on black military-age males. My denominator estimate for military-age males (ages fifteen to thirty-nine) includes free blacks and those held as slaves in the loyal slave states, given the extensive service of slaves freed by joining the ranks. As expected, estimates for black Army service show the same overall positive relationships as for whites ($r = 0.46$), and unlike for whites, they are similarly large in free contiguous states ($r = 0.38$). Republican states had higher levels of war service from their black residents. County-level data provide a more localized test. I identify individual black soldiers by their service in USCT units or in one of the five state-organized regiments, for enlisted troops only. The full-war models here cover 1863–1865 for black soldiers. Table 4.6 presents the results of black voluntarism models for all fifteen states, for all but Kentucky, and for the free contiguous states.

TABLE 4.6 *Prewar white partisanship & black war participation*

	Total Black Volunteers 1863–1865 (MAM)			Total Black Desertion 1863–1865 (Prop. of Serving)		
	All States	All but KY	Free Contiguous	All States	All but KY	Free Contiguous
Republican votes (1856–1860 prop.)	0.34	0.86*	0.48	0.06^	0.07	0.07
	(0.25)	(0.31)	(0.40)	(0.03)	(0.06)	(0.06)
Total population (1860 in 50k)	−0.03*	−0.03*	−0.04*	0.002	0.002	0.002
	(0.01)	(0.01)	(0.02)	(0.002)	(0.002)	(0.002)
Immigrants (1860 prop.)	0.62	0.86*	1.29*	0.04	0.04	0.04
	(0.39)	(0.41)	(0.51)	(0.07)	(0.08)	(0.08)
Wealth per capita (1860)	0.16	0.13	0.17	−0.02	−0.02	−0.02
	(0.18)	(0.20)	(0.23)	(0.04)	(0.05)	(0.05)
Constant	0.05	−0.27	−0.13	0.02	0.02	0.02
	(0.18)	(0.18)	(0.21)	(0.04)	(0.04)	(0.04)
R^2	0.02	0.03	0.03	0.02	0.01	0.01
N	572	463	421	288	244	244

Note: Table entries are OLS regression coefficients with robust standard errors in parentheses, clustered by state, weighted by 1860 white voting-age males.

* $p < 0.05$, ^ $p < 0.10$, two-sided t-test.

Consistent with expectations and similar to partisan dynamics for white troops, the positive estimates indicate Republican counties sent larger shares of their African American men to war across the duration of the war. The model excluding slave-state Kentucky (which also gave virtually no votes to Republicans) reaches statistical significance. Substantively, a twenty-point rise in prewar Republican vote share (one standard deviation) is associated with a seventeen-point increase in the proportion of local black military-age males volunteering for service. By contrast, desertion rates among black soldiers were mostly unrelated to local white partisanship, as expected once those soldiers left local white political environments for the battlefields and camps.

Forty thousand black men died in U.S. military service during the war, three-quarters due to disease.[25] Assessments of black casualties as a proportion of men's service tell a mostly non-partisan story similar to desertion dynamics, as Table 4.7 shows, though the estimate for all states is similar to the white death estimate and just short of statistical significance. Once beyond the influence of local white partisan environments that contributed to black voluntarism, there is not much detectable influence of white partisanship on black military shirking or sacrifice.

In mobilizing soldiers to defend the nation in its most destructive war, Republican places sent more of their men to fight – black and white – than

TABLE 4.7 *Prewar white partisanship & black soldiers' deaths*

	Total Black Deaths 1863–1865 (Prop of Mil.)		
	All States	All but KY	Free Contiguous
Republican Votes	0.10^	0.07	0.07
(1856–1860 prop.)	(0.05)	(0.08)	(0.08)
Total Population	−0.002	−0.002	−0.002
(1860 in 50k)	(0.003)	(0.003)	(0.003)
Immigrants	−0.05	−0.05	−0.05
(1860 prop.)	(0.11)	(0.11)	(0.11)
Wealth per Capita	−0.08	−0.08	−0.08
(1860)	(0.06)	(0.07)	(0.07)
Constant	0.15*	0.17*	0.17*
	(0.06)	(0.07)	(0.07)
R^2	0.02	0.02	0.02
N	288	244	244

Note: Table entries are OLS regression coefficients with robust standard errors in parentheses, weighted by 1860 voting-age males.
* $p < 0.05$, ^ $p < 0.10$, two-sided t-test.

Democratic places. Although African American war motives and social positions surely differed from whites, these results suggest a key role for local partisan leaders and towns in galvanizing soldiers to suppress a partisan rebellion.

"You Will Probably Not See Our Names": Women at War

Give her the soldier's rite! She fought the hardest fight ...
She staunches his blood, cools the fever-burnt breath,
And the wave of her hand stays the Angel of Death.

Poems from *In Honor of the*
National Association of
Civil War Army Nurses (1910)[26]

Women had their own reasons not to aid in the government's salvation, given their second-class status in the nation and the home.[27]Nonetheless, tens of thousands of women volunteered as nurses, laundresses, and cooks. Even more made clothing and supported aid drives to collect supplies for the troops. Though legally barred from combat roles in the war, a few disguised themselves to fight. And, of course, many encouraged the men around them to fight or abstain. Most women in formal roles were white and middle class, with others excluded, but working class white and black women made critical war contributions as well.[28]

Many studies on women's political participation show that women's motives, their opportunity, and their recruitment into civic activity differ from men in important ways (e.g. Burns et al. 2001; Carpenter & Moore 2014; Corder & Wolbrecht 2016; McConnaughy 2013). That warrants caution in expecting similar dynamics for women's mobilization into war service. On the other hand, women's and men's partisan behavior is often more similar than different (e.g. Box-Steffensmeier et al. 2004; Corder & Wolbrecht 2016; Norrander 1999; Pew Research Center 2018). In the Civil War era and throughout much of the nineteenth century, historian Rebecca Edwards (1997) describes women's substantial participation in partisan politics, attending meetings, canvassing voters, and giving speeches. In many ways, women's partisan culture looked much like men's in their community, despite lacking a vote. More broadly, Edwards argues the war's intervention in women's traditional home and family spheres helped facilitate women's broader involvement in politics.

I have no equivalent location data with which to analyze women's participation. Similarly, women did not control the press, and editors often excluded their voices from the news, which thwarts other tests

similar to those for men in this book. But, what women said about the
war and their participation in it mirrors rhetoric from leaders and men,
which makes partisan views a plausible motivator of voluntarism for
women as well. Republican newspapers and leaders advocated women's
war service as well, more so than Democrats, providing more reason to
expect partisan motives for women and partisan gaps in their war
participation.

Historian Jane Schultz (2004) documents women's essential war service in military hospitals. An "army of relief workers" over 21,000 strong
labored for the Union doing physically and emotionally difficult work as
matrons, nurses, laundresses, and cooks (p. 3). Women comprised about
a third of hospital staff in otherwise male military environments, and one
in ten were black women. Many women overcame resistance from
acquaintances and administrators who doubted their propriety in serving,
but that social pressure deterred others. Hospital worker voluntarism was
strongest in the first two years of war when national partisan divides over
the war were weaker.

Like men, they sought war service out of patriotism, Christian duty,
adventure, financial need – and, plausibly, political views. Schultz (2004)
writes, "The zeal with which young men enlisted in the first year of the
war was matched by women seeking hospital positions" (p. 12). Some,
like Elizabeth Wheeler of Massachusetts, even equated their motives with
those of a soldier: "When the first company enlisted from Worcester, and
my brother went with them, my whole soul was aroused, and had I been a
man I should have counted one of the number" (p. 47). Another woman
shared soldiers' deep contempt for the Confederates she sometimes had to
treat: "How I hate my rebel wounded. I don't think I can dress their
wounds anymore" (p. 79). Many women died of disease, like the men
they cared for, and enemy fire killed others in combat zones (Schultz
2004).

Women also galvanized local social groups into women's aid societies –
a vast network with tens of thousands of tiny ad hoc supply factories for
troops, knitting socks, collecting food donations, and raising money to
purchase items for sick and wounded soldiers. Eventually organized
under the unified banner of the U.S. Sanitary Commission, the groups
contributed the modern equivalent of nearly half a billion dollars in
supplies (Schultz 2004). On Election Day 1862, the *Chicago Tribune*
(IL-R) printed a letter by "6 ladies" who identified their party loyalties
as they denied that donated goods were *sold* to soldiers. "The tories
[Democrats] started this story in order to make loyal people think, that

it would not be worth while to send anything for the sick." Mary Livermore, a Republican journalist, organized the first U.S. Sanitary Fair in 1863 Chicago to raise money to supply troops and encourage patriotism (Lawson 2002). Other women followed her lead, running Sanitary Fairs around the country that raised millions of dollars from tens of thousands of attendees. Leading women shared credit for the fairs with men, even as they did most of the work. The fairs were formally nonpartisan, but their late war support made them inherently partisan.

Historian Judith Giesberg (2009) writes how loyal working class women sustained local economies by managing farms, working in factories, supplying the military, and caring for military men and the dead – what she calls an "army at home." Wealthier women contributed their own money to local bounties incentivizing military voluntarism, as the *New York Sun* (NY-I, July 1864) reported. Women also lobbied officials and formed groups like the National Women's Loyal League to rouse women into active Union war support. Women's rights activist Elizabeth Cady Stanton was a key advocate. In one of the group's tracts, Caroline Kirkland decried the wickedness of rebel women, whom she dehumanized as "fish-women . . . in times of war and commotion, bad women, like bad men, find an opportunity of coming to the surface" (quoted in Giesberg 2009, p. 125).

DeAnne Miller and Lauren Cook (2003) recount the lives of many women who surreptitiously joined the Union army, among hundreds who did so, despite the challenges of keeping their secret in close quarters with their comrades. Predating modern recognition of transgender people, some kept their biological sex hidden for decades after the war. Others may have gone undetected entirely. The motives of these fighting women were probably similar to those of enlisting men, as with the young women who wished to join them but who were restrained by their sex.

In sum, despite the dearth of data for more systematic tests, women likely shared their community's partisan views, and those individual and local forces probably spurred their service in ways that resembled local men, to the extent allowed. The scholarship here supports the idea that women and men joined the war for similar reasons, even as their social positions set them apart.

CONCLUSIONS

To put down the rebellion, Americans needed the will to sustain the Union with their votes while transforming themselves into agents of death, with hundreds of thousands dying to secure those ends. The revolutions wrought in the Civil War era – Union, abolition, equal protection, and more – were impossible without the military strength to sustain the United States against the armed rebellion rejecting the 1860 elections that empowered Republicans. "The progress of our arms, upon which all else chiefly depends," as Lincoln said in his Second Inaugural Address. How did ordinary partisanship mobilize the war's violence? This chapter tested those relationships, building on prior studies of Civil War participation motives from extensive anecdotal accounts and systematic quantitative tests (Costa & Kahn 2008; Frank 1998; Matsui 2016; McPherson 1997; White 2014).

Having already found greater war support among Republican leaders in the news, wartime soldier votes showed that individual Republican voters were likelier to fight. State- and county-level data indicated some combination of individual and local partisanship differentially mobilizing three stages of war participation among white residents in state, county, and local data – war voluntarism, lower desertion rates, and higher casualty rates. The last may be the first statistical evidence of lethal *partisan* differences in the costs of the Civil War. Partisan war voluntarism differences were especially large in the last year of the war, when Republican and Democratic leaders disagreed most.

Together, the results indicate static and dynamic partisan opinion leadership conditioning who bore the burdens of war and who abstained over time. In other words, ordinary partisanship systematically mobilized partisan warfare, though the differences are not absolute – many Democrats fought and many Republicans shirked their opportunity to serve. Opinion leadership is the most plausible primary mechanism given the elite and mass level evidence, with reinforcement from individual perceptions and social influence. Although observationally equivalent in my data, opinion leadership stands out in light of cross-temporal evidence on wartime public opinion and general limits on public reasoning (e.g. Berinsky 2009; Converse 2000). Politics is too complicated for most people to make choices without guidance, let alone life-and-death decisions for themselves. Is there a threat worth going to war over? Is it worth me *killing* and *dying* for? Few people are equipped to make those judgments without guidance from group leaders they trust.

I concluded by examining war service among African Americans and women, whose contributions have often gone untold. The question was whether the partisan dynamics driving white men to volunteer for the Union military shaped the voluntarism of these disenfranchised groups, despite diverging social positions. The answer seems to be a tentative yes for black men and plausible but uncertain for women. Local war voluntarism by African American men generally followed the contours of local white partisanship in the free states, likely due to local white partisan leaders who facilitated enlistment opportunities and encouraged local black men to join in concert with black leaders. Local partisan influences seem to have dispersed once black troops were in the ranks. The materials for evaluating women's war service are far more limited. Nonetheless, women's stated motives seem to align with those of men, and partisan leaders, communities, and newspapers surely differed in encouraging women's war participation, in line with shifting partisan war divides.

In bearing the costs of the nation's most destructive war, Republicans served and sacrificed more than Democrats did, especially late in the war. Documenting these partisan differences is historically important, showing the uneven costs of war paid across political geography. It also helps to explain the intensity of partisan resentments after the war between those who bore the brunt and those who abstained – not just in service but also in death – let alone hatred of the white Southerners who caused their deaths. The enlistment mechanisms may have been formally non-partisan, and war-supporters generally eschewed casting war motives in explicitly partisan terms, but party war positions polarized military action among partisans in the public. Likewise, the lopsided soldier vote (and their violent vitriol against Peace Democrats described elsewhere) attest to how much the people actually fighting the war viewed anti-war Democrats as destructive and dangerous.

These violent partisan disparities align better with historical arguments highlighting corrosive Northern partisanship (e.g. Weber 2006) than competing claims of resistance confined to rhetoric (e.g. Neely 2017; Smith 2006). Democratic war opposition hindered U.S. efforts to fill the ranks during an existential crisis. More broadly, partisan polarization in civil war participation shows the lethal potential of ordinary partisanship when party leaders call their followers into extraordinary violence. That recognition dramatically expands our understanding of mass partisan potency, far beyond the dislike, distance, and discrimination found in recent American political behavior studies.

The next chapter traces partisan news patterns shaping Northern voting behavior during the war, including extreme rhetoric that incited low-level violence *within* the North, and which nearly produced *widespread* partisan violence – even rebellion – in the ostensibly loyal states.

PART II

BALLOTS IN A PARTISAN CIVIL WAR

5

Election News during Wartime

Loyalty, Racism, Retrospection, & Violence

with Tim Klein & Elias Shammas

A vote for [Republican] Arnold is a vote to avenge the blood of our dead – a vote for [Democrat] Sherman is a vote to insult their memory.

Chicago Tribune (IL-R)
November 4, 1862

Our friends in the field look to the voters at home to support their bullets with our ballots. Shall we not do it?

Berkshire County Eagle (MA-R)
October 30, 1862

Every bullet fired in this unholy rebellion at the hearts of our loyal countrymen ... was fired by a disloyal Democrat; for a man has to be a Democrat before he can be a traitor. ... the brave and devoted men ... who now sleep in their bloody shrouds, went down by shots and shells fired by disloyal Democrats...Fathers and mothers who are mourning over lost sons were made childless. ... Wives made widows. ... Orphan children. ... The flags of the Republic riddled and torn by shot and shell ... aimed by rebel Democrats ... who howl with fiendish joy when their Democratic sympathizers hurl their fierce malediction against the Government.

Sen. Henry Wilson (MA-R)
U.S. Senate speech[1]
February 21, 1863

The electoral stakes have never been as high, before or since, as they were during the Civil War, as the fate of the nation hung in the balance. Northerners were dying by the hundreds of thousands in the war, Republicans increasingly viewed slavery as a war target, and both parties were acutely aware of Democrats' recently severed ties with the partisans now at war with the United States. The choices set before voters were momentous. How did partisan leaders frame those choices in wartime elections amidst epochal national events, mind-boggling casualties, and extreme partisan conflict? We expect party loyalty from editors backing their party's candidates and policies, along with motivated reasoning that frames war progress, blame, and casualties in line with partisan war views. We test those expectations with election dates in our representative sample of twenty-four newspapers.[2]

Modern voting research and historical accounts are surprisingly consistent in attributing voting behavior to three fundamental factors: (1) party loyalty, (2) racial orientations, and (3) retrospective voting.[3] Party loyalty is utmost, minimizing persuasion in partisan campaigns. But racial attitudes and national conditions (retrospective voting) present opportunities for winning over ambivalent voters. We argue the partisan press – an arm of each party's campaign – reinforced partisan loyalty at the polls by emphasizing partisan enmity and encouraging motivated reasoning about the war, setting the stage for stable voting behavior that looked almost mundane, as if nothing significant was changing. This opinion leadership helped voters rationalize habitual partisan votes when asked to sustain or extinguish the war and the nation at the ballot box.

Beyond the majority of loyal partisans, campaigns sought to attract the few undecided and conflicted voters with clashes over the country's well-being, each party's ability to achieve peace and national reunion, and the status of African Americans. For Democrats, this meant encouraging negative views of national well-being and appealing to white supremacy. Republicans focused on the importance of national salvation, war successes, and Democratic disloyalty to the Union. With an eye toward upcoming chapters on voting stability and war casualties, we are especially interested in representations of the war's progress, how party leaders differently framed the war's human costs, efforts to link the war with voting, and the distribution of blame.

Election campaigns also enflame partisan conflict as leaders try to mobilize their supporters through the mobilizing and reinforcing emotions of anger and outrage (Valentino et al. 2011). Intergroup competition between strong social identities fuels heated rhetoric and intense animosity in most election cycles (Sood & Iyengar 2016). But campaigns during a partisan civil war threatened to produce mass violence between partisans *in the North*. We evaluate that danger here. These last tests further isolate the *partisan* nature of violence in the Civil War era, apart from the sectional divisions between Republicans and Southern

Democrats that conflated so many other factors. We begin, however, by setting expectations about the power (and limits) of partisan campaign messages.

Weighing Campaign Effects

Campaigns influence vote choice and turnout, but top-down messages generally have small electoral effects. The sound and fury on both sides tends to cancel out. Only when one side's message volume overpowers the other do small shifts in voting appear – a few percentage points at most (Darr & Levendusky 2014; Erikson & Wlezien 2012; Gerber et al. 2011; Huber & Arceneaux 2009; Sides & Vavreck 2013; Zaller 1992). Party strongholds during the Civil War naturally had more lopsided messaging. Partisan campaigns are also limited when people opt out of reading opposing partisan sources, and others avoid politics entirely (Arceneaux & Johnson 2013; Holzer 2014; Zaller 1992). Non-partisan election news today has similarly small vote effects in the general election (e.g. Sides & Vavreck 2013). By contrast, conversations had between ordinary people tend to have the most influence on voting through persuasion and mobilizing appeals (e.g. Beck et al. 2002; Mutz 2006; Sinclair 2012; Walsh 2004). Perhaps the best chance for leaders to influence the public, then, was to activate social networks to spread the party's mobilizing and persuasive messages from person to person (Druckman et al. 2018; Lazarsfeld et al. 1944; Nickerson 2008). All that tempers expectations of direct partisan message effects in Civil War elections, but party leaders still worked to move those margins and to reach non-activists indirectly through enormous canvassing efforts.

REINFORCING PARTY LOYALTY

The main function of campaigns is to reinforce the loyalty of partisans and mobilize them to vote (Gelman & King 1993; Lazarsfeld et al. 1944). Most federal elections have few undecided voters to persuade from the start, and so campaigns focus on turning out their loyal voters. Nineteenth century elections were much the same (Edwards 1997). "[C]ampaigns centered around the ability of each military organization to mobilize its full strength on election day" (Silbey 1977, p. 11), with messages "designed to activate and reinforce long-standing partisan predispositions" (p. 166). Democrats "rallied the voters long since identified with their cause to their familiar banner by invoking memories of their party-nation" (Neely 2017, p. 82). And the *Boston Journal* (MA-R, Nov 1864) instructed, "It is not of much use to talk politics now with inveterate opponents. They are joined to their idols for this campaign at least. What we want now is to get out our own strength."[4]

Both parties talked of setting aside party in favor of the national interest in 1861, and they even fielded a few fusion tickets that fall, combining their forces (Smith 2006). Democrats shifted to caustic criticism of Republicans before the next year's midterm votes, however, and thereafter. Republicans continued no-party rhetoric in 1862, but they deployed it as a cudgel against Democrats. Both parties made positive appeals and negative attacks, but negativity dominated, like today. Attack messaging is effective, even though voters say they dislike it (e.g. Albertson & Gadarian 2015; Ansolabehere & Iyengar 1995; Krupnikov 2011; Krupnikov & Easter 2013; Smith & Searles 2014).

Newspapers were explicit about the need for party loyalty and strong turnout on Election Day, like the *Cheshire Republican* (NH-D, March 1863), which thundered, "[t]he Democrat whose failure to vote enables the enemy to gain an important advantage, is just as censurable as one who joins the enemy." The *La Crosse Democrat* (WI-D, July 1864) prescribed, "Hang the Christian who will not stand up for his church or the man who will not fight for his party." The *Chicago Tribune* (IL-R, Nov 1862) exhorted Republicans: "Vote yourself, and then see that your neighbors vote. . . . No shirking to-day; meet the issue manfully." And the *Cincinnati Enquirer* (OH-D, Nov 1864) wrote, "We trust every Democratic elector will vote early today, and then rally out his McClellan neighbor."

The papers described local and national electioneering events paralleling the organization and content of war mobilization, just as war mobilization had paralleled prewar political campaign activities. Mass meetings, rallies, and parades were common. Coverage emphasized massive turnout to impress readers of their party's popular strength, motivation, and organizational prowess. Mentions of opposing events compared crowd size unfavorably, derided speakers, and counterargued. For example, the *Cincinnati Enquirer* (OH-D, Nov 1864) described a Democratic rally in Kentucky as "the greatest ever held in the county. . . . The torch light procession was the result of twenty-four hours' notice, and although the Lincolnites had one at the same time . . . it fell far short of the Democratic display." The *Louisville Journal* (KY-D, July 1864) said Republican meetings "are all thinly attended and by no means enthusiastic."

In a time when parties distributed ballots to their supports, many newspapers warned supporters to watch for mixed party tickets, made by the opposition to gain votes on the sly. They also accused the other of suppressing soldiers' votes (with each claiming the troops favored them), using soldiers at the polls to suppress voters, and fraud by ineligible voters or others casting multiple of ballots. All the while, both sides confidently predicted victory if the election went off fairly.[5]

Naturally, all papers backed their party (as listed in Rowell's directory). We coded party support on a five-point party scale (–1 explicit Democrats to +1 explicit Republicans). For the midterm dates, five of seven Democratic papers scored –0.5 or lower for the midterm dates, but two were much closer to neutral. Nine of 12 Republican papers were equally clear in their Republican endorsements.[6] Beyond in-text endorsements, several newspapers printed partisan banners above their editorial columns endorsing whole party tickets. Half the newspapers did so in the 1864 contest – all the Democratic papers and 42 percent of the Republican papers. None of the independent papers printed full-party endorsements. In short, the partisan papers were clear about for whom their readers should vote.

Partisan Moral Disengagement

Throughout the war, the two parties reinforced loyal us-vs.-them partisanship with the extreme rhetoric of moral disengagement (Bandura et al. 1996). They represented their opponents as disloyal, evil, national threats, and less than human – the same language war supporters used against rebels. That made violence against *Northern* partisan opponents easier to accept, as we detail later.

Treason

The lines between legitimate opposition, disloyalty, and treason were murky in a partisan civil war. Talk of disloyalty was common in the news. Across the war, Republican papers mentioned disloyalty in Union states (coded 0, 1) in 61 percent of war pages, more than Democratic papers at 44 percent ($b = 0.16$, *s.e.* = 0.06, $p < 0.01$). Roughly one in three loyalty mentions accused a *party* of disloyalty. For the midterms, 64 percent of Republican pages and 17 percent of Democratic pages called their opponents disloyal. By the presidential election, that rate rose to 81 percent for Republicans and 42 percent for Democrats. These accusations appeared much more often at election time than other points in the war. (In a few cases, the accusations against Democrats were true.)

For the presidential election, the *Boston Journal* (MA-R, Nov 1864) wrote, "Have you voted? ... We ought to bury secret conspiracy, treason and anarchy at the North under such a majority that it will not dare to lift a finger," and they blasted the Democratic "platform constructed by the convicted traitor Vallandigham." Likewise, the *Berkshire County Eagle* (MA-R, Nov 1864) alleged, "The Copperhead [Democratic] ticket receives the support of all who desire the dismemberment of the Republic." And the *Chicago Tribune* (IL-R, Nov 1864) claimed "every disloyal man in Chicago" would vote for Democrats. Republican voters were "men whose loyalty and patriotism have never been impeached! ... On which side are you? Vote the Union War Ticket." This they repeated dozens of times across their pages that day.

Democrats responded in kind. The *Louisville Journal* (KY-D, July 1864) wrote illogically and deceptively:

Mr. Lincoln is working for the rebellion as clearly as they are working for Mr. Lincoln ... we will wage an undying hostility to both these rebellions, one against the integrity of the Union, and the other against the principles of the Constitution. ... The rebel declaration in favor on Lincoln ... ought to open the eyes of those supporters of the ticket who are not themselves conscious traitors.

Republicans also emphasized Democratic disloyalty by highlighting their party ties to rebels. Republicans identified the rebels as Democrats in 6 percent of midterm pages on the war ($p > 0.10$) and 14 percent of the 1864 election pages ($b = 0.14$, $s.e. = 0.06$ $p < 0.05$), but minimally on other dates. For one, the *Detroit Advertiser & Tribune* (MI-R, Nov 1864) quoted Senator Sumner's speech: "A sham Democracy has been the slave of slavery, and Democrats inaugurated the rebellion. All the States now in rebellion were at its outset Democratic States, while all its leaders were Democrats. ... And now at this moment the Democratic party are but guerilla bands – in fact, the Northern wing of the rebellion."

Evil & Inhuman

Republicans painted Peace Democrats and other war opponents as evil in 14 percent of midterm war pages ($p < 0.01$). For example, the *Chicago Tribune* (IL-R, Nov 1862) blasted "the modern Democracy, whose efforts and wickedness almost surpass belief." And the *Berkshire County Eagle* (MA-R, Nov 1864) reported this exchange: "'Three cheers for Lincoln' shouted a Union man. 'Three cheers for the devil' growled a copperhead."

War supporters (e.g. Republicans) were rarely called evil (7 percent, coded 0, 1), but the few cases were always Democratic papers. The pro-war *Missouri Republican* (MO-D, July 1863) saw wickedness on both sides: "The wrath of the [abolition] radicals and the insane gibberings of secessionists will pass away, or only be remembered as instances of human weakness and depravity."

Partisans also dehumanized the other side. The *Cincinnati Enquirer* (OH-D, Nov 1864) conflated Republicans and abolitionists: "Such creatures are not human – they are worse than brutes even – fiends, whom it would be a vile libel on the human race to call men." Republicans routinely called Democrats "Copperheads" – a venomous snake – and the *Boston Journal* (MA-R, Nov 1864) called that party "a breeding-nest for traitors."

National Threats

Civil War partisans saw their opponents as existential threats. The *Chicago Tribune* (IL-R, Nov 1862) printed a local soldier's letter: "we find a majority of those who stayed at home, are opposed to us; and are not only willing to see us defeated, but are on the eve of commencing a war on our rear." A win for Democrats, he said, risked a second rebellion. In the midterm, the *Cincinnati Enquirer* (OH-D, Oct 1862) warned of a Republican "system of espionage and terrorism" around the election and declared "our free institutions ... were never in so great danger as at this moment. ... If the election shall result in the return of a Democratic majority ... we may, afterward, breathe freer and hope, whatever our losses and sufferings, that all is not lost. ... [But] If we lose this election in these Central States, the country is gone – gone as a Union, and gone as a habitable part of the globe for real freemen." Threat assessments could be even more partisan: 9 percent of war pages in Democratic papers at the 1864 election claimed the war's main purpose was to hurt Democrats.

In sum, party news went to negative extremes to bind their own partisans at the ballot box.

WHITE SUPREMACY AT THE BALLOT BOX

Racial attitudes and identities influenced voting during the Civil War, much as they do today, with effects over and above those for partisanship (e.g. Acharya et al. 2018; Jardina 2019; Kalmoe & Piston 2013; Kinder & Kam 2010; Kinder & Sanders 1996). Naturally, those effects are stronger when campaigns emphasize race (e.g. Mendelberg 2001; Sides et al. 2018;

Sides & Vavreck 2013; Tesler 2016; Valentino et al. 2002; White 2007; White et al. 2014).

Democrats were the party of white supremacy in the nineteenth and early twentieth centuries (Edwards 1997). The Southern wing of the Democratic Party dominated the national organization, making it strongly pro-slavery. Northern Democrats advocated slavery's westward migration and supported "Black Codes" in their states that stripped civil rights from black residents and barred others from moving into the state. Many of the most bigoted white voters were already Democrats as a result. Long-standing Democratic efforts to depict "Black Republicans" as radicals reached feverish levels after Lincoln deployed emancipation as a war measure against the rebellion. That's not to say white Republicans weren't racist – most probably were.[7] But their racial views were generally less hostile than those among Democrats.

Civil War Democrats saw the potential for the public's widespread racial prejudices to pull support away from the Republican majority, and perhaps to realign those voters into a Democratic majority. Republicans were less confident that their racial views could hold public support on their own, and so they sought to defend emancipation as essential for the war and as a means to punish traitors, with less attention to the moral case for freeing the slaves. Historian Mark Neely (2017) acknowledges the 1864 Democratic campaign was racist, but he says everybody was at that time, and he denies any explicit white supremacy advocacy.[8] The evidence here from representative papers shows white supremacy was *central* to Democratic appeals in the midterm elections and again in 1864, and not for Republicans.

Republican newspapers were more likely than Democratic ones to endorse Lincoln's Emancipation Proclamation freeing slaves in rebellious areas, or even favor national emancipation through the 13th Amendment. Eleven of twelve Republican papers endorsed ending all U.S. slavery by war's end, and the twelfth endorsed emancipation in rebel areas. Democratic papers split between accepting emancipation in rebelling states and rejecting it everywhere. By the 1864 election, 29 percent of Democratic papers argued abolition had become the main war goal, versus 8 percent for Republicans.[9]

What did partisan views on race sound like? For Democrats, any gain in status for black men, however small, threatened white supremacy. The *Cheshire Republican* (NH-D, Mar 1863) alleged Republican plots in jarring terms for midterm elections: "In the name of the nigger they obtained power; in the name they will use their power to rob the people of their liberties." That was under the headline "Subjugating the North," as the paper rejected enlisting black men. The Democratic paper quoted a soldier's father: "I have always been a Republican. . . . We have letters from my son in the army saying that, if you could see your first born wading in the mud half leg deep, with sixty pounds upon his back, with a nigger by his side on horse-back with his gloves on, you would never vote the Republican ticket again; and we have taken heed to his advice." Taking the same tack, the *Cincinnati Enquirer* (OH-D, Oct 1862) wrote, "The doctrine of the Abolition-Republican party ... is to cast four millions of negroes among the working people of the North, and thus ruin free white labor." And the *New York Herald* (NY-I, July 1862), which backed Democrats in fall elections, castigated Republicans advocating for black troops: "The *Tribune* wants to elevate them to the level of white men, by putting arms in their hands," which the paper called "radical treason against government" for its potential to enflame the enslaving Union states.

Democrats enlisted white supremacy again in 1864 to boost partisan support and war opposition. A month after Lincoln's nomination, the *La Crosse Democrat* (WI-D, July 1864) described the war as "a murderous abolition crusade for cotton and niggers." The *Davenport Democrat* (IA-D, Nov 1864) wrote that casting Democratic ballots was a civic duty "to serve your country and your race." The *Democrat* asked, "Will you sustain the man who would barter away your country for the freedom of a few Africans? ... do you support the white man's Democratic party to Lincoln's nigger party?"[10] The *Missouri Republican* (MO-D, Nov 1864) said Republicans sought white "enslavement." And the *Cincinnati Enquirer* (OH-D, Nov 1864): "Stand to the front, white man! Vote while you have a chance to vote! Once for all – once in a life time – be in the foremost line of battle today!"[11]

Republicans tried to blunt Democratic attacks by calling out their racial demagoguery. On Election Day 1862, the *Chicago Tribune* (IL-R) wrote:

If, by reason of the lies which are told by the Tory Democracy, in relation to the cause and end of the war for the preservation of the Union; if by reason of an unworthy fear that a black man liberated from slavery, may come North to look for his bread; if as the result of the countless lies that the tories have told, and the mad appeals that they have made to popular prejudice, fear and hate – they have a triumph, we have little hereafter to expect but anarchy or despotism.

Two years later, Republican Senator Charles Sumner similarly sought to thwart Democratic race baiting over emancipation in a speech to an Irish-American audience, printed by the *Boston Journal* (MA-R, Nov 1864):

"It is a mistake to suppose that if the slaves are liberated they will compete with the labor of the North. They will not come North." In the same issue, the *Journal* endorsed the 13th Amendment, which they thought would require electing more Republicans to Congress: "It is extremely desirable that the Union men should gain new members enough – only three or four more – to give them two-thirds of the new House, and the ability, therefore, to carry the amendment of the Constitution abolishing slavery."

Republicans advanced a practical case for emancipation, and they equated Democratic opposition to it with treason. In November 1862, the *Boston Journal* (MA-R) quoted from a Republican speech: "It is not as an Abolitionist that I demand at all the emancipation of the slave; I demand it – if I demand it at all – as a war measure, necessary for the suppression of the rebellion and to restore the integrity of the national territory, and to preserve the national life. . . . [It is supported by all] not in secret sympathy with the rebels." The *Chicago Tribune* (IL-R, Nov 1862) and *Berkshire County Eagle* (MA-R, Oct 1862) wrote much the same, aligning with the Lincoln Administration's position.[12]

WAR VOTES & CASTING BLAME

The Civil War directly affected nearly every American, and partisan campaigns made the war a singular electoral focus.[13] How did party newspapers represent war views, connect the war to voting, frame the war's progress or stagnation, and direct the credit or blame that might follow?

War Views on Election Day

The parties campaigned clearly on their war positions, even when opponents muddied the waters. Republican papers in both elections emphasized support for the war and Democratic disloyalty in failing to share that view. Democrats initially criticized Republican war *leadership* and the war's emancipatory expansion while backing the war, then later moved against the war itself (Chapter 3). Five of seven Democratic newspapers backed the war to some extent at the midterms. Only one – the *Cheshire Republican* – expressed more negative than positive views overall. Even the *Nashua Gazette*, which took just one pro-war stance across seven dates, did so for the midterm. In contrast, *all* seven Democratic papers took anti-war positions in November 1864, leading the *Rutland Herald* (VT-R, July 1864) to call them the "peace and surrender" party. Democratic papers characterized anti-war partisans as morally righteous on 55 percent of 1864 Election Day pages mentioning the war, compared with none for Republican and independent papers. It was a big change from the midterms when no newspapers portrayed anti-war partisans that way. Independent papers espoused pro-war views in both elections – even the four that endorsed Democrats in one or both election cycles.

Linking Ballots & Bullets

Both parties' newspapers portrayed elections as fundamental determinants of the war's undecided outcome. Republican papers described midterm elections as critical for war success on 49 percent of their pages mentioning the war. Democrats often claimed the same (34 percent) – not quite as often, but not statistically distinct. By November 1864, a whopping 84 percent Democratic pages mentioning the war framed elections as a war referendum, along with 61 percent for Republicans ($p < 0.10$). Newspapers widely conflated voting with violence using metaphor, as the *Chicago Tribune* (IL-R, Nov 1862) did:

To-day, the freemen of Chicago and the whole State must fight the bloodless but no less important battle of the ballot box, and determine whether our gallant boys in the field shall be encouraged, whether the Administration shall be sustained in its efforts to crush the rebellion, and the Government maintained integral and harmonious in all its parts. . . . Remember that Jeff. Davis and his rebel crew will hail with delight the success of the Democratic ticket. The rebel papers so proclaim it. . . . If the opposition carry Illinois to-day, it will do the loyal cause more harm than the loss of a great battle, and knowing this to be so makes the tories work so desperately to carry the State.

For the Kentucky midterm, the pro-war *Louisville Journal* (KY-D, Aug 1863) wrote similarly:

If our people perform their whole duty today, the fame of their doings will echo as loudly and as far as the thunders of Shiloh and of Gettysburg. . . . Every vote today against the secession ticket will be worth a keen bayonet against the rebels in the field. . . . Let us give them another lesson at the ballot-box, lest they madly create the necessity of being taught a far severer one by the military authorities. . . . Daybreak has been a favorite hour with our brave boys for attacking the enemy in the field. We cannot, at so early an hour this morning, make an assault upon secessionism at the polls, but we can make it at half-past six, and let us be up to time. . . . Our armies have scotched the snake of the rebellion in the field; let us now kill it at the polls.

In the presidential election, the *Iowa State Register* (IA-R, Nov 1864) wrote, "the Union soldiers are to-day resting their arms, waiting for the Union victory which it is your duty to aid in gaining at the ballot-box. They are waiting for you to vote for the candidate for whom they cheer, and against the candidate for whom the rebels cheer." The *Chicago Tribune* (IL-R, Nov 1864) described soldiers voting in town while on their way to war, "and thus begin their campaign by helping to extinguish rebel sympathizers at home." Soldiers wanted it known: "every vote polled to-morrow in opposition to the government, will be hailed as a God send by the rebels, and will be as a bullet aimed at the heart of the nation's defenders." And the *Boston Journal* (MA-R, Nov 1864):

While the soldiers are fighting the rebels with bullets, the least that patriotic men at home can do is fight them with ballots. ... In the election of McClellan and Pendleton, and in the defeat of Lincoln and Johnson, is the only hope of Rebellion, Disunion, and Slavery. ... The question at stake not only concerns the success of the Government over the Southern rebellion, but it appeals to us to frown down and extinguish the beginnings of anarchy here at home ... the question to-day was whether [Confederate President] Jefferson Davis should triumph in Boston.

Soldiers' votes were a common source of party disagreement. The *Cincinnati Times* (OH-R, Oct 1862) claimed, "Every soldier in the army, if he was in Cincinnati, would vote for the Union ticket. ... For the sake of your brethren in the field, vote the Unconditional Union ticket." Two years later, the *Boston Journal* (MA-R, Nov 1864) asked, "Why is it that so many of our highest officers in the army and navy who, at the beginning of the war, were earnest Democrats, are now zealously in favor of the re-election of Abraham Lincoln?" For Democrats, the *Cheshire Republican* (NH-D, Nov 1864) claimed "a large majority" of one unit would vote McClellan. The *Nashua Gazette* (NH-D, Nov 1864) and *La Crosse Democrat* (WI-D, Nov 1864) also described soldiers voting for Democrats. The party's efforts to ensure soldiers were unable to vote suggested less confidence about systematically winning their votes, however.

In sum, the link between the war and its elections was inescapable.

Reporting the War's Progress

Politics is complicated, and voters struggle to make sense of the details. Beyond partisanship and group prejudices, some voters rely on retrospective assessments on national conditions to judge whether to support the party in power or the opposition (e.g. Achen & Bartels 2016; Baker 1983;

Fiorina 1981; Renda 1997). A cataclysmic civil war bears heavily on that judgment, even as partisanship biases perceptions (e.g. Bartels 2002). Civil War Democrats North and South hoped voters would punish Republicans for horrific national conditions, even as part of the party was causing the carnage.

Republican news consistently presented more positive views of war progress (on average) than Democratic papers, by about 20 points (b = 0.21, *s.e.* = 0.12, p = 0.10). However, huge gaps opened for the 1864 election, when Republicans were sure the war was going well and Democrats printed apocalyptically negative views (b = 1.17, *s.e.* = 0.19, p < 0.001). Midterm dates had a much smaller but detectable gap (b = 0.33, *s.e.* = 0.17, p < 0.10). In sum, party gaps in progress views were larger at election times, even for the midterm elections when Democrats largely supported the war while criticizing its administration.

Highlighting progress, the *Toledo Blade* (OH-R, Nov 1864) wrote on Election Day, "[t]he rebellion has been deprived, by three years of war, of two-thirds of its original area. ... as the war proceeds, the resisting powers of the rebellion diminish in a constantly accelerated ratio, and there is every reason to believe that it will not take the same proportionate time to overcome the last stage of the rebellion." Democratic biases were even more apparent in November 1864. The prospects for Union victory were obviously improved, but Democratic papers presented even direr views of the war then than they did in July. For example, the *Louisville Journal* (KY-D, Nov 1864) wrote, "We may, however, contrast our military position now with what it was about this time one year ago, and draw encouragement from it." Republican views in November were slightly more positive than in July.

Blame for War

Incumbents try to shift blame for any national troubles in hopes of avoiding electoral penalties, with varying success (e.g. Sides & Vavreck 2013). Given enormous casualties, some might expect voters to punish any party seen as responsible, for bringing those deaths and other cataclysms upon the nation. Successfully casting blame onto one party could drag down their electoral prospects. Partisan papers were equally likely to cast blame for the war, but with different targets, of course.

Republicans blamed the catastrophe on Southern rebels, more so than Democratic papers by more than twenty points in November 1864 (b = 0.23, *s.e.* = 0.07, p < 0.01), but there was no such partisan difference in the midterms (b = 0.08, $s.e.$ = 0.10, p = 0.43). The *Boston Journal* (MA-R, Nov 1864) noted, "The opposition ... are noticeably sparing of condemnation of the crime of rebellion, which has carried mourning into thousands of families and desolated many fair portions of our land and burdened the country with debt and taxation. ... without justifiable cause they trailed the flag of the Union in the dust, alleging for it as a pretext the election of Mr. Lincoln." Republicans blamed slaveholders in 7 percent of midterm papers ($p > 0.10$) and 8 percent on presidential election day (b = 0.08, $s.e.$ = 0.05, $p < 0.10$). The *Chicago Tribune* (IL-R, July 1862) argued, "While all deplore the war, the sentiment is universal that this wicked slaveholder's rebellion must be put down at any cost of treasure and life." And the *Albany Journal* (NY-R, Nov 1864) declared, "Slavery is the mainspring of the Rebellion."

Many Democrats were just as insistent that blame for the war should fall squarely on Republicans. The Democratic press was forty-two points more likely to explicitly blame Republicans for the war in November 1864 than other papers ($b = -0.42$, $s.e.$ = 0.10, $p < 0.001$), but not so in the midterms two years prior. Democratic papers were also twenty-one points more likely to blame abolitionists – Republican cousins – in the presidential election ($b = -0.21$, $s.e.$ = 0.05, $p < 0.001$), but not in the midterms. For example, the *Cincinnati Enquirer* (OH-D, Nov 1864) wrote, "It was the fanaticism of New England that caused the war with the Southern States and brought desolation and sorrow to the hearth stones of our people. She ransacks the entire country for negroes to fill her quotas in the army, and, while crying for a vigorous prosecution of the war, fattens on the blood of Western men." Interestingly, Republican papers did *not* return the favor by explicitly blaming Democrats in either election cycle. Some relatively moderate Democratic papers took a "both sides" approach to blame in November 1864 ($b = -0.12$, $s.e.$ = 0.06, $p < 0.05$), but not in the midterms.

REPORTING & INTERPRETING THE DEAD

Civil War deaths were intensely political and personal, all at once. They weighed heavily in the rhetoric of partisans for and against the war, and their implications for national salvation or disaster might have swayed retrospective-minded voters. It is easy to imagine how deaths of loved ones could overcome the pulls of party and prejudice, though partisan rationalization might diffuse those identity threats. Noting the presence of the dead in war news is our task here, particularly how newspapers represented and interpreted them for their electoral purposes.

In a war with seemingly innumerable deaths, there were many ways to die. Wasting away from disease did not fit the heroic narrative (Faust 2008), but disease ultimately claimed twice as many lives as war violence did.[14] Newsreaders were less likely to read about them, however – disease deaths appeared on just 16 percent of pages mentioning casualties. Press coverage tended to focus instead on battle casualties, presented initially in exclusively heroic terms, and later intermingled with matter-of-fact lists and counts. A small proportion of dead soldiers were murdered, committed suicide, or died in drownings or accidents. Rarely did news audiences read the gruesome realities of combat, though it was not entirely absent. Casualty lists often noted wounds, including the carnage after Bull Run: "shot in the throat," "shot through the hips; missing," "shot through the head; brought off, and recovery possible," "head cut off by a grape shot" (*Chicago Tribune*, IL-R, July 1861). Sometimes gory details accompanied an emotional narrative. As the war went on, breathless reports on the first few soldiers killed gave way to news routines that revealed the banality of killing: "Our losses for the day were no larger than usual" (*Boston Evening Traveller*, MA-R, July 1864). The *Detroit Advertiser & Tribune* (MI-R, Nov 1864) likewise reported, "We have suffered, but it will hardly amount to more than 100 killed and wounded, while the enemy's loss must reach from 150 to 300."

Reporting Casualties

Political scientist Scott Althaus and colleagues (2014) examined *New York Times* coverage of the five largest American wars between World War I and the Iraq War. They found relatively little coverage of war dead in those pages – in 10–20 percent of stories – with little variation across wars despite huge differences in the number of dead. By contrast, Civil War newspapers talked constantly about the war dead. An average of 72 percent of pages during the war mentioned any casualties (on either side).[15] Democratic papers were no more likely than Republican ones to mention casualty news, and on some dates, Republicans were *more* likely to do so. Republicans were much likelier than Democrats to mention any kind of casualties in midterm elections (80 percent vs. 59 percent of pages, $b = 0.21$, $s.e. = 0.08$, $p < 0.05$) but not more so in November 1864 elections due to rising Democratic casualty coverage. *Local* casualty reports were similarly split for midterms (42 percent vs. 6 percent, $b = 0.36$, $s.e. = 0.12$, $p < 0.01$) but not 1864 elections (both ~8 percent).[16] The deaths of black troops received attention on roughly one in ten pages mentioning African American service for midterms and one in five pages for 1864 elections. The low rate of mentions for black troops, however, reduces that casualty coverage to just 1 percent of pages in the midterms and 5 percent in 1864, compared with two of every three pages for white combatants.

Depicting enemy losses is another way to boost war support by showing progress, especially relative to one's own losses. The parties did not differ significantly in reporting recent rebel casualties in the midterms, though Republicans did this 23 percentage points more often than Democrats for 1864 elections (56 percent vs. 33 percent). Anecdotally, pro-war papers often compared Union and Confederate casualties to emphasize greater enemy losses, as when the *Rutland Herald* (VT-R, July 1863) wrote of Gettysburg: "our loss is comparatively small – say seven thousand killed and wounded; rebel loss (killed and wounded) from twelve to fifteen thousand." The *Herald* (VT-R, July 1863) took a wider view of morbid progress when it keenly observed: "every great battle is to [rebels] necessarily a defeat ... a loss of ten thousand men, more or less, in battle, even supposing they retain possession of the battlefield and gain what is technically termed a victory, brings them so much nearer the end of their resources; it is a loss which is irretrievable."[17]

What about news of *total* Union casualties across the war? That's a different view of human costs that computes more easily than a running tally. News of total losses was initially quite rare – on just 2 percent of pages mentioning casualties for the midterms, with no partisan differences. The presidential election looks much different, however. Democrats totaled the Union dead for readers on 39 percent of pages mentioning casualties, versus 2 percent for Republican papers ($p > 0.10$). Democrats clearly wanted readers to remember the dead when casting their ballots. For example, the *Cincinnati Enquirer* (OH-D, Nov 1864) wrote, "Four hundred and twenty-five thousand men a year, 200 men every day, are sacrificed. How long will this expenditure go on before our homes are made desolate? Every rolling month carries from 30,000 to 40,000 our sons to their graves or the hospitals. Yet the Administration still demands victims. If Mr. Lincoln is reinstated in power, new and greater drafts will be necessary." Local casualties did not get comparable cumulative treatment from any papers, and so any public reactions to total *local* deaths among voters must have arisen from the accumulation of recent local reports or from information sources beyond local newspapers. This finding has important implications for local casualty effects on voting found in Chapter 6.

Overall, Republican newspapers did not shy away from reporting deaths. That suggests they found ways to frame those dead in ways that sustained the war and its Republican leaders.

Interpreting the Dead

Civil War deaths posed monumental psychological challenges for Republicans and other war supporters. How could they continue to support a fight that cost so much? On the other side, Democrats opposing the war could view casualties – particularly of friends and family – as more cause to oppose, even as they ignored the sacrifice of Union and democracy to get peace.

Republicans had to transform deaths into martyrdom for some higher purpose. Some historians argue our present-day focus on the war's noble abolition ends are post hoc efforts to justify the enormous human and moral costs of a war killing three-quarters of a million Americans. But we have many contemporary examples of noble meaning making during the war, including President Lincoln's Gettysburg Address heralding "a new birth of freedom" (Wills 1992). Likewise, loyal Americans fought to maintain the Union and its democratic elections from the start (e.g. Gallagher 2011). Those frames helped maintain Republican war support by representing the dead as heroic martyrs whose spirits demanded resolve to finish the violent work they began.

For example, the *New York Herald* (NY-Ind, July 1862) eulogized a dead captain: "The blow to the family, as it has been to his friends, will be terribly severe, but they have the great consolation of knowing that they do not grieve alone. Every loyal heart beats in unison with theirs, and many are the prayers that will be sent to the throne of the Almighty for the salvation of one who fell while nobly defending the honor and integrity of his country and her flag against rebels who would blindly destroy the Union of this bright and glorious land. ... The government has lost a noble officer, and an able defender of its rights, and his family a loving and devoted husband and father." Democrats said the war dead were lost for nothing, as when the *Detroit Advertiser & Tribune* (MI-R, July 1864) reported it was shocked by a Democratic paper that wrote Grant "can let more blood, and lead more innocent white men to the Lincoln slaughter pens than any other."

Republican newspapers were immensely likelier to cast deaths as noble sacrifices (+1) and not senseless losses (−1) in the 1864 election, compared with Democratic papers (b = 0.83, *s.e.* = 0.19, p < 0.001). They were no likelier to do so for the midterms when Democrats were indistinguishable in their war support ($b = 0.13$, *s.e.* $= 0.14$, $p = 0.36$). The first panel in Figure 5.1 shows the partisan gap in martyr/senseless frames through the war, which grows largest in 1864. Republicans occasionally mentioned senseless deaths, but mostly just when criticizing individual Democratic military leaders for failures that needlessly cost lives.

Republicans were also more likely to cite the dead to justify continuing the war rather than quit, in the midterm ($b = 0.17$, *s.e.* $= 0.07$, $p < 0.05$) and especially in the presidential election ($b = 0.52$, *s.e.* $= 0.12$, $p < 0.001$). For example, the *Chicago Tribune* (IL-R, July 1862) printed an Oliver Wendell Holmes poem: "Now while the foremost are fighting and falling / Fill up the ranks that have opened for you!" And, for the presidential election, the *Albany Journal* (NY-R, Nov 1864) wrote, "The battle thus waged in this case cannot fail. Even if it could fail, the field which was lost would forever be a holy sepulcher." The second panel in Figure 5.1 shows this relationship over time.

Finally, Democrats implored voters to remember the dead in their voting choices on 58 percent of pages mentioning casualties in the presidential election (coded 0, 1), far more so than Republicans (13 percent, $b = -0.44$, *s.e.* $= 0.15$ $p < 0.01$), but no difference in the midterms. The third panel in Figure 5.1 shows this trend for the full war. Naturally, each party argued the dead were reason to vote for their own party. The *Chicago Tribune* (IL-R, Nov 1862) warned a Republican midterm election loss would mean "the country is lost! and that the 100,000 lives sacrificed to save it have been of no avail." In opposition, the *Cincinnati Enquirer* (OH-D, Nov 1864) alleged some regiments had lost 90 percent of their men and added, "If you want to make sure of getting out of the world quickly, vote for Lincoln Tuesday." The paper endorsed McClellan to "restore the Union and end the war without further shedding of blood." Democrats' strong rhetorical link between the dead and voting – three times more than Republicans in November 1864 – may have made casualties more electorally potent in the places where Democratic messages were loudest – Democratic bastions.

Taken together, we see enormous differences in how the parties framed the war's dead, with implications for partisan vote choice. These frames provide vital context for interpreting the influence of national and local casualties on election results in Chapters 6 and 7. Civil War Democratic newspapers also differed from most modern non-partisan war news in their efforts to highlight the dead for purposes of war criticism (Althaus et al. 2014).

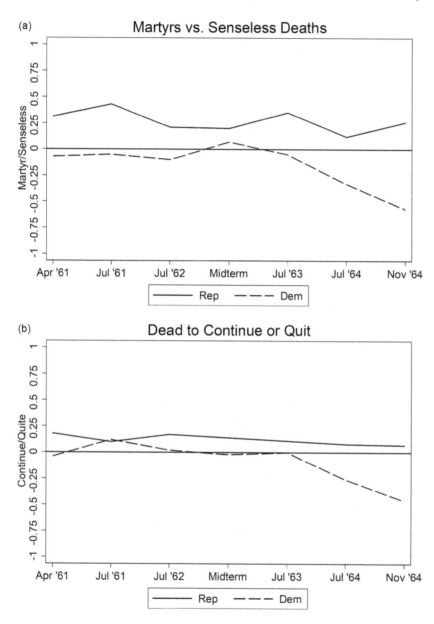

FIGURE 5.1 Framing the dead over time

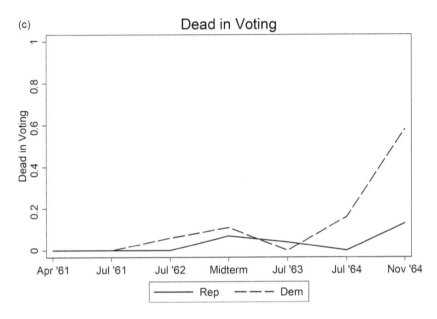

FIGURE 5.1 *(cont.)*

PARTISAN VIOLENCE IN THE NORTH

Extremely negative campaign messages helped bind partisans together in voting loyalty. But Northern partisan animus went far beyond acceptable bounds for electioneering in a democracy, even beyond allegations of treason, to include widespread violent threats and low-level partisan violence. When the *National Intelligencer* (DC-I, Nov 1864) endorsed Democrat George McClellan for president, they added, whoever wins "may rightly ask to be upheld in the discharge of his constitutional functions by citizens of all parties alike." That they deemed such a statement necessary helps to show the furious conflict *within* the Union as well as against the rebels, though the latter remained far greater.

Democratic elections reduce violence in society by selecting leaders through non-violent mechanisms (e.g. Collier & Vicente 2014; Przeworski 1991), but election campaigns are contentious (Sood & Iyengar 2016), and election seasons can *produce* violence in fractious contexts (e.g. Rappoport & Weinberg 2000; Wilkinson 2006). We see that same dynamic at work in the American Civil War. Civil War elections brought Northern Democrats and Republicans into direct political conflict. The election cycle continued unabated fair and free, despite the enormous ongoing rebellion, and that in itself was a huge national achievement. However, those campaigns also stoked party conflict in a nation already violently split by partisanship. Mid-nineteenth century partisans were accustomed to low-level violence against the opposition (Grimsted 1998), but these acts went further as the legitimate violence of war made violent threats and actions against political enemies seem more acceptable.

Civil War historian Mark Neely (2017) asks a fundamental question in a civil war – "whether partisanship drives one party to the brink of disloyalty and the other, the one in power, to flirt with tyranny" (p. 1). There is no doubt *Southern* Democrats were violently treasonous, so the only question left relates to Northern parties. Neely argues any widespread Northern disloyalty was in rhetoric only, not behavior, with violent action limited to few Democrats. Historian Jennifer Weber (2006) vehemently disagrees, presenting the most extensive case for Peace Democrats as a dangerous force in Northern politics, not just an annoyance to Republican war-leaders.[18]

Here, we cite explicit calls from our newspaper sample advocating violence against opposing Northern partisans. These are consistent with many Civil War histories recounting violent partisan expressions in newspapers, speeches, and letters, providing substantial evidence of widespread views among elites and citizens alike (e.g. McPherson 1997; Weber 2006). We also describe many cases of partisan violence and insurrection plans, the worst of which came in the months before the 1864 election. These snapshots affirm the violence from *partisanship* in particular, apart from the partisan-regional war. The language of violent partisanship in newspapers reflected elite views and public attitudes, but, like military enlistment, party leaders were key in mobilizing those views and acts in the public.

Identifying the Partisan Threat

In 1861, defeated Democratic presidential candidate Stephen Douglas acknowledged the danger of violence between *Northern* partisans:

The [Southern] conspirators have been led to hope that, in Northern States, it would be made a party question, producing civil war between Democrats and Republicans, and the South being united, could step in with their legions and help the one destroy the other, and then conquer the victor. Their scheme was bloodshed and all the horrors of civil war in every Northern State! There is one way to prevent it; united action on the part of Illinois; closing up the ranks, renders it impossible that war should rage on our soil.

Douglas admitted the degree of enmity between Northern partisans impeded unified efforts, and that is what gave the rebels hope:

I am aware that we have had some difficulty and prejudice to encounter in producing unanimity. It is not surprising that such should have been the case. We must remember that it has been but a few short months since we came out of a fierce political strife [the 1860 election], which engendered much bitterness of feeling. It takes some little time to banish those passions from the human heart, and substitute unalloyed patriotism in their place.

Douglas prescribed non-partisanship as the salve. Recognizing the power of language to enflame hostile partisanship, he said partisans must avoid all references to parties:

How are we to overcome partisan antipathies in the minds of men of all parties so as to present a united front in support of our country? We must cease discussing party issues, make no allusions to old party tests, have no criminations and recriminations, indulge in no taunts one against the other as to who has been the cause of these troubles.

Ultimately, efforts toward non-partisanship did not survive more than a year of the war.[19]

Calls for Partisan Violence in the North

Most early-war calls for partisan violence were Republicans targeting anti-war Democrats. The *Burlington Free Press* (VT-R, July 1862) reported on an ex-Democrat's speech: "He now thinks there are some of his old partisans in New Hampshire who ought to be hung, and we might add in Vermont too." For the fall elections, the *Iowa State Register* (IA-R, Oct 1862) printed a pro-war Democrat's letter, which called for punishing anti-war Democrat Clement Vallandigham with "a common destiny with such traitors as Jeff. Davis and his colleagues South." The *Albany Journal* (NY-R, Nov 1862) transcribed a campaign rally with Secretary of State William Seward. When he described lenient treatment of "open and defiant enemies" in the North, the crowd reportedly shouted, "better if they had hung Vallandigham and the rest of them."

Union soldiers seemed especially apt to threaten violence against anti-war Democrats back home. Having shot down many Southern Democrats engaged in rebellion, they had fewer qualms about shooting Democrats back home who wished rebel success, and who made rebel victory more likely by opposing the war. The *Chicago Tribune* (IL-R, Nov 1862) printed a local soldier's letter:

You may say, for this army, that we are thoroughly in earnest in crushing out every spark of rebellion, whether found in South Carolina or Illinois, and that we endorse every measure of the president to weaken and destroy the enemies of our country … and that we hold every man in the North as a tory and a traitor who opposes [Lincoln's Emancipation Proclamation] at this time, and that it will be our duty, if this opposition should continue till our return, to put it down as we have been taught to put it down in Virginia. … At present we are engaged in the South; but we will be home one of these days, and then, gentlemen tories, will come your turn, and I assure you our feeling towards our open enemies in the South is lenient and forgiving to what it will be towards you. A solider can tolerate anything but treachery and deception.[20]

The balance of calls for violence swung toward Democrats in the war's last year, but they used oblique expressions to avoid suppression by authorities. For example, the *Cincinnati Enquirer* (OH-D, Nov 1864) seemingly adopted the words of rebels to represent its own violent views. Alongside brief Democratic endorsements, the *Enquirer* devoted the rest of its front page to articles from rebel newspapers. One read: "there is but one means for a thorough reunion, and that is by a combination between the Confederates and the Northern Conservatives, cemented by the blood of the Black Republicans. … But nothing short of the blood, the extermination of the monsters who have made this war will suffice." The paper also advertised an election night meeting to resist the draft: "Help One Another: All the drafted men of the Sixth Ward, and all others who are willing to keep the Ward out of the draft, will meet tomorrow evening. … There should be a general turn out." Whether they planned violence is unclear. The *Davenport Democrat* (IA-D, Nov 1864) was most explicit: "It is better that Lincoln die and the nation live and those who thus believe will vote for the unconditional union candidate – George B. McClellan."

Each party criticized the other's violent incitement. In the midterm, the *Cincinnati Enquirer* (OH-D, Oct 1862) quoted abolitionist Cassius Clay, who recommended, "ropes round the necks of those traitors," citing notorious Peace Democrats. The *Enquirer* cried, "This, then, is the banner under which the [Republican] Wadsworth campaign is to be conducted – The Banner of Blood! … hung out by the hands of the most notorious leader of the Abolition party. … Alas! That we have come to this – that a political campaign is instigated by a proposition of murder – of a reign of terror – of a carnival of blood!" For its part, the *Boston Journal* (MA-R, Nov 1864) warned readers of Democrats "blustering about revolutionary violence, in case of Mr. Lincoln's reelection … roll up such a tremendous majority in support of the Government, that these audacious propagandists of fraud and violence will never dare to repeat their attempts during this generation."

Acts of Partisan Violence & Rebellion in the North

Partisan conflict in the North went far beyond words, intensifying long-standing patterns of low-level violence. Historian Jennifer Weber (2006) provides the best treatment on Northern political violence during the Civil War. She describes partisan murders and countless partisan brawls between individuals and informal groups. Some on Election Day continued a long history of electioneering violence. On a larger scale, Weber describes dozens of violent and sometimes deadly anti-draft riots, partisan militias, quasi-legal coups, and violent plots to overthrow local governments. Not all Democrats were anti-war and certainly not all were violent, but most anti-war people were Democrats, as Republicans were fond of noting.

As the war began, the *Chicago Tribune* (IL-R, July 1861) described partisan killings in southern Illinois, the state's most Democratic and anti-war region: "Political excitement has for some time been running very high in that region. ... [Davis] rushed into the room and made several declarations against all Republicans. A fight with knives ensued. ... Davis was killed, and the floor reeked with the blood of five others, all respectable citizens, seriously, and it is thought mortally wounded." At midterms, the *Chicago Tribune* (Nov 1862) reported that a Republican news editor in Dayton, Ohio, had been shot and killed. And when a deserter murdered a soldier, the *Albany Journal* (NY-R, July 1863) wrote, "We regard the affair as the natural result of the teachings of the Copperheads leaders, who refused to extend the aid of either men or money to the Government, and talked of 'a free fight or a free ballot!' The blood of Col. Butler rests heavily upon their shoulders."

New York City – a hotbed of anti-war Democrats – produced the largest anti-draft riot, composed mostly of Irish immigrant targeting black residents and federal offices. Over several days, the mob killed more than one hundred people, wounded thousands, and burned dozens of buildings. They even burned the Colored Orphan Asylum and prevented fire fighters from extinguishing the blaze.[21] At the riot's peak, the Republican *New York Times* put a Gatling gun in its print shop to protect the paper from the mob (Holzer 2014). Republicans accused Democratic Governor Horatio Seymour of inciting the mob by giving a speech to an assembly of them in which he identified with them. Democrats said he only tried to relate as a way to persuade them to stop. Police and state militia could not stop the violence, and so Lincoln sent several regiments of the U.S. Army and Marines straight from battle at Gettysburg to restore order by force. Weber (2006) describes anti-draft riots throughout the North during "a riot-filled summer" (p. 114).[22]

Given the unrest, President Lincoln had to station thousands of Union soldiers in hot spots around the loyal states to keep the peace, including on Election Day. General Halleck called on General Grant to send combat troops from the battlefield to help maintain order against Copperheads, but Grant said the state militias had to handle it – the Army couldn't sustain fights on two fronts simultaneously (Weber 2006, p. 153). Democrats accused Republicans of using troops to intimidate Democratic voters, harass local Democrats, and arrest speakers, editors, and sometimes ordinary people for discouraging military enlistment, encouraging desertion and anti-draft resistance, and openly praising the Southern rebellion – or statements interpreted as such by local commanders.

The most infamous case involved Congressman Clement Vallandigham, the unofficial leader of Peace Democrats. He was tried and convicted of making treasonous statements, banished to the Confederacy, and then made his way to Canada to run for governor of Ohio (and lose) in exile. While in Canada, Vallandigham met with Confederate commissioners to discuss fomenting a revolution in Midwestern states to form a second confederacy. The Confederate government appropriated $500,000 ($14 million today) to buy weapons to arm a secret society of anti-war Democrats. The rebellion was to begin upon Vallandigham's arrest when he illegally returned to Ohio in mid-1864, but Lincoln wisely declined to arrest him. A backup plan to stage a coup during the Democratic convention also evaporated when Democrats changed the date (Weber 2006, p. 151). Vallandigham went on to write the anti-war Democratic platform for the 1864 presidential election, calling for an immediate cease-fire to open negotiations with the Confederacy and end the war. Since the rebels had no interest in reunion, this would mean accepting an independent Confederacy.

Weber describes two other rebellious plots by Democrats that received substantial weapons funding from the Confederate government. One by an Indiana printer sought to take over Midwestern arsenals, free rebel prisoners of war, and lead the southern Midwest out of the Union. The plan was to attack several cities simultaneously, in coordination with rebel invasions of Kentucky and Missouri. In concert with the plan for Midwestern unrest, the editor of the *New York Daily News* took $25,000 from rebels to fund an armed riot in New York City (Weber 2006, p. 151). Democrats abandoned these plots in August when they began to think they could beat Lincoln fairly at the polls without resorting to mass violence.[23]

Nearly all Republican papers carried 1864 Election Day stories about a plot by Democrats in Chicago to spring rebel POWs from a prison camp nearby, then "fire the city and control the election" (*Boston Journal*, MA-R, Nov 1864). In disrupting the plot, authorities found huge caches of weapons. The paper wrote: "the order was composed entirely of Democrats. ... Is it not high time for every honest, patriotic Democrat, to quit a party which has fallen into such corrupt hands and become a breeding-nest for traitors?" The *Albany Journal* (NY-R, Nov 1864) reported the ringleader had "evidence enough against him to ensure him swinging."

Armed groups of army deserters and draft-dodgers banded together by the hundreds and the thousands in some counties in Pennsylvania and Indiana, occasionally killing local and military officials (Sandow 2009). Although their war views aligned with Democrats, they were not overtly partisan. Other armed groups robbed Unionists and ransacked Republican newspapers. In central Illinois, Democrats ambushed U.S. soldiers, kicking off a two-hour gunfight in a town square. Draft officers also faced frequent attacks. Partisans on both sides made concerted efforts for their own party to populate the state militias so they could have effective control over the state's military force and access to its weapons, even if the state's governor was of the other party. Democrats and Republicans also formed independent militias within secret societies to protect themselves and to plot against opposing partisan groups. Collectively or informally, these groups frequently attacked local newspaper offices of the opposing party (Weber 2006). U.S. soldiers on furlough often participated in Republicans mobs. Neely (2002) also found extensive coordinated efforts by soldiers to act on violent threats made in their letters. Dozens of regiments collectively passed resolutions, mailed to their governors, explicitly tendering military services as whole units to suppress Democratic plots, mob violence, and anti-war advocacy.[24] Finally, there was Lincoln's assassination in April 1865 and the broader plot to decapitate much of the president's cabinet in one night.

In sum, the Civil War North was a violent place for partisans, who sought to suppress each other politically and lethally. Though far more limited than our focus on the predominant partisan violence of a war fought disproportionately by Republicans against Southern Democrats, we cannot forget that violent partisanship ranged much farther. The *Rutland Herald* (VT-R, July 1863) summed it up: "So is presented this strange phenomenon – the culmination of the plottings of northern dis-loyalists in local and temporary but destructive and murderous insurrec-tion, while Southern treason is receiving its death blows at the hands of our gallant armies."

CONCLUSIONS

Like modern-day campaigns, Civil War parties focused mostly on reinfor-cing and mobilizing their own partisans by emphasizing the righteousness of their own group and the wickedness of their opponents. Republicans and Democrats also sought advantage among undecided voters and wavering partisans by alternately attacking their opponents and defending themselves. Unlike most modern campaigns, Civil War elec-tions stoked hostility to the point of outright violence, even threatening outright insurrection in the North.

Election news focused almost wholly on national politics.[25] Both parties presented wartime elections as referenda on the war and national existence – points they emphasized to readers repeatedly. Republicans in particular envisioned a fusion of ballots and bullets, with electoral actions and outcomes having as great an impact on the war's outcome as the war's most consequential battles. Leveraging retrospective voting dynam-ics, Democrats sought to portray the war and its Republican leaders as failures, especially by emphasizing the war's human costs. Republicans defended themselves by painting a rosier picture of progress while shifting blame for the cataclysm onto rebels.

Democrats also extensively deployed white supremacy appeals in hopes of drawing away the most racist white voters. Republicans responded by emphasizing the military necessity of abolition against the rebellion. Republicans went on offense against Democrats, accusing them of disloyalty and even treason for their war opposition (and more nefari-ous plans). Democrats countered that opposition to emancipation and the war was an expression of their national loyalty, and they accused Repub-licans of rampant authoritarianism in actions against the most vitriolic Democratic war critics.

Republican papers were no less likely than Democratic ones to repre-sent the war's human costs in their pages as incomprehensible numbers of dead accumulated day after day. However, they differed on interpret-ations and implications of the dead, especially in the final year of the war.

Democrats emphasized the total number of casualties on Election Day 1864 in hopes that those dead would sap Republican votes. Democrats also framed those dead differently – senseless losses and reasons to stop the war – as explicit rationales for casting Democratic votes in the fall elections. Republicans, in contrast, represented the dead as heroic martyrs demanding the war continue until victory was won – and therefore remade those dead into reasons to vote for Republicans.

Like modern-day campaigns, Civil War elections stoked partisan hostility (Sood & Iyengar 2016), but political competition amidst a partisan civil war led to unusually greater national dangers. Vilification far exceeded democratic bounds with widespread accusations of treason, threats of violence, brawls and murders, arson and riots, rebellious plots, and government crackdowns. Here, we see the war's violent partisanship extended much farther. Violent partisanship *within* the North highlights the lethality of *partisanship* as its own independent force. Clearly, though, partisan violence in the North never came approached the violence seen in the white Southern rebellion itself, and it is hard to know for sure the risk Democrats posed for a full-scale Northern rebellion.

The next two chapters investigate the influence of casualties and wartime events on voters. There, we see the electoral product of partisan campaign efforts detailed above. Given what we know of voting behavior, we expect the rhetoric here to reinforce partisan loyalties to produce stable partisan voting patterns, but we also look for the possibility that partisan frames of war experiences may have peeled some voters away.

6

Weighing the Dead

Partisan Reasoning at the Ballot Box

The attempt of a successful faction at the South to impair our national unity, is a sacrilege. ... Hence it is, that one soul, one will, inspires the Northern States in this terrible crisis, and that, as Senator Baker exclaimed, "Seven hundred and fifty thousand men and three hundred millions of money," will be readily sacrificed in behalf of such a vast and precious interest.

New York Herald (NY-Ind)
April 22, 1861

It is rather for us to be here dedicated to the great task remaining before us – that from these honored dead we take increased devotion to that cause for which they here gave the last full measure of devotion – that we here highly resolve that these dead shall not have died in vain – that this nation, under God, shall have a new birth of freedom, and that government of the people, by the people, for the people, shall not perish from the earth.

President Abraham Lincoln
Gettysburg, PA
November 19, 1863

The sheer scope of Civil War death was and is staggering: over three-quarters of a million Americans died fighting each other, a per capita proportion equaling nearly eight million today.[1] Half as many more escaped death with disabling wounds, including one in thirteen missing limbs.[2] Two-thirds died of disease – an especially disheartening reality for men and their families who assumed their potential death would at least be heroic, from battle and not typhoid or dysentery from contaminated water.

One in eleven military-age males from loyal states died. That was *six* times deadlier per capita than World War II, *sixty* times deadlier than the Vietnam War, and *ninety* times deadlier than the Korean War. Union forces at Gettysburg and Spotsylvania saw more of their own men killed in a few days of each battle than in two decades of twenty-first century combat in Afghanistan. On *fourteen* occasions in just four years, a single battle killed, wounded, or captured more than 10,000 Union soldiers.[3]

The sweeping human losses of the Civil War permanently changed American society and culture, as Drew Gilpin Faust (2008) movingly illustrates in her book *This Republic of Suffering*. The public demanded government take responsibility for those deaths, which led to new federal, state, and local organizations and institutions to care for the dying, to bury the dead, to locate and reinter hundreds of thousands of hastily buried Union soldiers in new national cemeteries, and to honor their memory. Half the graves were marked "Unknown," and the Missing Soldiers Office answered nearly 70,000 postwar inquiries from families seeking information on still-absent relatives. Theda Skocpol (1992) similarly writes of how the needs of widows and mothers who lost husbands and sons, and the needs of infirm veterans, led to the world's first mass welfare state. These loyal Americans sacrificed more than any generation before or since.

Here, I investigate the *mass* political impact of their deaths – whether and how national and local casualties influenced voters as they weighed partisan and national loyalties against the war's human costs. I begin by describing how Civil War voters were as critical to U.S. military victory as the nation's armies, and then I outline how modern political analysts have accounted for the political impact of wartime casualties. Did national or local war casualties depress Republicans vote shares – either from total or recent losses – as the monstrous death toll grew? Several studies on modern wartime opinion predict they would. In contrast, I expect partisan stability to predominate but with *polarized* casualty effects on the margins, depending on partisanship. Democrats used the dead to argue for an end to Republican rule, even as Republicans presented the slain as reason to redouble devotion to the cause, like the quotes that began this chapter. The election news analysis in Chapter 5 systematically showed these partisan framing differences. I investigate the electoral effects of national and then local deaths in turn, as framed by those partisan opinion leaders.

Ordinary Americans in a War of Wills

The Civil War was ultimately a contest of wills. Relative military might – key to the South's "Lost Cause" narrative of noble, inevitable defeat – surely contributed to Union victory, just as the rebellion's substantial military strength prevented its immediate failure, unlike many past rebellions. Military strength only matters when joined by the will to bear the human and financial costs, however, and that made it a war the Union could easily have lost had its resolve failed – what Democrats advocated in 1864. An Iowa soldier recognized the *political* danger when he lamented wavering war support back home: "it is a common saying here that if we are whipped, it will be by Northern votes, not by Southern bullets" (quoted in Weber 2006, p. 69). As horrific and unprecedented casualties mounted, how did citizens at home respond when offered the choice to sustain or extinguish the war at the ballot box?

Southern leaders had few illusions about winning a clear military victory. Instead, their aim was to make the choice for Union so costly that Northerners would give up. The American Revolution was their explicit model: Britain's military forces were vastly superior to the Continental Army, and yet Britain acquiesced when the conflict grew long and costly. Explaining this goal while cheering rebel invasions of the North, the *London Times* "hoped that Gen. Lee will at least make this invasion sufficiently effective to disgust the Northern people with the war, and to shame their leaders out of their boasting and conceit."[4] Thus, *political* victory over the North was key to the rebellion's hopes, by dispiriting Northern voters through mass violence.

Confederates counted on Northern elections to reflect dissatisfaction with the war and guarantee Confederate independence (Faust 2013). Confederate General Robert E. Lee wrote that a rebel proposal to the U.S. government for peace and separation in 1862 "would enable the people of the United States to determine at their coming elections whether they will support those who favor a prolongation of the war, or those who wish to bring it to a termination."[5] Similarly, Lee wrote to Confederate President Jefferson Davis in June 1863, "the most effectual mode of [dividing and weakening our enemies] ... is to give all the encouragement we can, consistently with truth, to the rising [Democratic] peace party of the North."[6] The reason: Democrats aimed to capture the House of Representatives, from which they planned to take charge of the war and negotiate for its end (Smith 2006, p. 52). Beyond military strategy, Confederates gave direct financial support to Lincoln's Democratic opponents as the war continued, including funds to launch Northern insurrections.

While public will has decided many wars, the American Civil War was unique: for the first time, the decision to continue fighting or accede to national dismemberment was in the hands of voters as well as military volunteers. The 1864 elections and the 1862–1963 midterms served as referenda for continuing the fight, more so than any other elections in U.S. history. McPherson (2002) writes, "Southerners interpreted Democratic gains in the states that held their elections in October ... as 'a matter of more serious interest than military news'" (p. 148). The Republican *New York Times* likewise said Democratic victory "would be regarded everywhere ... as an indication that public sentiment had turned against the war" (quoted in McPherson 2002, p. 93).

In sum, the Lincoln administration needed votes to sustain the war in the face of partisan opposition, as much as it needed arms and men to shoulder them. The public's votes were decisive, first for Republican Party successes and then for the Union and American democracy. Those victories required voters to view the innumerable war dead as martyrs in those essential causes.

WEIGHING THE NATIONAL DEAD

Many past studies find national casualties reducing support for wars and their leaders. That work began with political scientist John Mueller (1973), who showed U.S. war support and presidential approval declining as total national casualties rose during the Korean and Vietnam wars. Initial casualties were especially impactful. Others have found similar results in reanalysis of those wars (e.g. Althaus et al. 2012; Gartner et al. 1997). Many retrospective voting models account for costly war alongside economics as national conditions that disadvantage incumbents when either are going badly (Fiorina 1981). Other scholars argue instead that *recent* casualties matter more (Althaus & Coe 2011; Gartner & Segura 1998), or an increasing *rate* of casualties (Gartner & Segura 1998), or casualty effects that depend on whether the war is going poorly, or lacks moral justification (Gelpi et al. 2006; Kriner & Shen 2014). The partisanship of voters evaluating war deaths may matter too – whether they align with the party leading the war or not (e.g. Gartner et al. 1997). In short, casualties seem to shape public opinion, but scholars hotly debate exactly *how* they do.

Cumulative casualties theories described above would predict declining Republican vote share over the course of the war, and that would certainly conclude with Lincoln losing his reelection in 1864. After hundreds of thousands of Union deaths in four short years at an ever-increasing rate, Lincoln's support should have been so low by late 1864 that no combination of military successes would save his sinking electoral chances. Similarly, if *recent* national casualties are key, the enormous losses in 1864 equaling half the war's dead should have led to Lincoln's election loss as well. These modern expectations mirror the worries expressed by U.S. officials during the Civil War and the strategic plans made by Confederate leaders in advance of Union elections. Yet, Lincoln and Republicans won.

Other scholars point instead to opinion leadership to explain war attitudes in the public along with their policy views in other domains. People turn to trusted political leaders – usually prominent partisan leaders – for cues on where they should stand. Casualties (and major events) produce mostly *indirect* effects on public opinion through leaders, and that only happens if casualties cause partisan leaders to change positions on the war and related interpretations (Berinsky 2009; Kriner & Shen 2014; Zaller 1992). The public lacks detailed knowledge of wartime events, and when directly given information about casualties, citizens are surprisingly unresponsive to it. For example, public support for World War II remained high in the face of *overwhelming* U.S. deaths – second most to the Civil War. And, although a war's noble purposes might reduce casualty sensitivity, laudable goals combating the evils of the Nazi regime did not materialize broadly until *after* Allies won the war (Berinsky 2009). That suggests a much different relationship between death and war support – one that may help explain Lincoln's reelection, and one that might explain Republican electoral success at other points in the war as well.

Staggered Election Returns as National Partisan Barometers

To judge the partisan impact of national casualties over time, we need something like a regular tracking poll across the duration of the Civil War. In their stead, nineteenth century politicians used election returns to evaluate their national standing and to predict the partisan trajectory in upcoming contests. Historians similarly report elections as indicators of public mood, because these results provide the only *representative* evidence of local partisan sentiment in that place, better than what could be gleaned from local political reports. Lincoln and others knew that local election results were most useful in judging the trajectory to victory when viewed *in relation* to previous votes. Put differently, the *change* from one cycle to the next was more revealing about *national* climate than the absolute party vote share. Here, I slightly improve on those methods with a more systematic approach to track partisan stability and change over time.

I leverage a quirk in nineteenth century election calendars. Unlike today when federal elections mostly take place on the same day in early November, each cycle of U.S. House elections before 1872 sprawled across seventeen months. Gubernatorial elections were often held on (or near) the same day, with several states holding *annual* elections for governor. I focus on *shifts* from a partisan baseline by subtracting Lincoln's 1864 local vote share from House and governor elections, making movement toward or away from Republicans more comparable in each place. When viewed in relation to staggered votes by all other states, these election results roughly provide a continuous tracking poll on each party's *national* standing. Many factors influenced how individual candidates fared, but each party's average performance across hundreds of elections tells much about the American public's partisan views at each point in the war.

Without House and governor elections, we would have only Lincoln's vote in 1860 and 1864. With them, we have partisan data points from twenty-four of the forty-eight months of the war, often with many states voting together and thereby increasing the reliability of the national estimate at that time. However, this estimation strategy only works as a *national* barometer if votes for all three offices generally reflected the same partisanship and not major differences across levels of government and individual candidates. Like today, most voters in the 1860s cast straight-party votes due to strong partisan loyalties and other persuasive factors (Bensel 2004; Campbell et al. 1960; Hopkins 2018; Silbey 1977). Partisan news with widely circulating content also served to nationalize politics. Thus, a voter choosing Lincoln for president would usually choose Republicans for House and governor as well.

Political scientist Daniel Hopkins (2018) argues that twenty-first century partisan politics is far more nationalized than it was in the mid-twentieth century. Historians identify other nationalization peaks in the 1830s (McCormick 1973), during Reconstruction from the war's end until 1877 (Foner 1988), and in the Gilded Age ending the nineteenth century (Klinghard 2010). What about the Civil War era? For starters, Joel Silbey (1977) alludes to partisan synchronicity in his county-level vote tests in several states.

To more broadly test whether presidential, gubernatorial, and House votes aligned in each place, I examine county-level correlations between presidential votes and other elections for all states that remained loyal during the war (see Online Appendix, Table A6.1). Prewar votes show high levels of nationalization for Republican and Democratic vote shares, even in the convulsive partisan environment between 1856 and 1860, with correlations greater than 0.80. In fact, nationalization and synchronization equal or surpass present-day levels with near-perfect correlations in presidential election years. House and governor votes also serve as good leading indicators of upcoming presidential votes years in advance. The same partisan synchronicity appears in wartime elections, especially in the free contiguous states. In sum, voters chose mostly based on parties and not candidates when voting for state and federal elections (Holt 1978).

"Every Drop of Blood" in Wartime Elections

With a validated partisan barometer in hand, I examine the trend over time for any evidence of declining Republican vote shares as casualties mounted. Figure 6.1 shows remarkably stable national Republican vote share throughout the war from state-level data. Contrary to "cumulative casualties" theories, there was no decline in Republican vote share over time as national casualties grew. The figure depicts election results from January 1, 1860, through December 31, 1865, for free contiguous states, subtracting Lincoln's 1864 state-level vote share from Republican state-

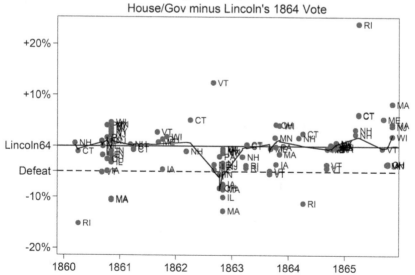

FIGURE 6.1 Republican vote share barometer in House & governor elections
Note: Contiguous free states. Trend line weighted by 1864 presidential votes cast.

level vote share in House and governor elections.[7] Lincoln's 1864 *national* popular vote share was 55 percent. A five-percentage point shift from Lincoln to McClellan would have created a popular vote tie. If Lincoln lost that much in every state, McClellan would have won the Electoral College and the presidency. Thus, the dashed line is the level at which Lincoln's reelection was in danger. A local regression line shows the national trend over time, weighted by state presidential votes in the 1864 election.[8] Lincoln's 1860 vote share essentially equaled his 1864 vote in these states. This evidence of partisan electoral stability throughout the nation's deadliest war is consistent with similar stability in war support during World War II, America's second deadliest (Berinsky 2009).

What about "recent casualties" theories? Republican votes dropped briefly in the fall of 1862, which I investigate further in Chapter 7. Otherwise, the trend is at zero throughout the war – no change. Fall 1862 is the only point when Lincoln appears in danger of losing reelection, and he seems to be on track again in 1863, if not earlier. A pattern like this would only fit recency theories if casualties were minimal across the war except for mid-1862. We already know that is decidedly *not* the case. The dead in 1863 exceeded the previous two years, and 1864 deaths overshadowed all other years. Success-based predictions for casualty effects do not fit either. Fall 1862 was not a low point in Union military performance – it immediately followed Antietam and Corinth victories. As for morally conditioned effects, the fall 1862 losses occurred *after* Lincoln announced the Emancipation Proclamation that may have added more value to victory beyond Union and democracy, and a substantial portion of the country *derided* that move.

In sum, there was almost *no* partisan electoral change in most loyal states during the war, except for the fall 1862 period. This was a shockingly stable electorate amidst national chaos. Chapter 7 continues this investigation of state-level voting trends in response to particular events.

No Differences in Partisan Bastions

Another possibility remains, more in line with my general partisan expectations: polarized reactions to national casualties based on state or local partisanship. State-level heterogeneity would manifest with heavily Republican states like Vermont and Minnesota growing more Republican over time and Democratic states like Delaware and New Jersey souring on Lincoln's party. Polarizing effects could wash out in the national trend,

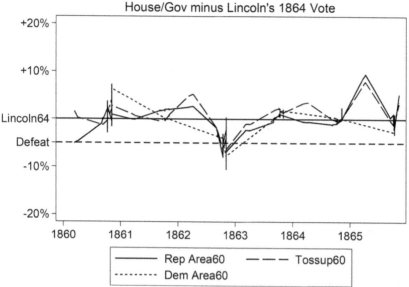

FIGURE 6.2 County-level Republican vote share in House & governor elections
Note: Contiguous free states. Democratic Area (<45% Lincoln in 1860),
Republican Area (>55%), or toss-ups (in between). Trend lines weighted by
1864 presidential votes cast.

giving the appearance of no change. That kind of pattern seems absent in
individual state data points in Figure 6.1 at first glance. However, a
clearer picture might emerge in *county*-level votes covering a wider range
of party vote shares. Polarization there might partly cancel at the state
level.

Instead, partisan bastions were just as stable in vote share as states.
Figure 6.2 replicates state-level tests with county-level data grouped by
prewar partisanship: heavily Democratic (<45 percent Republican,
lowest third), heavily Republican (>55 percent, top 42 percent), or toss-
ups.[9] The three partisan groups move together through the war with each
trend line following the state-level pattern in Figure 6.1: high stability
over time, a dip in late 1862, and a return to a balance near Lincoln's
1864 vote share in 1863.

In short, national casualties did not seem to hurt Republican vote
shares overall, and no difference materializes when looking for polarizing
effects by prewar partisanship at the county level. National casualties did
not correspond with partisan voting patterns predicted by any of the

theoretical casualty-based frameworks described – cumulative, recent, success-based, or party-contingent. Alternatively, voters might primarily respond to *local* casualties instead.

WEIGHING THE LOCAL DEAD

In many towns, the extent of wartime death meant the gradual annihilation of an entire population of able-bodied young men by combat and disease. For others, disaster came in an instant of destruction from a single calamitous attack. Military units enlisted and deployed by locale, full of neighbors, and so a field of death could instantly envelop a town's men in battle, by misfortune or heroic design. Still other places managed to escape higher death rates by luck or abstention.

We can try to imagine how these communities felt as they gathered outside newspaper and telegraph offices, anxiously awaiting word on whether friends, neighbors, fathers, sons had survived the latest battle alive and whole. Millions learned the worst. The huge numbers of Civil War dead meant that virtually every American lost people they knew *personally*. President Lincoln similarly waited through the night for battle and casualty reports at the War Department's telegraph office, some of which named his own friends among the dead. Results above showed unwavering partisan commitments despite unfathomably vast *national* deaths. But how did variation in horrendous *local* deaths shape partisan voting behavior in these most consequential elections? The immediacy of local losses should carry more weight than abstract national sums in the news.

More recent war opinion studies find robust evidence of *local* deaths eroding public support for wars and their leaders *beyond* any impact of national deaths (Gartner et al. 1997; Gartner et al. 2004; Grose & Oppenheimer 2007; Kriner & Shen 2007; Kriner & Shen 2012). *Recent* local deaths may be especially impactful (e.g. Althaus et al. 2012). Scholars posit local casualty effects arising from closeness to the dead through in-group identity and personal acquaintance (e.g. Gartner 2008).

In contrast, many public opinion scholars find no direct influence for local deaths on wartime public opinion at all, with all casualty effects mediated by partisan opinion leadership (e.g. Berinsky 2009; Karol & Miguel 2007; Kriner & Shen 2014; Zaller 1992). I argue that citizens processed *local* deaths through local and individual partisanship. Party leaders and communities provided polarized lenses for understanding wartime events, as seen in Chapter 5 news tests. Democratic newspapers were especially likely to tie the dead to vote choice, making potential effects strongest in Democratic places. That mechanism, if correct, would produce more polarized voting as local casualties grew.[10] War deaths are polarizing – even radicalizing – leading to intense hostility against the people responsible (e.g. Lyall et al. 2013). I expect partisanship adjudicates who blamed rebels and who blamed Republicans.

I know of only one study that quantitatively tests casualty effects on Civil War voting. Political scientists Jamie Carson and colleagues (2001) examined the influence of local war dead in 1862–1863 midterm elections. They concluded that congressional district dead hurt Republican candidates in 1862 but not in 1863. Like others, they argue this difference is due to the war going poorly for the Union in 1862 but better in 1863. However, their characterization of relative Union success in those years does not comport with the Civil War Sites Advisory Commission's evaluations of Union success.[11] Those midterm tests also have some measurement weaknesses that can be improved upon, namely, (1) they measured deaths for the *entire* war (not just up to 1862–1863 when the votes were cast); (2) they used a less geographically precise measure with *regimental* deaths in congressional districts (not individuals in counties), and they had local measures for only 71 of 184 districts (39 percent), distributing other dead evenly throughout the state. The tests below provide more precise casualty measures across all of the war's elections for president, U.S. House, and governor.

State-Level Deaths & Wartime Voting

I begin with state-level tests. Figure 6.3 shows the relationship between Dyer's (1908) total state war dead (black, white, and naval alike) as a proportion of military-age males and the change in Lincoln's state-level vote share between 1860 and 1864. Technically, this includes the relatively few war dead in the five months of war after the election, but county-level below address this timing problem. These state-level tests are aggregations of local processes above the level at which I expect deaths to influence voter decision-making.

Figure 6.3 shows a negative overall relationship between state casualties and change in Lincoln vote share, which might suggest direct casualty effects. However, notice the minimal change in Lincoln's votes in the free contiguous states (pyramids) where casualties were highest, clustered around zero. All low-casualty states with substantially *greater* Lincoln vote were either slave states or western states (x's) with few 1860 Lincoln

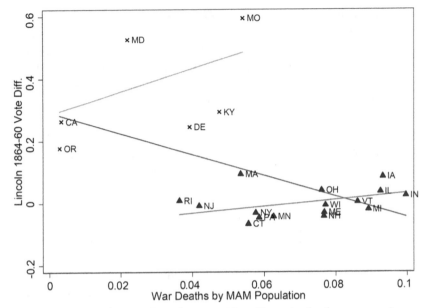

FIGURE 6.3 Lincoln vote share & state-wide military deaths (by state type)
Note: Pyramids are free contiguous states; x's are slave states or western states.

votes to begin with. These places had low war service rates too, which makes it difficult to disentangle participation from deaths.[12] The bivariate linear regression is negative ($b = -3.37$, *s.e.* = 1.24), but separate estimates for the two state categories suggest otherwise. Put simply, states with fewer deaths voted relatively more for Lincoln in 1864 than four years earlier, but we need more focused tests to consider alternative explanations.

County-Level Deaths & Presidential Voting

County-level tests move closer to the level at which I expect local deaths to register and the level more suited to influence by local party leaders and communities. I turn to American Civil War Research Database's individual soldier details (see Chapter 4 & Online Appendix). These records include death dates to measure local deaths only up through the month before governor, House, and presidential elections and tests for whether *recent* local deaths matter more for elections. I measure county deaths as a proportion of local military-age males in 1860.[13] The several hundred counties from fifteen Union states provide sufficient leverage for multi-variate models with controls to statistically rule out alternative explanations. I use six months before the election as the temporal criterion for recent deaths compared with those that occurred before that point. That date differs across states for each House and governor election staggered across calendars throughout the war.

I begin by testing the relationship between total pre-election county deaths and presidential votes with an OLS model regressing the county-level change in Lincoln's presidential vote share (1864–1860) on the total dead as a proportion of military-age males before November 1864, scaled so that moving from 0 to 1 equals a five-point rise in county dead per capita. The model controls for population, immigrant levels, and wealth per capita, weighted by 1860 voting-age male population, and it includes the proportion of military-age males enlisted before the election and the same for men drafted. These war participation measures reduce the chances of spurious attributions since local war participation correlates with local deaths, and they show the broader impact of local war experiences on votes. Draft rates might be an especially negative drain on the president's support given anti-draft animus in many places.

The left column of Table 6.1 shows a large average decline in Lincoln's vote share in counties with higher death rates. A five-percentage-point rise in local death rates corresponded with an eleven-point drop in Lincoln's votes from 1860 to 1864. The difference is substantially smaller when the model is limited to free contiguous states – a drop of about three percentage points – but the estimate remains statistically significant. Draft rates also had a corrosive impact on Lincoln's support in these counties, but the substantive impact was much smaller, given that the range of death rates was five times larger than for draft rates, making similar coefficient sizes misleading.

The right column of Table 6.1 shows recent local deaths (within six months of the election) had greater influence on voters than deaths occurring in the years before. Notably, this particular six-month period was the most sanguine of the war, including the enormously costly battles of the Overland Campaign. The losses in the six months before the election were equal to more than half the losses of the previous *three years combined*. It was a stunning escalation of death. However, these votes were also cast when most Americans were confident those deaths would lead to Union victory. Results show the average relationship between war deaths and the change in Lincoln votes is substantially and significantly larger for recent deaths compared with older deaths, by a factor of four. Recent deaths were about twice as impactful on presidential voting as total deaths before the vote.[14]

TABLE 6.1 *Local war dead & change in presidential vote choice*

	Change in Lincoln's Vote Share (1864–1860)	
	Total	Recency
Total Pre-Election Dead	−0.11*	−
(5% MAM)	(0.02)	
Dead May–October 1864	−	−0.22*
(5% MAM)		(0.04)
Dead before May 1864	−	−0.05*
(5% MAM)		(0.02)
Total Pre-Election Volunteers	0.002	0.002
(5% MAM)	(0.002)	(0.002)
Total Pre-Election Draftees	−0.15*	−0.12*
(5% MAM)	(0.05)	(0.05)
Total Population	−0.002^	−0.002
(1860 in 50k)	(0.001)	(0.001)
Immigrants	−0.05	−0.05
(1860 prop.)	(0.05)	(0.05)
Wealth per Capita	−0.07*	−0.06*
(1860)	(0.03)	(0.03)
Constant	0.15*	0.15*
	(0.03)	(0.03)
R^2	0.13	0.15
N	681	681

Note: Table entries are unstandardized OLS regression coefficients with robust standard errors in parentheses, weighted by 1860 voting-age males. "Dead" is the county-level proportion of 1860 military-age males who died in the military within the specified time (0–1 = 0 to 5% MAM). The correlation between them is 0.15. N declines from a lack of Lincoln votes for counties in KY (8), IA (3), and MN (5).
* $p < 0.05$, ^ $p < 0.10$, two-sided t-test.

Polarized Casualty Effects by Local Partisanship

Average local casualty effects might hide effects polarized by party. To test whether prewar partisanship moderates the relationship between local war dead and Lincoln votes, I sort counties into equal thirds by Lincoln's 1860 vote share (cut points at 38 percent and 55 percent). Table 6.2 replicates the total and recency models separately for each partisan third.

Casualties greatly reduced Lincoln's votes in Democratic bastions, as the left-most columns show, with local casualty effects almost wholly dependent on prewar partisanship. In contrast, places with strong support for Republicans before the war were wholly unmoved by the total local

TABLE 6.2 *Local war dead & change in presidential vote choice by prewar partisanship*

| Model Type | Change in Lincoln's Vote Share (1864–1860) | | | | | |
| | Total | | | Recency | | |
Prewar Rep. Votes	Low	Mid	High	Low	Mid	High
Total Pre-Election Dead (5% MAM)	-0.40* (0.08)	-0.04* (0.02)	-0.01 (0.01)	—	—	—
Dead May–October 1864 (5% MAM)	—	—	—	-0.77* (0.15)	-0.30* (0.05)	-0.08* (0.04)
Dead before May 1864 (5% MAM)	—	—	—	-0.27* (0.08)	0.05* (0.02)	0.03 (0.02)
Total Pre-Election Volunteers (5% MAM)	0.018* (0.005)	0.007* (0.003)	0.005^ (0.003)	0.019* (0.005)	0.008* (0.003)	0.005^ (0.003)
Total Pre-Election Draftees (5% MAM)	-0.19* (0.07)	-0.16* (0.07)	-0.09* (0.04)	-0.19* (0.07)	-0.09 (0.07)	-0.05 (0.05)
Total Population (1860 in 50k)	-0.005* (0.002)	0.03* (0.01)	0.02^ (0.01)	-0.005* (0.002)	0.04* (0.01)	0.02* (0.01)
Immigrants (1860 prop.)	-0.06 (0.05)	-0.02 (0.07)	-0.11* (0.05)	-0.01 (0.08)	-0.03 (0.06)	-0.12* (0.05)
Wealth per Capita (1860)	-0.09^ (0.03)	-0.03 (0.03)	-0.02 (0.03)	-0.08 (0.05)	-0.01 (0.03)	-0.01 (0.03)
Constant	0.26* (0.05)	-0.02 (0.03)	0.00 (0.03)	0.25* (0.05)	-0.03 (0.03)	-0.01 (0.03)
R^2	0.34	0.25	0.13	0.38	0.35	0.15
N	213	235	233	213	235	233

Note: Table entries are unstandardized OLS regression coefficients with robust standard errors in parentheses, weighted by 1860 voting-age males. "Dead" is the county-level proportion of 1860 military-age males who died in the military within the specified time (0–1 = 0 to 5% MAM). "Dead 6 Months" is the MAM proportion dead in the 6 months prior to the 1864 presidential election (May). "Dead earlier than 6 Months" counts all dead before the 6-month window.

* $p < 0.05$, ^ $p < 0.10$, two-sided t-test.

dead at the polls. In other words, Democratic places succeeded in under-mining support for Lincoln as local casualties grew, whereas Republican places staved off vote losses and kept support despite those local human losses. That strongly supports my expectations for partisan motivated reasoning, local opinion leadership, and local social influence, in line with the very different ways partisans interpreted the war and its dead.

The rightmost columns replicate the recency tests by prewar partisan-ship and find roughly the same partisan and recency patterns. Local casualties in Democratic places weighed most heavily on Lincoln's sup-port, with smaller effects in toss-up places. Recent casualty effects were smallest of all in Republican places, though they still reached statistical significance and cost Lincoln some votes. That shows Republican strong-holds weren't fully immune from the political fallout from recent local deaths. In all places, recent deaths were several times more impactful on voting than more temporally distant deaths.

Local war service effects also depended on prewar partisanship, with stronger relationships in Democratic bastions and much weaker ones in Republican strongholds. The impact of the draft differs especially by prewar partisanship, with higher draft levels eroding Lincoln vote share most in Democratic places. The result fits Horowitz and Levendusky's (2011) finding that conscription reduces modern war support. In sum, the *local* costs of war – deaths and involuntary war service – cut into Lincoln vote shares more deeply in Democratic places than in Republican ones. Average local effects primarily reflected the responses in places that were predisposed to blame Republicans.[15]

Governor & House Elections during Wartime

Wartime voting was highly synchronized across partisan offices, even in years when the president was not on the ballot. That local-national continu-ity implies similar forces shaping elections for governor, Congress, and president, including the effects of local war costs. Each state voted twice for House and at least once for governor during the war. Thus, these elections can show whether changes in the fortunes of war affected the shape of casualty effects (Carson et al. 2001; Gartner & Segura 1998; Gelpi et al. 2006) or if early-war deaths mattered more than late-war deaths (Gartner et al. 1997). My governor and House outcomes subtract prewar Republican vote share index (1856–1860 president, governor, and House) from Repub-lican vote share in the relevant election. These tests help to generalize the partisan consequences of war dead beyond late-1864 votes for the president in ways that add confidence in the presidential tests.

Results in Table 6.3 mirror presidential results. As expected, both early-and late-war voting patterns for governor and House elections largely replicate those for president in direction and magnitude. Local dead in Democratic bastions (and draft rates) consistently eroded Republican vote share, but those relationships fade and then disappear as we move into toss-up areas and Republican strongholds. This is true even though the levels of deaths were changing in each place in each period. For governors, the relationship looks stronger later in the war, when party leadership cues diverged to the greatest extent. House elections show the pattern in both halves of the war.

Although the estimates differ somewhat across offices and war stages, there are no clear differences that correspond with changing Union military progress. This robustness across offices and time is more remarkable because the measures of pre-election dead, volunteers, and draftees differ in each model, staggered across several months in each year of the war. Overall, the results provide consistent evidence of local casualty and draft effects moderated by local prewar partisanship in votes for president, governor, and Congress throughout the war.

WAR DEATHS & VOTING PARTICIPATION

How did local war experiences – felt at home as friends and family who were absent, wounded, dead, or missing – shape voter *participation* in wartime elections? Voter turnout is important to understand in its own right, but it also addresses a potential mechanism driving vote share results above. Casualties could depress Republican votes by persuasion, by changing turnout rates, or a combination of both. To my knowledge, no casualty studies account for turnout. Soldier deaths and disenfranchisement during the Civil War were large enough that those alone could depress turnout rates, but I adjust for those differences in these tests focused on civilian behavior.

Modern voting studies identify institutional factors, mobilization efforts, and individual traits as far stronger predictors than events or conditions (e.g. Burns et al. 2001). However, massive local deaths might motivate more negative local messaging from leaders and citizens during the campaign, leading to marginal shifts in voter behavior. Campaign negativity can mobilize or demobilize voters depending on whether voters have made up their minds before messaging exposure (Krupnikov 2011). Alternatively, local deaths might generally mobilize participation by raising the perceived stakes of wartime elections, regardless of how partisans framed those local war deaths (Blattman 2009).[16] For these tests, I re-estimated the models in Tables 6.2 and 6.3 with voting rates as the outcome, adjusted for absent and dead soldiers from prewar electorates. Table 6.4 presents the results.

TABLE 6.3 *War deaths & change in House & governor vote choice, 1861–1864*

Early War: 1861–1862

Prewar Rep. Votes	Governors			U.S. House		
	Low	Mid	High	Low	Mid	High
Total Pre-Election Dead (5% MAM)	-0.29	-0.20*	0.19*	-1.60*	0.16*	0.07
	(0.38)	(0.10)	(0.09)	(0.39)	(0.07)	(0.06)
Total Pre-Election Volunteers (5% MAM)	-0.03	0.01	-0.01^	0.00	-0.01*	-0.004
	(0.02)	(0.01)	(0.01)	(0.01)	(0.005)	(0.004)
R^2	0.44	0.18	0.11	0.38	0.11	0.07
N	69	146	184	217	214	215

Late War: 1863–1864

Prewar Rep. Votes	Governors			U.S. House		
	Low	Mid	High	Low	Mid	High
Total Pre-Election Dead (5% MAM)	-0.69*	-0.03	0.00	-0.69*	-0.04	0.01
	(0.09)	(0.03)	(0.02)	(0.10)	(0.02)	(0.02)
Total Pre-Election Volunteers (5% MAM)	0.02*	0.00	0.00	0.02*	0.005	0.00
	(0.01)	(0.01)	(0.00)	(0.01)	(0.004)	(0.00)
Total Pre-Election Draftees (5% MAM)	-0.37	-0.03	0.02	-0.52^	-0.09*	-0.01
	(0.25)	(0.04)	(0.05)	(0.28)	(0.04)	(0.05)
R^2	0.54	0.22	0.11	0.50	0.25	0.15
N	218	236	236	218	236	237

Note: Table entries are unstandardized OLS regression coefficients with robust standard errors in parentheses, weighted by 1860 voting-age males. Models include the same controls listed in prior tables. Dependent variables are the difference between Republican vote share in this election relative to average prewar Republican vote share. Early war excludes spring 1861 votes in NH and CT, before the war began.

* $p < 0.05$, ^ $p < 0.10$, two-sided t-test.

TABLE 6.4 *Local war deaths & change in voter turnout, 1861–1864*

1864

Prewar Rep. Votes	President		
	Low	Mid	High
Total Pre-Election Dead (5% MAM)	0.12	−0.11*	−0.02
	(0.08)	(0.04)	(0.03)
Total Pre-Election Volunteers (5% MAM)	0.01	0.01^	0.01
	(0.01)	(0.01)	(0.01)
Total Pre-Election Draftees (5% MAM)	−0.07	0.05	0.08
	(0.06)	(0.07)	(0.05)
R^2	0.30	0.21	0.05
N	213	235	233

Early War: 1861–1862

Prewar Rep. Votes	Governors			U.S. House		
	Low	Mid	High	Low	Mid	High
Total Pre-Election Dead (5% MAM)	0.06	−0.31^	0.01	−0.27	−0.03	.15^
	(0.32)	(0.17)	(0.09)	(0.29)	(0.14)	(0.09)
Total Pre-Election Volunteers (5% MAM)	−0.02	0.03*	0.01	0.03*	0.02*	0.02*
	(0.02)	(0.01)	(0.01)	(0.01)	(0.01)	(0.01)
R^2	0.08	0.16	0.22	0.19	0.19	0.16
N	69	149	184	178	224	214

(continued)

TABLE 6.4 (*continued*)

Late War: 1863–1864	Governors			U.S. House		
Prewar Rep. Votes	Low	Mid	High	Low	Mid	High
Total Pre-Election Dead (5% MAM)	-0.85	-0.05	-0.18*	-1.16	0.00	-0.10*
	(1.62)	(0.04)	(0.04)	(1.53)	(0.04)	(0.04)
Total Pre-Election Volunteers (5% MAM)	.014	0.05*	0.05*	0.14	0.04*	0.06*
	(0.14)	(0.01)	(0.01)	(0.13)	(0.01)	(0.01)
Total Pre-Election Draftees (5% MAM)	-0.71	-0.14*	-0.05	-0.97	-0.13^	-0.26*
	(0.64)	(0.06)	(0.09)	(0.63)	(0.07)	(0.10)
R^2	0.05	0.60	0.32	0.06	0.51	0.28
N	214	235	234	178	226	233

Note: Table entries are unstandardized OLS regression coefficients with robust standard errors in parentheses, weighted by 1860 voting-age males. Models include the same controls listed in prior tables. Dependent variables are the difference between voter turnout for each election relative to the latest equivalent prewar election. For states with annual governor elections, I used the first of the two years in the period (i.e. 1861, 1863).
* $p < 0.05$, ^ $p < 0.10$, two-sided t-test.

In 1864 presidential voting, local deaths corresponded with less voting in competitive areas, and they had no relationship in Republican places. The potential mobilization effect from causalities in Democratic strongholds is positive but not statistically distinct. However, the fourteen-point difference between Republican and Democratic estimates is marginally significant ($p = 0.10$). That suggests some asymmetric mobilization in the presidential election due to local dead, stronger in Democratic areas, which could be one explanation for declining Republican vote shares in those places. Higher overall turnout would hold more benefits for the predominant party. On the other hand, that explains only a small part of the relationship between casualties and partisan vote choice. When I add change in turnout as a control in the partisan vote choice models, results hardly change.

Equivalent models for early- and late-war votes for governor and House provide inconsistent results, which may reduce confidence in the presidential election turnout estimates. Alternatively, mobilization dynamics in House and governor elections may have differed. We know, for example, that turnout was lower in those contests than in presidential elections, though not by a large degree. Local military voluntarism consistently corresponded positively with higher local voting rates in places of all political stripes. This could be due to the community's greater civic commitment due to having more of its men away at war, or it may reflect a more general trait of community participation in public life. Local draft exposure seems to have broadly had the opposite effect, demobilizing potential voters. That might be because public officials used voting registration as a means to find individuals who were evading the draft – draft participation obligations accompanied voting rights as a citizen. Registering to vote meant adding your name to the draft list if it wasn't there already. Republican newspapers crowed about this requirement before elections. In places with higher draft rates, those who wanted to avoid a similar fate may have stayed home from the polls rather than risk the draft themselves.

In sum, local war casualties and war participation influenced voter turnout along with vote choice, with evidence of mobilization and persuasion operating together in response to war experiences.

CONCLUSIONS

How did the public respond to incomparably large war death rates when given the chance to sustain or end the war at the ballot box through partisan votes? Learning how war costs shaped voter behavior is important for understanding the political history of the Civil War, but it also tells us more about how citizens respond generally to the carnage of war, especially given casualty rates unmatched in any other U.S. elections. I first tested the impact of national casualties over time with a measure of national partisan mood using staggered House and governor elections to test reactions to casualties throughout the war. That measure works because partisan nationalization and synchronization across offices in the antebellum and wartime period were similar to what we see today. That partisan barometer showed cumulative national casualties did nothing to hurt the governing party despite the greatest bloodletting the nation has ever seen. Partisan vote share stability challenges the casualty theories that predict declines in public war support due to national totals, recent dead, success-based accounts, and indirect effects of the national dead conditioned by local partisanship.

Local war costs had far greater effects on wartime voting, though their influence was still marginal, not massive. The result was partisan polarization to a startling degree. Voters who processed local war deaths and conscription through partisan lenses polarized voting in wartime elections. Reactions in Democratic bastions drove the *average* local effects that eroded votes for Lincoln and his fellow Republicans. In contrast, voters in Republican strongholds mostly remained electorally unmoved, consistent with expectations based on motivated reasoning, opinion leadership, and social influence. That fits well with Chapter 5 evidence showing Democratic newspapers explicitly linking war deaths to vote rationales far more than Republicans did. Recent deaths were especially impactful, with small Republican vote losses even in the most Republican places. Local conscription effects depended similarly on local partisanship. Finally, I found some slight evidence of greater vote mobilization in Democratic places compared with Republican ones with heavier local death rates.

In sum, the war experience made a profound mark on voters, but that mark depended on *local* rather than *national* costs, more on recent experiences, and dependent on local partisanship in ways that completely refracted consequences for voting. The results therefore attest to the striking power of partisanship – the ability to process even the most extreme national events and conditions in ways that reinforce long-standing partisan identities and views, with the help of local leaders and community members. In the face of maximal local losses, Democratic places became more convinced that empowering Republicans was a mistake, while Republican places saw no reason for change. That fits well with historical accounts emphasizing the importance of partisanship in guiding mass behavior during the Civil War and causes trouble for narratives that downplay partisanship.

The heterogeneity in these results comports with scholarship on casualty effects in modern American wars, including the conditioning effects of partisanship (e.g. Berinsky 2009; Karol & Miguel 2007; Kriner & Shen 2014; Zaller 1992), and the importance of local and recent casualties (Althaus et al. 2011; Gartner & Segura 1998, 2000; Kriner & Shen 2014). That consonance is remarkable given differences in scale between the American Civil War and the wars that formed the evidentiary basis for these theories. On the other hand, the evidence did not support scholarship arguing emphasizing moderating effects based on how the war is going (Carson et al. 2001; Gartner & Segura 1998; Gelpi et al. 2006), or whether the judgment is cast early or late in the war (Gartner et al. 1997). In both directions, this analysis provides a fuller understanding of public reactions to war by introducing evidence from the most lethal American military conflict. With findings placed in context, this chapter adds to the tangled cyclical relationship between partisan electoral politics and violence.

The public interpreted the war's human costs – with guidance from leaders – in ways that reaffirmed prewar views, despite a more extreme election context than any other in our history. In Chapter 7, I dig deeper into election results in search of events-based explanations for 1862 Republican midterm losses, and I put conventional wisdom to the test on the electoral impact of wartime events, including the most remarkable such claim in American history involving the capture of Atlanta by Union troops.

Partisan Stability & the Myth of Atlanta

The Electoral Inconsequence of Wartime Events

You think I don't know I am going to be beaten [in the election], *but I do*
and unless some great change takes place *badly beaten.*
President Abraham Lincoln
1864[1]

I claim not to have controlled events, but confess plainly that events have
controlled me.
President Abraham Lincoln
1864[2]

Lincoln is the most truly progressive man of the age, because he always
moves in conjunction with propitious circumstances, not waiting to be
dragged by the force of events or wasting strength in premature struggles
with them.
John Forney, editor
Washington Daily Chronicle
1863[3]

Americans venerate Abraham Lincoln by acclamation today, but in mid-
1864, the president was a deeply polarizing figure. In fact, much of the
political class was sure he was doomed to lose reelection a few months
later, including the president himself. Seemingly, all thought the public
was despairing after three years of immense casualties and increasing
death rates with no end in sight. Near-constant battles in June and July
killed more men than any year prior, and then U.S. armies stalled outside
rebel strongholds in Atlanta and the Confederate capital of Richmond,
Virginia, making precious little visible progress. Republican leaders worried their own electoral fortunes would fall with Lincoln, and that these

calamities would produce a Democratic-led peace deal surrendering the Union and emancipation forever. Some prominent Republicans even maneuvered to replace him as the party's nominee.[4] Republicans thought they needed Union armies to win a major military victory. Only that would revive the public's war spirit and fortify resolve to see the conflict to a Union victory.

Then, at summer's end, U.S. troops commanded by General William T. Sherman captured Atlanta. The war's endgame suddenly became clear, and Lincoln went on to win reelection handily over former General George McClellan – the popular vote by ten points and a tenfold Electoral College majority. Politicians and journalists interpreted the Atlanta victory (and subsequent military success) as the principal cause of Lincoln's reelection – trading certain defeat for certain victory. Historians have largely deferred to those contemporary judgments. If so, it's the biggest, most consequential "game-changer" in electoral history. But there are good reasons for doubt – politicos, journalists, and pundits as a group are *terrible* judges of what moves public opinion, especially regarding the impact of campaign events.[5] That's true today, even with polls and research available to correct false claims. Nineteenth century politicians had no better means for judgment. On the other hand, despite skepticism about the electoral power of events today, the Civil War was the most extreme election context imaginable – creating environments in which unprecedented events would plausibly change votes, if ever they could.

So was Lincoln *really* doomed without Atlanta – was that military victory an epic "game-changer"? Or is that drama a campaign myth, like many events-based claims in campaign news today? The Atlanta narrative is also consistent with widely reported general volatility of public mood throughout the war following big shifts in war politics and progress. Chapter 6 already cast doubt on national casualties depressing Republican returns, but how volatile was public response to particular war events? What does systematic evidence say about tumultuous wartime opinion and its voting implications?

I tackle those questions here and narrate the war's history-in-brief for readers less familiar with its key contours. These sections compare historians' impressions of volatile public mood with systematic electoral evidence, looking for signs of public volatility in each state. James McPherson's work serves as a representative benchmark for the balance of scholarly views. I attend most to claims linking fall 1862 events with those midterms and the Atlanta victory to the presidential vote. I test the stability of partisan votes under the most extreme circumstances imaginable, with the surprising conclusion that *nothing* national seemed to move *partisan* votes in the Civil War, even if public mood swung wildly. The evidence rebalances narratives about America's most momentous elections.

A Volatile or Unflappable Electorate?

Nineteenth century politicians, journalists, other contemporaries, and the historians who write about them tend to describe a volatile Civil War public whipsawing between agony and ecstasy in response to military and political events. The empirical case for *electoral* volatility hinges on whether local observations by these sources – even those aided by the national distribution of major newspapers – were capable of making valid predictions about electoral support and the forces that move it (or don't), distinct from public *mood*. Without sound evidence and methods of inference, the conventional wisdom on Civil War public opinion, then and now, could be flat-out wrong.

Historians' accounts of the war – drawn firsthand from leaders and ordinary people – present a Northern public swinging from bitter despair after Union battle defeats to euphoric highs following victories. James McPherson (2002) writes, "The roller coaster ride of public opinion in response to events on the battlefields, both in the North and South, was a crucial factor in the war. Victory pumped up civilian as well as army morale and sustained the will to keep fighting; defeat depressed morale and encouraged defeatism" (p. 48). Similar narratives multiply in the aftermath of momentous policies like the Emancipation Proclamation and the military draft. From this perspective, every major event threatened or bolstered the odds of Republican majorities in Congress and Lincoln's second term. Financial markets were similarly volatile, jumping or falling based on the valence of war-related news (e.g. McPherson 1988; Neely 2002; Schwert 1989; Willard et al. 1996).[6] Public volatility is plausible given the unprecedented nature of the Civil War. Even political scientists skeptical of events-based electoral explanations allow for some exceptions. For example, Donald Green and colleagues (2002) write, "To argue that political events seldom impact partisan identities is compatible with the claim that events do matter under certain circumstances" (p. 11).

On the other hand, political scientists consistently find little evidence of aggregate or individual shifts in vote choice in most modern campaigns due to the anchor of partisanship and campaign reinforcement effects (Gelman & King 1993; Lazarsfeld et al. 1944; Sides & Vavreck 2013).

Some Civil War historians emphasize the stability and loyalty of Civil War partisans, as noted in previous chapters. Ultimately, those historical accounts have a two-headed quality, alternately emphasizing stability and maximal partisan disruption, sometimes within the same works.

The preceding chapters already provide direct evidence on the stability of Civil War–era voting. Chapter 2 found strong correlations between 1860 and 1864 presidential votes, and Chapter 6 found the same between presidential votes and others cast during the war. However, those correlations could still mask consistent net shifts across states and counties. More telling, Chapter 6 seems to show voters' insensitivity to *all* national Civil War events. In dozens of data points scattered across the four years of war, the national average in partisan voting patterns was largely stable for the duration of the war, and Republican and Democratic bastions were similarly unresponsive. I dig deeper here with a state-by-state stability evaluation juxtaposed with a narrative of wartime events. I focus again on the contiguous free states given the tumult and shifts in enslaving and western Union states.

EVENTS IN EARLY-WAR ELECTIONS

South Carolina claimed secession in December 1860. All six Deep South states followed in the next six weeks, and Lincoln took office on March 4. Did Northern partisan votes shift after the first wave of secession and Lincoln's inauguration? Voters may have feared further Republican gains would exacerbate tensions and therefore switched their votes in appeasement. Alternatively, they might have gained more resolve in the face of Southern treason.

The answer is almost perfect stability in early 1861 voting compared with 1860. Connecticut voted for governor and House of Representatives, and New Hampshire chose House members in March and early April, at Republican levels equal to their votes the year before.[7] Figure 7.1 shows Republican vote shares from 1860 through 1865 (normed by the difference from Lincoln's 1864 state vote share), along with Rhode Island for later reference. Much changed between spring 1860 and spring 1861, but partisan votes in these states did not. Chapter 6 shows state election results usually moved in tandem with national trends, so we can probably generalize from these to suggest minimal partisan change across the Union.

In July, Union troops moved from Washington, DC, aiming to capture the Confederate capital at Richmond, Virginia, which lay tantalizingly

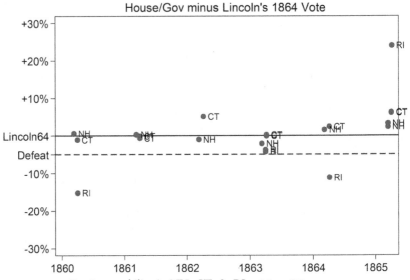

FIGURE 7.1 Partisan stability in NH, CT, & RI, 1860–1865

close to the U.S. capital. The opposing armies clashed beside Bull Run Creek along the way. What appeared early on to be a Union victory became an embarrassing defeat as Confederate reinforcements arrived by train to turn the tide. Casualties were light relative to later tolls, but the nearly 500 Union soldiers killed and 2,500 wounded or captured shocked the public, politicians, and press. Under a new commander, General George McClellan, the Eastern army regrouped, and then regrouped some more. So much regrouping, in fact, that they remained immobile for the rest of 1861. That built soldierly skills and morale, but it did not deploy the army's substantial advantages against the rebellion. Far from northern Virginia, the war kindled on multiple additional fronts spanning half the continent. Union forces in Missouri lost the Battle of Wilson's Creek, the first major fight west of the Mississippi River. By any measure, 1861 was a bad year for Union forces.

Meanwhile, Republicans pressed their advantage in Congress with new super-majorities following the departure of Southern Democrats turned Confederate, adjusting quorum rules to proceed with legislative business in their absence. The 37th Congress passed two major pieces of legislation in late 1861: the Revenue Act introduced the nation's first federal income tax, and the first Confiscation Act authorized taking property (including

1860–1865 Change in Republican Vote Share
House/Gov minus Lincoln's 1864 Vote

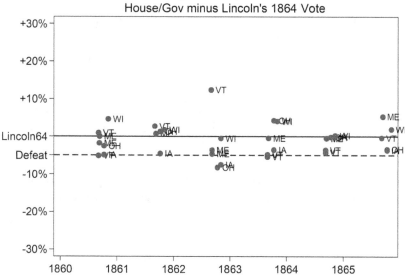

FIGURE 7.2 Partisan stability in VT, OH, ME, IA, & WI, 1860–1865

slaves) from Confederates who used that property to further the rebellion. They also retroactively endorsed Lincoln's localized suspension of habeas corpus in sites of active rebellion, which he had done while Congress was out of session and therefore unable to act on the crisis.

McPherson (1988) describes a "winter of Northern discontent" as the year ended and 1862 began (p. 15). Did these events affect Republican support in the fall 1861 elections? No. Figure 7.2 shows election results for free contiguous states that voted between September and November in 1861: Vermont, Ohio, Maine, Iowa, and Wisconsin. All states but Iowa cluster tightly together, centered on the same vote share Lincoln would get three years later. Republican 1861 vote shares aligned with those the year before, when the group was dispersed around a similar mean. Despite secession and the first year of partisan civil war, there is little electoral evidence of strengthened resolve favoring Republicans or, conversely, that disappointment in the face of military defeats and inaction hurt them.

By all historical accounts, Democrats were never in greater disarray than in elections between fall 1861 and spring 1862 (e.g. Silbey 1977). The usually robust Democratic campaign apparatus was almost wholly unorganized, with widespread failures to meet, canvass the public, hold rallies, and mobilize their supporters to the polls. Many Democrats at this time seemed to agree with Republicans that electioneering was inappropriate in a civil war. Despite this lack of party effort, the elections in this period show minimal evidence of Republican vote gains that should follow from a one-sided campaign against inert opponents. Although Republican vote share dips in fall 1862 when Democrats resumed vigorous oppositional campaigning, the 1861 "no-party" votes align with all those in 1863 through 1865. In other words, even when Democrats exerted maximal effort, their performance was little different from when they reportedly abandoned campaigning all together. That's surprising. It is possible, of course, that several electoral forces perfectly counterbalanced, offsetting gains and losses. A more parsimonious explanation is that Civil War voting was surprisingly stable – that local partisanship remained remarkably robust, even in the face of national tumult *and* party inaction.

Gains in the West, Losses in the East: Early 1862

The mid-1862 fighting season produced the first mass-casualty battles – thousands dead on each side – the sort of colossal, sudden death that became routine as ever-larger armies clashed more frequently and intensely. Several of the year's fiercest battles killed, wounded, or captured one in five men who participated in them. That was three times the casualty rate endured by Allied forces on D-Day in World War II.

Congress passed the Legal Tender Act in February, which introduced federal paper money ("greenbacks") for the first time. In February and early March, Union soldiers and sailors won the first important Union victories at river forts Henry and Donelson in Tennessee, where an obscure general named Ulysses S. Grant led the capture of 12,000 rebel troops and then seized Tennessee's capital at Nashville downriver, the first rebel state capital to fall. A similar victory at Island Number Ten on the Mississippi River yielded 7,000 rebel prisoners and greatly extended federal control down that strategically vital waterway. Each river fort that fell opened hundreds of river miles for U.S. naval gunboats to wreak havoc on supply lines and troop transports in the heart of the Confederacy. Likewise, victory at Pea Ridge gained U.S. forces surer control over Missouri and northern Arkansas.

After Fort Donelson, James McPherson writes "Almost overnight the Northern mood vaulted from despondency to ecstasy," and Union victory at Pea Ridge shortly after "had a profound effect on home-front morale" (2002, pp. 15, 19). Early 1861 *votes* show little sign of jubilation favoring

Republicans, however. Figure 7.1 shows New Hampshire dipped ever so slightly in 1862 relative to the previous years, and Connecticut rose about 5 percent over 1861. Was that elation over the western victories? Probably not. The fact that New Hampshire didn't respond similarly suggests idiosyncrasy rather than a national shift, and it was small in any case.

In the first half of 1862, the Republican Congress abolished slavery in the national capital, created the Department of Agriculture, accelerated western settlement with the Homestead Act, and banned slavery in U.S. territories. The last ended decades of contention that had wrecked two major parties and led to the war. Next, they passed the Anti-Bigamy Act targeting Latter-day Saints ("Mormons") in Utah Territory with limits on church finances and a ban on polygamy, enacted the first progressive income tax, established land-grant colleges, accelerated the transcontinental railroad, and enlisted African American laborers and soldiers in a national war effort for the first time in decades. Few periods in Congress' 225-year history were more consequential than these few months.

The April battle of Shiloh in Tennessee was the first with mass casualties comparable to the worst that would come. Grant won a strategic victory consolidating control of Tennessee and dooming the vital rebel rail crossroads nearby at Corinth, Mississippi. The human costs of those gains were staggering: 13,000 Union casualties. As April ended, the U.S. Navy captured New Orleans, Louisiana – the largest Confederate city. The state capital of Baton Rouge fell soon after. Union armies lost an important series of battles in Virginia's Shenandoah Valley in May, and Union troops under McClellan lost the Seven Days' Battles in June at a loss of 16,000 Union troops.

Confederate victories in Virginia "caused a temporary panic in the North," and "came as a huge shock to the North. The plunge of Northern morale was all the greater because expectations built on almost uninterrupted success over the previous four months had been so high" (McPherson 2002, pp. 42, 47). Unfortunately, we have no elections in this span with which to gauge voters, though the Chapter 5 newspaper analysis includes mid-July issues to give rhetorical purchase on party elites, showing steady, but slightly negative outlooks compared with 1861 after Bull Run, rather than a sharp decline. At the same time, Kentucky faced invasion by Morgan's Confederate cavalry. Secessionists in the state "begged him to leave the State as rapidly as possible – that his coming at this time would utterly ruin their cause at the August election, if it had not already done so," according to the anti-war *Louisville Democrat* (quoted in *Boston Evening Traveller*, MA-R, July 1862). Both sides hoped and feared war events would shape 1862 elections. Union forces in the East lost again in late August at the Second Battle of Bull Run, adding another 10,000 Union casualties to the toll. McPherson (2002) writes, "These were dark, dismal days in the North – perhaps the darkest of many such days during the war" (p. 85).

Fall 1862 Battles & Emancipation

Confederates under Lee followed up their Virginia victories with an invasion of Maryland in an effort to refresh supplies, gain international recognition, and pressure the Northern public to move against Republicans in midterm elections. It ended with a costly Union win at Antietam, the first real victory for Union forces in the East. The insurgents retreated to Virginia. The Union lost 12,000 soldiers in the bloodiest single day of fighting in American history. Lincoln fired General McClellan for withholding Union military reserves that could have effected a more resounding victory and for letting the rebels escape afterward.

With a recent major victory in hand, Lincoln issued the preliminary Emancipation Proclamation. The executive order threatened to emancipate all enslaved people in states still in rebellion on January 1 of the coming year. It was enforced by U.S. troops as they slowly reestablished national authority throughout the South. Enslaved people had fled north for decades, and they escaped by the thousands into Union military lines during the war. These "fugitive slaves" put immense political pressure on the U.S. government as it tried to navigate Republican emancipation pressures and Border State calls to re-enslave people by sending them back to their rebel owners. Lincoln's order recognized that the rebellion sustained itself with slave labor. Ironically, a rebellion inaugurated to expand slavery enabled what the enslavers feared most, pushing an institution odiously protected by the Constitution into the legitimate sights of the U.S. military, for obliteration by massive force. The combination of military victory and emancipation staved off international intervention by Britain and France, which could have tilted odds in the Confederacy's favor (McPherson 2002).

The Proclamation changed the character of the war from one to reunite with rebellious states to one that included the permanent destruction of American slavery, though that end was not certain until Lincoln's reelection assured military and politica victory. Democrats violently opposed emancipation, especially in border slave states, but most Northerners came to support the policy as a means to punish the South and relieve the Union of its greatest threat. Some appreciated its importance for respecting the humanity of enslaved people. The *Burlington Free Press* (VT-R, July 1862) wrote, "The attempt of the South at revolution for slavery, has worked a portentous revolution in sentiment against slavery, in the border slave States and the free States. ... Slowly and reluctantly, but certainly, the mind of the nation opens to the apprehension that slavery and the Constitution cannot live together, and that slavery must perish." While pleased with the policy, Republican leaders worried the announcement of impending emancipation would cause the party to lose support in fall elections and perhaps even push nominally loyal border slave states into rebellion.

The Antietam victory boosted the public. "The Northern press broke out in a paroxysm of exultation, all the more exuberant because of the pessimism that had preceded it" (McPherson 2002, p. 135). The victory "reversed a disastrous decline in the morale of Northern soldiers and civilians" (McPherson 2002, p. xvi). Had it gone the other way, McPherson suggests "the willingness of the Northern people to keep fighting for the Union" might have failed (2002, p. 94). He writes:

Before Antietam, Republicans and Democrats alike considered the prospect of Democratic control of the House all but certain. The Democrats nominated their candidates and adopted their "war is a failure" platforms during those August and early September days of "profound despondency" ... if the elections had been held any time during the three weeks after Antietam, however, Republicans might have defied the tradition of significant losses by the party in power in mid-term elections and retained their two-to-one majority in the House. ... But the post-Antietam euphoria – and its attendant political benefits – gradually wore off during those three weeks.

(p. 149)

Some historians say McClellan's failure to destroy Lee's army and public resentment about emancipation hurt the Republican Party in fall elections (Smith 2006, pp. 57, 63). On the contrary, Gary Gallagher (2011) argues emancipation had little effect on a public focused predominantly on the Union. McPherson (2002) also attributes Democratic gains in Pennsylvania to a Confederate raid that ended the day before (p. 150). Union forces managed to turn back the Confederate invasion of Kentucky and win another significant battle at Corinth, Mississippi, both in early October. Overall, Adam Smith (2006) writes that local Republican operatives thought fall battle victories "made a huge difference to their support, perhaps accounting for the better than expected showing" (p. 58).

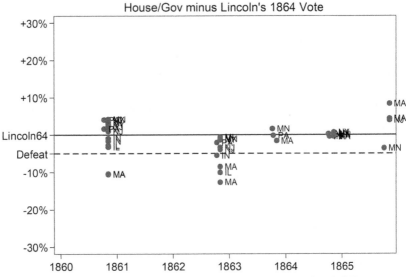

FIGURE 7.3 Partisan stability in MN, MA, IL, PA, MI, IN, NY, & NJ, 1860–1865

Republicans lost substantial vote share in fall 1862 compared with prior and future returns. Figure 7.2 above shows several of the voting states. Vermont and Maine provide useful referents with votes taken immediately before Antietam. Vermont's Republican vote rises from 1861, but Maine's shows a drop. Wisconsin and Ohio voted after Antietam, falling two and ten points below their 1861 Republican votes, respectively. New Hampshire and Connecticut also span this time – between March 1862 and March 1863 – with one- and four-point drops (Figure 7.1). Figure 7.3 shows the remaining non–Border States not included in Figures 7.1 and 7.2 – the ones that voted in fall 1862 but did not cast votes in 1861. Compared with 1860 votes, these states generally had similar declines in Republican support around 5 percent. Illinois falls even further, around 10 percent. Massachusetts is also low relative to Lincoln's eventual 1864 vote share but not much different from its 1860 votes. Individual states here roughly match the national average seen in Chapter 6.

Notably, even at this lowest moment of support across all five years, Republicans averaged only a little past the −5 percent tipping point for Lincoln to lose reelection in 1864. In other words, his reelection would have been close to a toss-up *at worst* even if held at this lowest point in wartime Republican votes. Of course, even this conservative comparison overstates the political danger for Lincoln if the decline was due to factors other than war pessimism, which I explore next.

INTERPRETING MIDTERM LOSSES IN FALL 1862

Republicans performed relatively well in 1861 and early 1862, but the party lost substantial vote share in late 1862. Republicans rebounded back to earlier levels in 1863 and sustained that average level through the 1864 elections, despite "increasing popular resistance to the draft and to emancipation" from 1863 onward (Smith 2006, p. 76). In terms of power, Republicans lost twenty-one House seats and majority control in a three-party chamber that included slave state Unionists as a separate faction that substantially backed the war but not emancipation. Republicans gained Senate seats elected by state legislatures. This section tries to explain the brief drop in Republican support. Was it due to battle outcomes or war progress views, the preliminary Emancipation Proclamation, midterm cycles, disenfranchised soldiers, or election interference?

Any explanation based on war progress is ultimately unsatisfying. The Republican decline comes right after a major Union strategic victory, and so we should see gains, if anything. Even if there were reasons to feel mixed about Antietam and its aftermath, there were certainly much darker days of the war in which a drop in Republican support should have been greater. Instead, we see no Republican losses outside this brief period. There is no reason why war mood in fall 1862 would be the exception in an otherwise stable national partisan electorate.

What about emancipation? That proves to be a dubious factor too. We should expect polar responses, with equal or rising Republican support in strong anti-slavery states and losses in pro-slavery ones. Instead, most states dropped together by similar amounts from prior vote levels. Figure 7.4 plots vote shifts in all states voting twice within about a year on either side of Antietam and the preliminary Emancipation Proclamation. The figure shows stability for Iowa, New Hampshire, and Wisconsin. Connecticut drops some and Ohio drops a little more, even though both states historically cast more substantially anti-slavery Free Soil votes than Iowa did. Maine and Vermont moved in opposite directions in votes cast just *before* the battle compared with the year before.

Next, I broaden comparisons to span from late 1860 to late 1862 (Figures 7.2 & 7.3). These show five- to ten-point Republican vote share

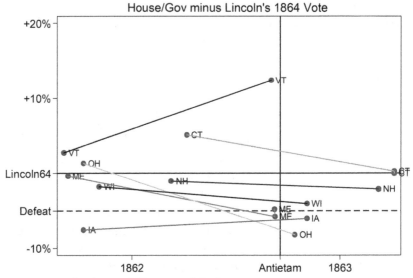

FIGURE 7.4 Partisan stability around Antietam

losses with surprising consistency. Massachusetts lost the most Republican votes despite its reputation as an anti-slavery stalwart. New York and Wisconsin had also cast substantial Free Soil votes in the past, but Republicans lost vote share there too, like other states. The enslaving states that hated emancipation most faced electoral chaos due to the war, making it difficult to interpret their votes, though Republicans generally did *better* in those states after the Emancipation announcement. Overall, it is hard to find patterns plausibly due to emancipation.

As a third explanation, McPherson (2002) observes that fall 1862 Republican election trouble may just be cyclical losses for the president's party, then and now, and that the losses in 1862–63 were especially mild by comparison. Table 7.1 illustrates McPherson's point. Net Republican seat losses in the House were the third lowest for the president's party across a forty-year span, and the party retained all but two Northern governorships (McPherson 2002, p. 154). Seemingly, then, the public responded *positively* toward Republicans, relative to its usual treatment of governing parties.[8] The problem with the cyclical explanation is that these tallies aggregate elections spanning well over a year, but vote share was *only* lost during fall 1862. If it were a midterm cycle, why does it only affect those fall 1862 states and not all the states voting for

TABLE 7.1 *Midterm losses for the president's party, 1842–1882*

Year	President's Party	House Seats Lost by President's Party	Seats Won of Total	Percentage of Seats After	Percentage of Seats Prior	Vote Change (%)	Seats Lost by President's Party (%)
1842	Whig	-69	73 of 223	33	59	-26	-31
1846	Democrat	-30	112 of 230	49	63	-14	-13
1850	Whig	-22	86 of 233	37	49	-12	-9
1854	Democrat	-75	75 of 234	32 (plurality)	69	-37	-32
1858	Democrat	-35	98 of 238	41	60	-19	-15
1862	Republican	-21	87 of 185	47 (plurality)	60	-13	-11
1866	Democrat*	+9*	47 of 224	21	21	0	0
1870	Republican	-34	137 of 243	56	72	-16	-14
1874	Republican	-89	106 of 293	36	69	-34	-30
1878	Republican	-10	131 of 293	45	46	-1	-3
1882	Republican	-29	121 of 325	37	54	-17	-9

*1866 was odd in that President Johnson, a Democrat, had been elected with Lincoln, a Republican. The seat total is low in 1862 due to Southern secession and withdrawal from Congress.

171

the same midterm class through 1863? Beyond that, why wouldn't voters treat 1861 votes and early 1864 votes like a midterm? None of those periods shows vote losses like those in fall 1862. By comparison, Democratic vote share during Buchanan's presidency was depressed in every non-presidential year for House and governor – 1857, 1858, and 1859 – but equal in 1856 and 1860, on average. That all seems to push against the cycle explanation.

A fourth potential answer comes from Bensel's (2004) study of Civil War vote irregularities, which calls election integrity into question. Federal troops and other officials policed the polls in the Union slave states and big cities, and they prevented some men from voting (see also Smith 2006, pp. 97–100). Loyalty oaths late in the war prevented secessionists from casting ballots (if unwilling to swear a false oath). Federal interference would have aimed to *improve* outcomes for Republicans in places where they applied pressure, but Bensel suggested to me that a backlash to intervention might have *hurt* Republicans in nearby places that saw less federal activity. Could federal election interference produce the voting changes limited to fall 1862? I'm skeptical. Republican losses were similar across most states, not just enslaving states, and they appear in all county types – from heavily Democratic through heavily Republican (see Chapter 6). Even if federal interference was a key factor in votes nationwide, the fall 1862 scope would need to be greater than at other points throughout the war. That seems unlikely based on most histories I've read describing wartime voting.

A final possible explanation is the absence of over half a million voters who were away at war – disproportionately from Republican localities, as Chapter 4 showed – and who did not have ballot access until absentee procedures were implemented, mostly after 1862. The Army furloughed some troops home to vote, especially those from vulnerable congressional or gubernatorial seats, but furloughs were not possible for most soldiers. Most states allowed absentee soldier votes by 1864, but several Democratic states refused. Democratic politicians were right to worry about soldiers' votes: they backed Lincoln by a margin twenty points larger than his national popular vote share.

Soldier votes could only explain the puzzling results if there were few soldiers away from home before fall 1862, huge numbers absent in fall 1862, and then immediate absentee voting making up the entire difference beginning a few months later. Military size did leap between mid-1861 and early 1862, and then largely leveled off.[9] That could explain the decline, but absentee voting didn't expand broadly until 1864, which can't explain the return to equilibrium throughout 1863.

Summary

Fall 1862 elections show a moderate decline in Republican support. If not reversed, the losses may have threatened Lincoln's reelection chances. However, the party rebounded in 1863 elections and remained stable afterward. Seen in context with McPherson's (2002) point about midterm losses for the president's party, this result is better than average. Periodic midterm cycles seem to explain the losses better than disgruntled voters moving against the war or emancipation, or the absence of Republican-leaning soldier-voters, though a big puzzle remains regarding why the losses did not extend to other off-cycle votes outside the fall 1862 window. Perhaps several factors worked in combination, making it difficult to arrive at any solid conclusions. Regardless, the evidence deflates several common explanations for Republican losses in these elections.

TURNING POINTS IN EAST & WEST: LATE-WAR ELECTIONS

December 1862 ended badly for the Union at Fredericksburg, Virginia, in a lost battle that netted 13,000 Union casualties in suicidal frontal charges. Though Union troops suffered twice the losses of the enemy, Lincoln recognized that rebel armies would be exhausted before Union ones, even at that awful rate. West Virginia joined the Union in December, seceding from rebel Virginia. In February 1863, Congress passed anti-fraud legislation for federal contractors selling "shoddy" military goods and introduced whistleblower laws still in force today. New laws in March began military conscription, delegated presidential authority for suspending habeas corpus in a rebellion, and restructured the judiciary.

Connecticut, New Hampshire, and Rhode Island were the next states to vote following Union losses at Fredericksburg and the inconclusive battle at Stones River near Murfreesboro, Tennessee, which cost another 13,000 Union casualties. These states continued the midterm election season, but they showed far less evidence of Republican struggles than those a few months earlier, despite two major battle losses and the formal enactment of emancipation. Connecticut was down four points for Republicans from the year before (but equaled Lincoln's 1864 vote share), New Hampshire was only down one, and Rhode Island was ten points *better* for Republicans than in its prior vote in 1860. Republicans soundly defeated Copperhead candidates in each state.

Chancellorsville, Virginia, was the site of the second major 1863 battle in early May – another Confederate victory – with Union troops losing

17,000 casualties. Also in May, and with far greater success, Union General Grant executed an end-run around the Mississippi River bluffs of Vicksburg after months of frustration, putting that city under siege and pressing its occupants toward a choice between surrender and starvation. The city relented on July 4, putting 29,000 surrendered rebels out of the fight. The U.S. victory there and another soon after at Port Hudson, Louisiana, ceded full control of the vital Mississippi River to the Union while dividing the Confederacy in two. Lincoln poetically remarked, "The Father of Waters again goes unvexed to the sea."[10] On the same day, another rebel invasion ended in retreat after Union victory at Gettysburg, Pennsylvania, costing 23,000 Union casualties over three days, the most of any battle in the war. On the third day, General Lee commanded Pickett's suicidal charge that greatly depleted rebel ranks. Later in July came the first major fighting for U.S. Colored Troops and the first Union military draft, which led to a week of white riots in New York City against black residents and federal authority.

September saw Union defeat at the Battle of Chickamauga in northern Georgia, costing 16,000 Union casualties, and rebels besieged U.S. forces in Chattanooga, Tennessee. Lincoln delivered his two-minute Gettysburg Address that November, recasting America's national purpose toward "a new birth of freedom" (Wills 1992). The president promoted Grant to U.S. western theater commander, who led troops in a breakout from Chattanooga, defeating rebels dug in on a steep ridge outside of town with an unplanned charge. Union troops lost 6,000 casualties. Overall, 1863 mixed Union victories and defeats, and Lincoln worried war troubles would cause losses like 1862 to recur. Doris Kearns Goodwin (2005) writes, "recent battlefield victories augured well for Republican chances," but "the divisive issues of civil liberties, slavery, and Reconstruction threatened to erode support in many places" (p. 573). Republicans ultimately gained sizable victories over anti-war Democrats.

In fall 1863 elections, Republicans fared substantially better than in fall 1862, and they equaled or exceeded Lincoln's future 1864 vote. Figure 7.2 shows states voting at this time. Besides Vermont, all states show moderate or large gains of 3 to 12 percent. If there was any substance to the 1862 dip beyond midterm cycles, it was gone in 1863. The national Republican vote share was back to its prior level, and it remained there through Lincoln's reelection the following year.

ATLANTA IN LINCOLN'S REELECTION

U.S. forces made momentous military progress in 1864, and the year's elections incalculably shaped the nation's political future. Lincoln promoted Grant to lead all U.S. forces as General Sherman took command in the West, starting a campaign that soon captured Atlanta.[11] Early in the year, rebels turned back the Union's Red River Campaign through central Louisiana, adding 5,500 Union casualties in a failed effort to subdue most remaining rebels west of the Mississippi. Early 1864 elections went well for Republicans, outperforming Lincoln's eventual vote share in three of four states. Connecticut and New Hampshire showed small Republican gains over 1863 levels (see Figure 7.1). Unsteady Rhode Island's vote was substantially lower than the year before.

May began the war's end in the East, though no one knew it at the time. Grant's Overland Campaign had several inconclusive, large-casualty battles condensed in under two months as his army maneuvered into collision after collision with the enemy – 18,000 Union casualties in the dense forests of Virginia's Wilderness, Spotsylvania Court House with 18,000 more, a suicidal assault on entrenchments at Cold Harbor sacrificing 13,000 Union casualties, most in under an hour. Grant was undeterred by heavy losses, recognizing the proportionally greater mortal costs for rebel armies and the need to attack relentlessly to win. Grant then outfoxed Lee by swiftly shifting his forces south to Petersburg. That cut off rebel supplies and pinned down Lee's forces for good. The Union's total loss for the Overland Campaign was 55,000 casualties. Union troops settled into a nine-month siege of Petersburg, interspersed with assaults, including the Battle of the Crater in July that cost another 4,000 Union casualties, after U.S. sappers dug tunnels under rebel lines and then exploded them. Meanwhile, Mobile, Alabama, fell to Union Admiral Farragut ("Damn the torpedoes, full speed ahead," he was later said to say) completing the Union blockade along the Gulf coast, and General Sherman led Union troops to the gates of Atlanta in a series of battles, where they were stymied until late August.

Despite that laudable progress, the best political minds thought Abraham Lincoln's reelection odds were slim in summer 1864, including Lincoln himself. The year had been especially brutal for Union arms, even compared with enormous losses in previous years, and the largest Union armies seemed to be stuck. To many, it was doubtful whether Union forces could win a military victory before the Northern public gave up on the war, and this made Lincoln's electoral defeat seem certain.

In late August, the Democratic Party nominated the Union's former top general, George McClellan, as its presidential candidate, along with the Copperhead George Pendleton for vice president. Copperhead Clement Vallandigham helped write the anti-war Democratic platform, which McClellan declined to endorse. Vallandigham was famous for fulminating against the war and abolition, encouraging soldiers to desert, and persuading draftees to dodge, which led to his arrest and banishment.[12] Given that peace platform, Lincoln's loss might have meant the death of the Union, the perpetuation of American slavery, and the faltering of democracy's prospects around the world.[13]

Then the political and military landscape seemed to change overnight. On September 2, rebels in Atlanta surrendered to Union troops under General Sherman – a major Union victory and the end of most rebel resistance in Georgia. Union forces lost over 30,000 men during the summer campaign. Over the next several weeks, Union troops in Virginia's Shenandoah Valley cleared out rebels there at the cost of 12,000 Union casualties. Another October victory for the Union cemented Union control of Missouri with 1,500 Union casualties. These victories, but especially Atlanta, seemed to convert Lincoln's prospects from defeat to victory (Donald 1995; McPherson 2002). But was that really so?

If Lincoln was in trouble before Atlanta, Republican vote share before that victory should be lower than after. On the other hand, little change in Republican votes would mean Lincoln was set for reelection without Atlanta. Figures 7.1–7.3 show fall 1864 House and governor Republican vote shares identical to Lincoln's, in line with 1863 and early 1864, with no upswing in national trends before Fall (see Chapter 6). Lincoln appears on track for reelection from early 1863 onward.

Within-state evidence also counters claims that Atlanta was a game-changer. Figure 7.5 examines twelve states that voted twice within a year of Atlanta's capture.[14] Five states had Republican vote shares rise slightly after Atlanta fell compared with the year before. Seven states saw Republican declines, mostly by insubstantial amounts. There is no clear rise in Republican support after that breaking point for the Confederacy.

To be sure, the evidence here is assailable. We have no elections in the critical summer months when Union morale may have been dangerously low. However, given clear evidence of national partisan vote stability throughout the war across major victories, defeats, and nation-changing political developments, it is unlikely that public opinion suddenly became volatile for these several weeks before returning *precisely* to the point where it held steady through most of the war. We can't rerun history to

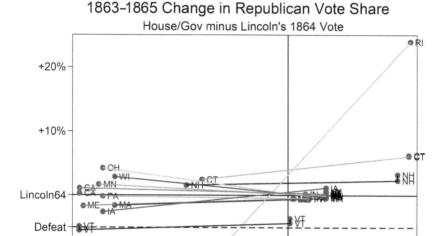

FIGURE 7.5 Partisan stability before & after Atlanta

see what would have happened if Atlanta had remained in rebel hands, but visible electoral trends show Lincoln on track for reelection for most of his presidency.

Lincoln won 55 percent of the popular vote in a two-person contest and dominated the Electoral College vote 212 to 21. Even so, shifting 5 percent of voters from Lincoln to McClellan in every state would have flipped the result. It is easy to imagine how, with relatively few states holding elections in early 1864 and the immense stakes, fears could multiply during a terrible fighting season despite a small but robust Republican advantage. The 1862 losses surely added to their fear. Although periodic midterm losses for the president's party are familiar now, that pattern may not have been clear to political observers in 1862.

Union Victory & Lincoln's Assassination

Following Lincoln's reelection, the Union army in Tennessee annihilated the rebel army in that region at the battles of Franklin and Nashville in late November and mid-December, accumulating 5,000 Union casualties. Simultaneously, Sherman's army in Georgia was on its famous March to the Sea, strategically destroying rebel infrastructure while operating deep in enemy territory, cut off from their supply lines. Congress formally proposed the 13th Amendment in January 1865 to abolish slavery nationwide and sent it to the states for ratification. Its approval later that year guaranteed that the war measure of emancipation would not be undone and extended abolition nationwide. Sherman's army continued to advance and win battles through the Carolinas. A final look at Figure 7.1 gauges New England votes in early 1865. Republicans rose slightly in Connecticut and New Hampshire, while Rhode Island was markedly higher. There is no sign of any substantial partisan shift, however, even when the war appeared won.

Grant's army defeated Lee's near Petersburg with 4,000 Union casualties, after which rebel troops abandoned Petersburg and burned their capital of Richmond. Rebel troops raced west with Union soldiers in pursuit, culminating in a final battle at Appomattox Court House. Lee surrendered his army to Grant on April 9. Remaining rebel forces around the country surrendered in the next few weeks. Instead of condemning all the insurrectionists to death – as John Brown had been for his treason – Lincoln allowed the rebel combatants simply to go home, allowed them to keep their horses even.

In March 1865, Congress passed legislation establishing the Freedmen's Bureau to administer policy related to emancipation for millions of slaves in the South, including aid for reuniting families torn apart by the slave trade, and programs promoting literacy. Lincoln used his second inaugural address to retrospect on the war and its roots in slavery, and he made his call for a generous Reconstruction policy toward the South: "with malice toward none, with charity toward all ... to bind up the nation's wounds." On April 14, Union soldiers raised the American flag to fly once again over Fort Sumter in Charleston Harbor, where rebels had fired the first shots of the rebellion at American troops. That evening, an assassin shot Abraham Lincoln, and the president died the next morning, one of the last deaths of the war. His vice president, Andrew Johnson, a slave-owning Democrat from Tennessee, assumed the office and soon thwarted congressional Republican postwar plans. Historians view him, along with Buchanan before Lincoln, as one of the worst American presidents, the two of them bookending the nation's greatest.

Fall 1865 elections continue to show partisan stability, with votes clustered around Lincoln's average in each state, but with greater spread than in 1864 (see Figures 7.2 & 7.3). In December, three-quarters of the states had ratified the 13th Amendment, and slavery formally ended nationwide. The war freed four million enslaved people, by their own ingenuity and strength and multiplied by the liberating force of the Union army violently crushing enslavers and their cursed institutions. The mass death ended with victory for the Union, but the rebellion fought on in other ways, through politics and terrorism, placing the war's broader outcomes in doubt.

Distinguishing Public Moods from Partisan Votes

Historical claims about public electoral volatility after Atlanta and other events are probably irreconcilable with this electoral evidence. Even so, that leaves plenty of room for real public volatility beyond voting. The evidence of public agony and ecstasy that led contemporaries and historians to worry about and diagnose electoral volatility may have reflected shifts in the public's views on the war's progress, which did not cause their votes or their war support to waver. Party newspapers clearly made those distinctions, and the public probably did too.

Newspaper representations of war progress moved in line with the progress of Union forces, including relative agreement between Democratic and Republican papers for most of the war. Figure 7.6 shows war progress claims by party over time. Union defeats at Bull Run in 1861 and the Seven Days battles depressed war progress views compared with April

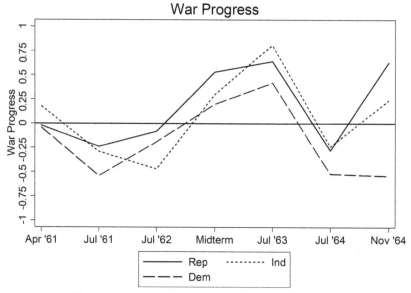

FIGURE 7.6 War progress in newspapers by date & party

1861, but they rebounded by the midterm elections after Antietam and Corinth victories. Progress views edged higher after the Gettysburg win but then dropped into negative territory in July 1864, even among Republican papers. After Atlanta, Republican and Independent papers were very positive again, while Democratic progress representations were slightly more *negative* than in July 1864, for electoral purposes.[15]

Recall, however, that Chapter 3 found unflagging *war support* in Republican and Independent papers in July 1864 despite these relative concerns about war progress. Likewise, levels of Republican newspaper support for Republican leaders in July 1864 were identical to July 1863 and July 1862 – and slightly higher than in July 1861.[16] Here, we see an ability to form separate judgments, at least among local party elites – Republican concern about war progress without losing support for the war or party leaders. Public mood was probably similarly volatile without upsetting partisan war support or voting behavior for most citizens.

CONCLUSIONS

While recounting the major military and political events of the Civil War, I looked for electoral signs of voters responding to these monumental events. There is little evidence for event-based effects on wartime *partisan* mood, casting doubt on historical and contemporary accounts about the influence of the war on elections. Those narratives read more like modern "game-changer" myths than real forces in these most consequential American elections. Cataclysmic events seemed to do little to help or hurt the governing party, likely due to partisan identities guided by local and national partisan leaders and communities.

At no point did Lincoln appear in danger of losing badly, as he worried. Even the grimmest interpretation of tough fall 1862 midterms showed little worse than a toss-up. The reason for these small, brief Republican vote share losses is unclear, but it probably was not due to casualties, war malaise, emancipation, nor absent Republican soldiers. Midterm cycles are a plausible but still insufficient explanation. Republican fortunes restored in 1863, which should have allayed Republican concerns. Public *partisan* mood was probably not against Lincoln before Atlanta – contrary to ubiquitous accounts – and his chances did not seem to rise substantially after.

Another sign of equilibrium in partisan voting comes from comparing Lincoln's 1864 vote share with the same in 1860. Even though the latter was technically a four-party contest and despite all that happened in those four years, Lincoln's vote changed hardly at all in the sixteen contiguous free states (excluding slave states, Oregon, and California). Only Connecticut dropped more than five points (−6.7) and only Iowa and Massachusetts rose by more than 5 points (+8.5 and +9.3), the latter due to native son Everett on the Constitutional Union ticket in 1860. Slave states changed more due to upheaval and substantial declines in their electorate. Newspaper views of war progress show shifts corresponding with war events, but those views did not cause partisan elites to shift their war position nor their electoral support. Ordinary people probably followed their party leaders in roller-coaster views of war progress, and followed their stable partisan war and election attitudes as well.

How did Lincoln and others get it so wrong? By many informed accounts, the president was the most brilliant political mind of his generation with a defter feel for public opinion than any of his contemporaries. Yet, pessimism about his electoral prospects in 1864 overcame him. What accounts for this? First, and most important, even the brightest political analyst struggles to know public opinion in the absence of representative data. Without well-designed opinion polls, that task is nearly impossible. While Lincoln and his contemporaries had access to the same election results analyzed here, patterns of election behavior known today may have been less clear then (or seemed less reliable in a new party system). Moreover, without hindsight, it would have been quite reasonable to think the first presidential election in the midst of a civil war might not hold to voting patterns observed in more tranquil times. Leaders may have misinterpreted real public depression over war progress as a harbinger of depressed Republican votes, without clear evidence that the two might not be closely linked.

Another possibility is that some voters, including Republicans may have actually wavered several months before the votes. It is common for some weak partisans to express uncertainty or preference for the other party before their party's campaign swings them back to their usual partisan habits by reminding them why their usual party is best (Lazarsfeld et al. 1944). Doom-saying Republicans may also have gained by strategically overstating the political danger. Those alerts might cause supporters to redouble their efforts to ensure a favorable outcome, like the dark warnings candidates sometimes send in fundraising appeals today. Finally, the stakes of these elections were plainly too high and the electoral margins too narrow to feel comfortable about national partisan control at any time during this period. Given the circumstances, it is no knock against Lincoln and others of his time to have imagined stories about the effects of Atlanta and other events on wartime elections, even if they now appear less founded. Lincoln's wartime contributions are sufficient without expecting unerring punditry from him too.

As a final point of clarification, some readers might wonder how I can make the case for highly influential party leaders guiding military mobilization and party loyalty from voters on one hand while claiming they did not know where the electorate stood on the other. I think this is less of a conflict than it might seem. I'm sure party leaders knew they had substantial sway over their own followers, but they would not have known *exactly* how persuasive they had been, especially in places where they needed to count on less party-committed voters to secure confident victories. In other words, leaders knew they had influence but could not know with certainty that they had the vote margin needed for victory in toss-up places and in the nation as a whole. Leaders did not need to know precisely where the public stood to influence their views.

* * *

All told, contemporary and historical accounts of mass partisan volatility before and during the war appear to be overwrought. Across several chapters in this book, we see partisan voting coalitions continuing from the Second Party System into the Third, and prewar electoral coalitions holding together during and after the war. Party positions and wartime circumstances shifted dramatically, but most voters were unmoved. National casualties did little to erode Republican electoral support, and likewise, the predominant "game-changer" election narrative surrounding Civil War events generally looks to be more myth than reality. Only local casualties seemed to hold some sway, and only on the margins in predominantly Democratic places. Saying so does not diminish the significance of prewar and wartime events and experiences, nor Lincoln's reelection and Union victory, all of which still shape our politics today. But it does inform our understanding of *how* Lincoln and his fellow Republicans won. Partisan stability, not change, was the order of the day, even when the days themselves were most unstable. As historian Joel Silbey (1977) concluded, "[t]he outstanding characteristic of Northern voter behavior in the Civil War was that the electorate had neither fragmented nor become volatile. ... When people cast their ballots, they remained in accustomed partisan grooves, and the pattern of electoral behavior remained, therefore, quite rigid" (p. 156).

PART III

LEGACIES OF PARTISAN VIOLENCE

8

Ghosts of the Civil War

Voting, Honoring, & Organizing

Opposed to you are arrayed the late Confederate army of the South, and their more treacherous allies the Copperheads of the North. ... But yesterday they were using the bullet to overthrow the government, to-day they are using the ballot to control it.

Executive committee address
1868 national veterans' convention[1]

We will vote as we battled in many a fight, for God and the Union for Freedom and Right. Let our ballots secure what our bullets have won – Grant and Colfax will see that the work is well done.

1868 campaign song
Boys in Blue veterans' group[2]

The last rebel forces surrendered almost four years to the day after the war began with the first shells fired at Fort Sumter, though the rebellion lived on in postwar racial-partisan violence and Jim Crow dominance. Union soldiers and civilians returned home by the hundred thousands as their terms of enlistment and employment expired over the next year. Approximately 2.2 million men had left to serve in the U.S. armed forces battling the rebellion, but only 1.8 million survived to return home. Those dead left gaping holes in families and communities that would never be filled. Chapter 6 presented evidence that local Union losses polarized wartime votes on the home front as voters chose to sustain Republican governance or sided with anti-war Democrats who sought peace at any price. Here, I examine the *enduring* influence of the war on postwar politics and society – the local dead in postwar elections, commemoration of their sacrifice, and organizing efforts by surviving veterans – all of which tied partisanship and violence together long after the war ended.

Scores of recent studies show that cataclysmic events – particularly lethal ones – pervasively alter local social and political attitudes and behaviors for decades (even centuries) after the trauma. The scope of Civil War death and its centrality in Republican rhetoric after the war – "waving the bloody shirt" – make it likely that the dead lingered in postwar elections, causing a permanent change in local political culture in the places that suffered the most. My affirmative results are the first systematic evidence I know of showing war casualties shaping postwar elections.

Next, I show how local prewar partisanship and wartime service shaped postwar commemoration – the political contours of local Civil War memory. Veterans of the war – soldiers and civilians alike – looked back on their traumatic and heroic experiences with horror and pride, but the meaning of those experiences differed dramatically based on their social positions and politics (Blight 2001). I test partisan influence in the formal state adoption of Decoration Day, the placing of local war statues, and state-level commitment to keeping more thorough bureaucratic records of their own veterans and war dead. Finally, I investigate the partisan origins and effects of the Grand Army of the Republic, the Union veterans' organization, first with its impetus from Republican politics and then its seeming local influence in a few key partisan elections.

Collectively, this varied set of postwar snapshots traces the interaction of local war experiences and mass partisanship on political culture in the war's aftermath – a behavioral view of American political development in the late nineteenth century. I begin with a brief review of postwar partisan politics.

From Civil War to a Broken Peace

President Lincoln was among the last to die in the Civil War. An assassin's bullet undid the work of four million ballots cast five months before, motivated most proximately by Lincoln's plan to enfranchise black war veterans with the vote. He was the first of three presidents shot down in a span of thirty-six years – the latter two war veterans. The war's toll could have been much higher, as in contemporaneous civil wars where the rules of war fell apart entirely (Sheehan-Dean 2018).

Had the rebellion been small, the surviving insurgents would have hung after the war. Instead, the size of the rebellion seemed to put justice out of reach in exchange for hopes of peace. In 1861, then-Senator Andrew Johnson noted, "It is said that treason becomes respectable from the number of traitors. If it be true, I suppose treason is now respectable, but if the traitors be many or few, I am resolved that I, for one, will endeavor to put them down."[3] A fate of execution or imprisonment might have delayed the rebellion's defeat, but either would have served justice and prevented subsequent rebel violence against black citizens, their white allies, and democracy itself during Reconstruction, Jim Crow, and beyond, when rebels regained control. The greatest cosmic justice may have involved imprisoning ex-rebels for life, with their captivity overseen by thousands of black freedmen working for the U.S. government as jailors of their former tormenters. Instead, virtually all rebels went entirely unpunished – an outcome championed by Northern Democrats (Baker 1983).

Vice President Johnson, a Democrat from Tennessee, was elevated to the presidency after Lincoln's murder, where he clashed with congressional Republicans who opposed his efforts re-empowering rebel leaders in state and national governments. Unreconstructed Southern Democrats reunited with their Northern brethren at the 1868 Democratic convention. Voters elected Republican war hero Ulysses S. Grant to two presidential terms, and he worked with Congress for a more substantial Reconstruction. For two postwar decades, federal government remained solidly in Republican hands. The party's presidential candidates won consecutive elections through Cleveland's victory in 1884, and Republicans held majorities in the U.S. Senate until 1879 and in the U.S. House until 1875. Wartime service elevated many military officers into presidential politics, including Sherman (declined), Garfield, Arthur, Harrison, and McKinley in addition to Grant and Hayes.

The U.S. military remained in the rebel states to enforce national laws and elections for a decade after the war, and those forces maintaining federal law and order were predominantly black men. One in three Reconstruction soldiers was black, which local whites despised (Berlin et al. 1998). Those U.S. forces sustained the effort to reincorporate states and citizens from rebellion back into the nation while preventing the practical reestablishment of slavery and preserving equal protection for newly enfranchised freedmen under the 14th and 15th Amendments, despite concerted efforts by white Southerners to reestablish servility in other forms (Du Bois 1935; Foner 1988).

African Americans throughout the South rapidly gained social, political, and economic status as democracy took hold (Gates 2019). Those gains failed, however, as northern political will to sustain African American civil rights faltered in the face of violent white resistance. The next president, Republican Rutherford B. Hayes, bargained away Reconstruction in exchange for his election over Samuel Tilden in 1877. That disputed election threatened to rekindle partisan civil war: Democrats even mobilized under the slogan "Tilden or Blood!" and President Grant had to call in U.S. troops to protect the nation's capital (Gates 2019).

White Southerners enacted a broad campaign of racial-partisan violence against black Southerners and other Republicans during and after Reconstruction, through the Ku Klux Klan and similar groups. In 1866, a white mob in New Orleans murdered hundreds of black residents during the Louisiana Constitutional Convention. In another case, white Democrats in Colfax, Louisiana, murdered dozens of black Republican residents who occupied the Grant Parish courthouse following the 1872 governor's election (Foner 1988). Continuing the gubernatorial unrest two years later, thousands of Democratic militiamen – mostly rebel veterans – fought New Orleans police and state militia in the streets to take over Louisiana's state government, killing dozens. Federal troops had to retake New Orleans. After federal abandonment of Reconstruction, whites in the city erected a monument celebrating the attack with the inscription "United States troops took over the state government and reinstated the usurpers but the national election November 1876 recognized white supremacy in the South and gave us our state." Rebel veterans in Wilmington, North Carolina, staged a similar violent coup in 1898, killing scores of black residents while overthrowing the legitimately elected local Republican government and replacing them with white Democrats (Gates 2019). Like much of the postwar white supremacist terrorism, the insurgents in North Carolina targeted successful black residents who defied white myths of racial superiority in their successful bid to disempower black citizens. Similar racial-partisan violence recurred in Arkansas, South Carolina, Tennessee, Georgia, and elsewhere. White mobs lynched thousands of black Southerners in the late nineteenth and early twentieth centuries as they erected monuments celebrating their rebellion and ended black voting with violence and laws (Cubbison & White 2016). Mass black imprisonment for arbitrary offenses and prisoner leasing essentially reinstated slavery across much of the South (Blackmon 2008).

Ultimately, Northern leaders and voters gave up on democracy and let rebels retake control, which they did by killing, disenfranchising, incarcerating, and subjugating Southern blacks in the Jim Crow era. Rebel descendants built upon that racial-partisan victory by consolidating a one-party white authoritarian enclave for the next century (Mickey 2015), still empowered in regional and national politics today. In short, postwar politics continued some of the immense changes wrought by war while reversing others, all shot through with racial-partisan violence. So how did the war continue to weigh on Northerners as they faced a rebel population actively fighting against democracy and for white supremacy, and now reunited with Northern Democrats?

Persistent Shifts in Local Political Culture

I argue that the Civil War's extreme destructiveness made a lasting partisan imprint on local political cultures that endured in elections for many years after. Recent scholarship has plentiful cases of long-term persistence following large societal shocks – a phenomenon political scientists Avidit Acharya, Matthew Blackwell, and Maya Sen (2018) call "behavioral path dependence." They identify the local political impact of slavery as it was in 1860 on white Southern partisanship and racial attitudes from the nineteenth century until today. Socialization and local culture transmitted those effects across generations and party realignment. Acharya and colleagues (2018) also review persistence research tracing similar effects around the world, including the lingering influence of the Crusades and anti-Jewish pogroms in Europe centuries later.[4]

The American Voter (Campbell et al. 1960) notes the strong regional persistence of Civil War partisanship, a century after the war, building on insights from political scientist V. O. Key (1949):

> The distribution of partisan attachments in the nation today, a century after the Civil War, follows the same regional lines laid down at that time. The South ... is still the citadel of the Democratic Party, with the Republican Party offering hardly more than token opposition in large parts of the area. The Northeast, including New England and the Middle Atlantic States, which was the center of abolitionist sentiment, is now the strongest Republican area of the country.
>
> (pp. 151–152)

Those patterns persist today in inverted form after Democrats ceded their active defense of white supremacy to Republicans in the late twentieth century, shifting white Southerners en masse to the Republican Party (Darmofal & Strickler 2019; Kuziemko & Washington 2018; Valentino & Sears 2005).[5] Similarly, the massive local war casualties that reshaped wartime voting in Democratic strongholds might continue to do so after formal fighting ceased. But, for that to occur, voting behavior would have to be fairly stable over that time.

The first question, then, is whether local partisanship persisted in the decades after the Civil War. The answer is a resounding yes. Figure 8.1

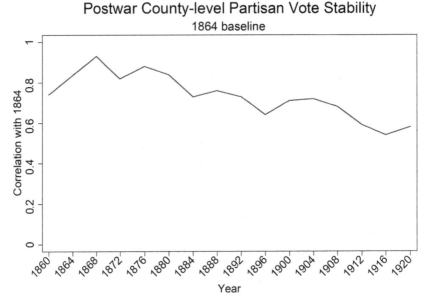

FIGURE 8.1 Presidential voting continuity across political eras
Note: Republican county-level vote correlations for president, weighted by
1864 total vote count. The year 1912 substitutes Democratic continuity
(1864–1912) due to the split between Republican Taft and former Republican
Roosevelt.

correlates 1864 county-level Republican presidential votes with the same
from 1860 through 1920 for the fifteen Union states analyzed in Chapter 6. This is a hard test of continuity from the Civil War era through
Reconstruction, the Gilded Age, and the Progressive Era, including the
transition from the Third Party System to the Fourth. Nonetheless, the
results show remarkable local voting stability across six tumultuous
decades.

The strongest relationship is naturally the closest to 1864 (1868
r = 0.93), and the weakest links are most distant (1916 r = 0.54, 1920
r = 0.58), with a roughly linear decline from one presidential election to
the next. Even then, Lincoln's 1864 vote share continued to predict more
than a third of the variance in Warren Harding's 1920 election. Bear in
mind that this simple test shows strong local continuity despite huge
population flows due to migration and immigration, near-total gener-
ational replacement in the electorate, and women's suffrage in 1920.
Local Civil War votes strongly persisted in postwar elections, and so
wartime electoral influences may have altered votes long after the war.

THE DEAD IN POSTWAR ELECTIONS

What mechanisms might sustain local casualty effects on partisan votes long after the war ended? Republicans kept war memory alive with "bloody shirt" rhetoric, like a portion of their 1884 slogan "Rum, Romanism, and Rebellion" blaming Democrats for the war (Edwards 1997). War holidays like Independence Day and Decoration Day provided opportunities for local speech-making and reflection focused on living and dead war heroes, including parades of veterans and picnics held in local cemeteries. The Grand Army of the Republic veterans' group organized many such events through local fraternal posts. Monuments commemorating local service and sacrifice also provided permanent reminders for all who saw them in town squares and fronting county courthouses. Other reminders were more poignant: hundreds of thousands of disfigured and disabled veterans with visible scars, and many others emotionally destabilized. Local widows and orphans were war reminders too. War-related policy debates and implementation kept war memory fresh, and even the bureaucratic machinery of local pension evaluations and disbursement continually called the war to mind.

Partisanship also persisted without explicit reference to Civil War politics or the dead. Family and community socialization, along with local partisan organizational strength, took on stabilizing lives of their own. New generations learn partisanship from preceding ones, and local organizations self-perpetuate, having overcome initial barriers to collective action. *The American Voter* makes a similar point when noting twentieth century continuities enduring from the war:

> We do not wish to suggest that these regions are still preoccupied with the issues of the Civil War. The participants in that conflict have long since passed from the scene, and slavery and secession now have only historic interest. But as [political scientist V. O.] Key has made clear, community patterns of party affiliation have a remarkable capacity to persist long after "the disappearance of (the) issues that created the pattern." The inheritance of the struggle between the states is unmistakably present in the distributions of partisan attachments as we find them across the country, not so sharp as it was in the 1860s certainly, but still clearly visible.
>
> (p. 152)

Long-term partisan effects from catastrophic events are not inevitable, however. The authors of *The American Voter* continue: "We have said that changes in long-term party allegiances tend to be associated with great national crises" (p. 534). However,

> [t]he stability of mass percepts depends, too, on how well they are bound into the social fabric. ... We have remarked that the world wars of the twentieth century

did surprisingly little to remake the partisan perceptions held by the electorate. . . .
The impact of the Civil War was very different, opening, as it did, issues of intense
partisan contest, which coincided very closely with enduring regional and racial
fissures in the social order. The stability of percepts arising out of the Civil War
experience undoubtedly was greatly reinforced by the fact that they became
enmeshed in conflict between enduring social groupings.

(p. 62)

Evidence of Postwar Casualty Effects

To test whether local war dead shaped postwar votes, I re-estimate
Chapter 6 casualty-voting models, now predicting the difference between
Republican presidential vote share in each postwar year and Lincoln's
1860 proportion. Deaths are a count of total local dead for the whole
war, proportioned by local military-age males (white and black alike).
The main panel of Figure 8.2 shows the impact of local dead on Republican voting from 1868 through 1920, estimated separately across prewar
partisan bastions. I also control for the change in Republican presidential
votes between 1856 and 1860 to account for local partisan trends unrelated to the war.[6]

The plotted coefficients indicate startling continuity of local casualty
effects on voting through Reconstruction and well into the twentieth
century. All elections show the same substantial and statistically significant depressing effects for Republican vote share in Democratic enclaves
due to local war deaths. A 5 percentage point increase in local dead
among military-age males reduces Republican vote share by about 20 percentage points in the years immediately after the war, and the impact
persists around 10–15 percentage points into the twentieth century. In
contrast, the postwar effects of local casualties are generally minimal in
contested places and Republican strongholds, as it was for wartime
elections. These Civil War casualty effects hold through Taft's 1908
election. They then transfer onto erstwhile Republican president Teddy
Roosevelt under his Bull Moose banner in 1912 before reappearing for
Republican presidential nominees in 1916 and 1920. This evidence suggests that casualties influenced elections well after the war, with lasting
effects on local political culture. At the same time, the local casualty
effects in Democratic places slowly lost some impetus over time.

Figure 8.2's other panels show the long-term impact of local draft
exposure and war voluntarism. The political costs of local drafting also
eroded Republican votes. Unlike casualty influences, higher conscription

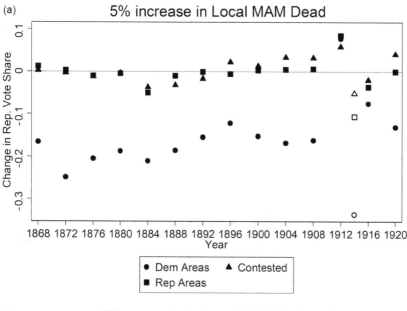

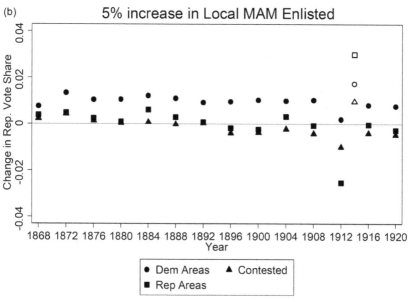

FIGURE 8.2 Local war experiences in postwar presidential votes, by prewar party
Note: County-level models, separate for each year and prewar party type. Change
in vote share subtracts Lincoln's 1860 vote share from each year's Republican
presidential vote share. Ordinary least squares (OLS) models include local dead,
local voluntarism, local draft, population, immigrant proportion, wealth per
capita, and 1856–60 Republican vote share change, all weighted by 1860 voting-
age male population. Hollow shapes are 1912 estimates for Progressive vote
share.

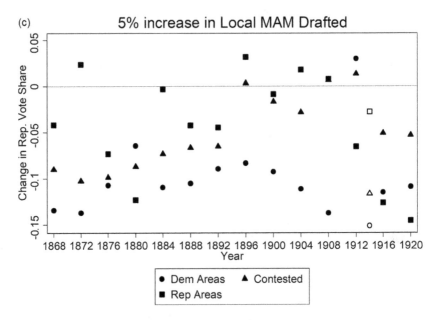

FIGURE 8.2 (*cont.*)

hurt Republican vote share even in Republican strongholds, though the relationship is strongest in Democratic places. Local enlistment in Democratic bastions generally corresponded with *more* Republican vote share relative to Lincoln's share, perhaps due to soldiers' increased Republicanism during the war and their local influence afterward. Thus, war voluntarism was both a function of prewar partisan voting and an influence on postwar partisan ballots.

The Dead in Postwar House & Governor Elections

Chapter 6 found evidence of local casualty effects in wartime House and governor elections, beyond presidential votes, and the tests above show decades-long endurance of those effects in postwar presidential voting. Did the dead still influence voting for lower-level offices as well? The result may depend on whether elections were highly nationalized and synchronized after the war, as they had been before and during the war (see Chapters 2 & 6). I examine votes through 1880, a few years after Reconstruction.

Governor and House elections remained aligned in the late 1860s. Figure 8.3 shows voting correlations weighted by presidential vote

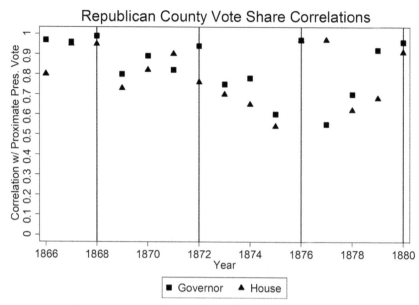

FIGURE 8.3 Partisan nationalization & synchronization in postwar elections

counts, with reference lines indicating presidential years. The high correspondence gradually fell as years passed, though the relationship remained nearly perfect in presidential election years and remained substantial in all. Estimates restricted to free contiguous states are much the same.

Partisan nationalization and synchronization patterns strongly predict local casualty effects in House and governor elections in the 1860s and in all presidential years, given the extent to which those votes corresponded with presidential ballots. By contrast, the falloff of presidential partisan alignment in off-year elections might limit the impact of war dead on these votes. Figure 8.4 presents the results.[7]

The evidence broadly supports those expectations. The presidential-level casualty pattern of Republican losses in Democratic strongholds replicates in gubernatorial elections in the 1860s and in presidential years thereafter, but not in off-year 1870s elections. The same is true for most House elections, though 1872 breaks the pattern. The off-year difference also adds confidence that the effects visible in presidential elections do not simply reflect some constant unmeasured factor. If it did, then that factor would likely express itself similarly across all elections. Instead, we see manifestations in the first batch of postwar vote and then only in

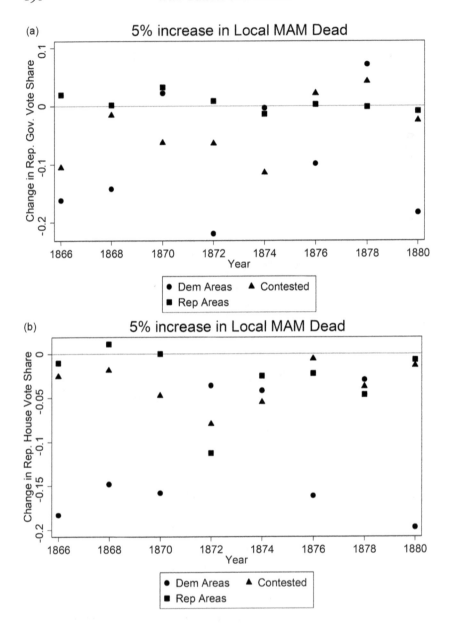

FIGURE 8.4 Casualty effects in postwar House & governor elections

presidential years afterward, suggesting a unique relation between presidential voting and war deaths.

In sum, the local dead altered national and state elections – but only when presidential and elections for lower-level offices coincided. When they diverged in off-year elections, the effects of local casualties faded, only to reappear in presidential election years for all three election types. This latter contingency makes sense given the social and political environments surrounding nineteenth century elections that conspired to encourage voters to back the entire party ticket consistently (Bensel 2004).

MEMORIALIZING THE DEAD

The soldier should not be dead, but mortally stricken. Whatever agony is thus caused should be expressed by his grasp at his death wound, supposed to have been received near his heart. His face should express exultation at the knowledge that victory crowns his efforts and that the sacrifice of his life to his country's cause is not in vain, which fact is made clear to him by Victory holding aloft the flag he carried, where, in his last moments, he can gaze upon it and glory in the comforting thought of victory won.

Instructions to the Sculptor
Wisconsin Monument at Shiloh
Remarks at the 1906 Dedication

The war's human costs made remembrance unavoidable, even for those who wished to forget. Many insisted on honoring the national dead for patriotic and partisan purposes. Immediately after the war, the federal government galvanized an extraordinary effort to disinter hundreds of thousands of U.S. soldiers hastily buried throughout the South for reinternment in new national cemeteries (Faust 2008). Those early postwar years saw the first Decoration Day observances – later called Memorial Day – as a means for communities to commemorate the fallen (Blight 2001). Then, in the late 1890s, veterans' groups persuaded the federal government to establish the first five national military parks on the most significant battlefields. Some veterans on each side began gathering at those sites and others to mark anniversaries of their battles with reminiscences and surprising camaraderie. Closer to home, local war monuments provided collective honors in public spaces throughout the North, and state bureaucracies memorialized the service and sacrifice of their men in Adjutant General reports. The product of those latter labors is the source for the individual-level soldier data analyzed in this book. That record-keeping honored veterans and the military dead by naming them, but it also helped adjudicate pension applications for aid to widows and infirm veterans (Skocpol 1992).

In this section, I assess how partisanship shaped Civil War memorial efforts, even as the rhetoric extolled national virtues. Across several expressions, I expect Republican places to show more commitment than Democratic ones to remembering the war and their people's sacrifices.

Remembering the Civil War

Historian David Blight (2001) identifies three competing lenses through which Americans remembered the war, each of which mobilized the dead in support – reconciliation, white supremacy, and emancipation. The first brought together soldiers and the dead from both sides in ostensibly apolitical recognition of mutual valor and sacrifice. The second joined with the first to erase race from the war, doing violence to black bodies and black memory. The third recognized the war's racial roots and its egalitarian consequences in emancipation, equal protection under the law, and a new birth of freedom. Reconciliation views soon won over emancipation in white national culture and remained dominant for well over a century as white Americans North and South sought racial solidarity to replace violent political difference. War veterans played important roles in solidifying the view. Thus, having won the war, they collectively failed to use their influence to sustain many of the war's most noble and hard-fought accomplishments earned through their sacrifices.

Decoration Day Commemorations

Decoration Day had several self-styled originators, but the African American residents of Charleston, South Carolina, organized the first observance commemorating the Union dead in 1865 (Blight 2001). The day gained national recognition in 1868 when General John Logan called on members of the Grand Army of the Republic veterans' group he led to organize events nationwide.

New York was the first state to make Decoration Day a state holiday, in 1873.[8] All Northern states officially followed by the 1890s.[9] Comprehensive dates of state adoption are hard to find, but an 1879 publication of *The People's Cyclopedia of Universal Knowledge* lists just nine of twenty-two prewar loyal states that had made the date a formal holiday.[10] Lincoln's 1860 vote share in those early-adoption states averaged 59 percent compared to 38 percent for those that didn't – a statistically significant difference ($p < 0.05$).[11] Put differently, half the states that gave Lincoln an 1860 majority had the holiday by 1879 versus 14 percent among other Union states. By contrast, war deaths and war service did not relate to early adoption. In sum, states with stronger Republican roots were more likely to recognize Decoration Day at an early date.

Monuments to the Dead

National cemeteries served as the first war memorials, holding the bodies of Union dead throughout the country (Faust 2008). In the South, the organized and consolidated cemeteries protected Union graves from desecration by rebels when they had been scattered across large battle sites. Before the cemeteries, local black residents worked to protect the scattered graves of the Union dead. The cemeteries were a bureaucratic turning point indicating the nation's newfound commitment to honoring and preserving the remains of its martyrs (Faust 2008). Then, when veterans organized for reunions in the 1880s, they lobbied the federal government to establish the first five national military parks at the sites of the war's most important battles – Gettysburg, Vicksburg, Shiloh, Antietam, and Chickamauga and Chattanooga. Those were established in the early 1890s during the peak of Union war commemoration. By then, veterans dominated political offices, and they found plenty of allies in government eager to help. Historian Timothy Smith (2008) casts those battlefield memorials as reconciliationist shrines to soldier valor and sacrifice, stripped of the war's political baggage. Veterans generally wanted those sites of intense struggle to show future generations what they had done, not why they had done it. The landscapes were naturally suited for apolitical narratives of heroism and loss. Northern states quickly populated those parks with state and regimental monuments to their troops, as had been done at Gettysburg before its formal nationalization (Smith 2008). Confederate monuments were generally disallowed until the early twentieth century, at the height of Jim Crow.

Union monuments also appear in thousands of town squares throughout the North, commemorating the service and sacrifice of local residents. The memorials seem ubiquitous, though modern passersby hardly notice them in parks and along thoroughfares, and fewer know their meaning. The Historical Marker Database (hmdb.org) records the locations of Civil War monuments throughout northern states. Fully half appeared after 1950. Almost all of those are informational markers or memorials for all wars including the Civil War. In contrast, almost all before 1930 are Civil

TABLE 8.1 *County monuments by prewar partisanship, service, & sacrifice*

| Prewar Rep. Votes | Pre-1930 Monuments (per 1k people in 1860) | | | |
	All	Low	Mid	High
Total Dead	0.02*	0.05	0.03*	0.01*
(5% MAM)	(0.01)	(0.03)	(0.01)	(0.01)
Total Volunteers	−0.002*	−0.003	−0.003*	−0.002
(5% MAM)	(0.001)	(0.002)	(0.001)	(0.001)
Total Draftees	0.12*	−0.02	0.15*	0.02
(5% MAM)	(0.03)	(0.02)	(0.03)	(0.02)
Prewar Republican	−0.01	−	−	−
Votes (prop.)	(0.01)			
Constant	−0.02^	−0.01	−0.03*	0.02
	(0.01)	(0.02)	(0.02)	(0.02)
R^2	0.27	0.19	0.50	0.04
N	567	91	239	237

Note: Counties in thirteen free contiguous states. Entries are unstandardized OLS regression coefficients, robust standard errors in parentheses. Model includes 1860 population, immigrants, and wealth per capita (not shown). Weighted by 1860 white voting-age male population.
* $p < 0.05$, ^ $p < 0.10$, two-sided t-test.

War–specific monuments, made apparent by names like "Civil War Memorial" and "Civil War Soldiers' Monument." I focus on the 663 pre-1930 monuments in the free contiguous Union states for which I have county soldier data.[12] To learn whether local partisanship helped produce these memorials, I summed the pre-1930 monuments in each county, divided 1860 population.[13] Table 8.1 presents results from models that consider prewar partisanship, local war service, and 1860 controls, like the casualty tests above.

The first results in the left-most column show prewar partisanship does *not* relate linearly to Civil War monuments, contrary to my expectation, and local war voluntarism was associated with *less* monumentation. However, places where larger fractions of their military-age males died in the war were more likely to memorialize their soldiers with monuments, as were places with larger shares of men drafted.

The second set of results tells a different story. These models test war experience effects conditioned by prewar partisanship. The constants show a significant *non*-linear relationship between partisanship and monuments after accounting for other factors. As expected, postwar monumentation is greatest in the places with the most stalwart support for Republicans before the war. However, monumentation is lowest in *middling* places, and Democratic places fall between. Why is not clear. The +0.05 substantive difference between Republican and toss-up places looks small, but that equals an additional monument in an average-sized county of 19,000 ($p <. 05$). Comparing the most Republican places to the other two combined shows Republican places significantly differed from the rest, supporting my expectation for more monuments per capita in Republican strongholds.

These models also show the effects of local wartime experiences conditioned by partisanship. Almost all move in the same direction across variations in local partisanship, but they differ in magnitude. Democratic places appear more responsive to local dead, similar to the effects of casualties on postwar voting. Local voluntarism looks similar across all three partisan areas.

Administrative Record-Keeping

Between 1865 and the early 1900s, states compiled and published comprehensive records of individual war service by their citizens. These served as honor rolls and as bureaucratic verification for pension applications. Even here, differences in documentation emerge by prewar partisanship. In a simple difference of means tests, the fifteen states with more complete and detailed soldier records for county-level tests in this book averaged 53 percent for Lincoln in 1860, while the seven states without sufficient records averaged just 33 percent ($p <. 01$) Put differently, Republican states were more committed to thoroughly documenting their citizens' war service than Democratic ones.

A GRAND ARMY OF REPUBLICANS

Returning veterans maintained their local bonds with comrades after the war with regimental and brigade reunions. The 12th Iowa Infantry regiment, for example, held regular reunions with speeches and war songs roughly every four years from 1880 well into the next century.[14] They preserved the memory of their exploits for themselves and for posterity in regimental histories that celebrated their epic accomplishments, recounted their supreme hardships, and memorialized comrades they had lost. The Grand Army of the Republic (GAR) veterans' organization bridged local regimental groups under its national umbrella, but it also played a key role in postwar electoral politics, pension advocacy for veterans and their families, patriotic civic education, and war remembrance.

In this final section, I examine the local forces that gave rise to GAR posts and look for evidence of GAR influence in local partisan elections. I expect the organization was strongest in places that had numerous veterans and Republican voting histories. GAR activism may have also produced more Republican votes than places with less GAR presence. I begin with a short GAR history followed by empirical tests. I conclude with women's postwar organizations, one in support of the GAR and the other of women who served as nurses during the war.

The GAR & Its Politics in Brief

Union veterans remained a major force in the political and civic life of the nation in the war's aftermath, some as elected leaders and many others as activists (Dearing 1952; McConnell 1992; Skocpol et al. 2000). The Grand Army of the Republic was their most robust organization – organized to support fraternal communion, to elevate veteran members into political office, to elect Republicans, to keep their service and their comrades' sacrifice alive in public memory, and to lobby for the nation's first large-scale social welfare programs aiding disabled and elderly vets and their families (Skocpol 1992). The last Civil War veteran died in the 1950s.

The predominance of Republican voters among soldiers made any veterans' organization a site for Republican politics. Although veterans' groups were involved in congressional and gubernatorial elections 1865–1867, they were especially active in promoting General Grant's 1868 Republican candidacy for president. GAR leadership was reluctant to publicly engage in partisan advocacy – though Democrats continually accused the group of partisan designs – and so GAR members separately organized as a national veterans' convention to endorse Grant, using the Radical Republican rhetoric quoted at the start of the chapter (Dearing 1952). GAR leadership and members primarily channeled their partisan energies into a group called the Boys in Blue, though individual GAR posts broke with leadership to explicitly endorse Republicans (Dearing 1952, p. 181).

Many Democrats worried about the threat of political violence posed by former soldiers participating actively in electoral politics – especially as efforts to organize their own veterans into white supremacy groups languished – and some Democrats hatched rebellious plans contingent on election outcomes in postwar years (Dearing 1952). Scattered low-level campaign violence did break out in the form of attacks on veterans' processions that injured and sometimes killed participants in a few places

(Dearing 1952, p. 181), returning to the low-level violence seen in prewar elections (Grimsted 1998).

The New York *Tribune* noted the organizational parallels between Republican militias before the war and Republican veterans after the war:

> Far more than the strength which was given to the Republican cause by the organization and turn-out of the Wide-Awakes in 1856-60 would now be derived from the introduction into the present campaign of grand processions of the Veterans of the war of the Union, reassembling clothed in the faded and worn army blue under the torn and tattered ensigns which they bore through the battle's blast.
>
> (June 9, 1868; quoted in Dearing 1952, p. 161)

Veterans' organized efforts may have been more important for Republican victories in 1868 than the work of any other group, especially in organizing campaign events (Dearing 1952, p. 181).

Local GAR posts collapsed and nearly disappeared after 1868, partly due to perceptions of partisanship in the group, with the heaviest losses outside the Republican-dominant Northeast (Dearing 1952, p. 189; McConnell 1992). Veterans and the Republican Party saw less need for veteran organization in Grant's 1872 reelection. Later in the decade, declining Republican vote share forced party leaders to seek veteran votes actively again, but done through veterans' organizations other than the GAR (Dearing 1952, pp. 191–194, 203).

The GAR revived again in the late 1870s under new organization, it peaked around 1890 with over one million members, and then it slowly faded as its membership disappeared through disinterest or death (Dearing 1952; McConnell 1992). Membership exceeded 2 percent of the adult male population during both peaks (Skocpol et al. 2000). Although the group was less partisan in its later form, it still helped elect five U.S. presidents, all Republicans. The new GAR focused more on fraternal activity, patriotic education, charity activities for war widows and orphans, and lobbying for pensions. Both parties backed pensions, though Republicans endorsed larger benefits and accused Democrats of being anti-veteran (Dearing 1952, pp. 258, 496).

Partisanship in GAR Posts

Given these organizational roots, I expect the Grand Army of the Republic was strongest in places with more veterans and more prewar Republican partisanship. That would manifest as more local GAR posts per capita, often with a few dozen members per post. Republican places provided more amenable ground for GAR organizations, even after accounting for

TABLE 8.2 *Prewar partisanship, war participation, & county GAR posts*

	Total GAR Posts, 1865–1920 (per 1k MAM)
U.S. Volunteers	0.47
(prop. MAM)	(0.30)
U.S. Draftees	0.23
(prop. MAM)	(5.34)
Republican Vote Share	1.42*
(1856–1860)	(0.24)
R^2	0.06
N	685

Note: Cells are unstandardized OLS regression coefficients with robust standard errors in parentheses, clustered by state, weighted by 1860 voting-age males. Control variables not shown.
* $p < 0.05$, two-sided t-test.

the Republican predominance in local war service. For evidence, I analyze an original county-level dataset of GAR posts from 1865 to 1920 based on data published by the Sons of Union Veterans of the Civil War, merged with local Census and election data, and county-level Civil War participation, with sufficient data for tests covering fifteen Union states.[15] Table 8.2 presents the results predicting the total number of local posts from 1868 to 1920 with the now-familiar suite of factors. I scale GAR posts relative to the 1860 military-age male population (in thousands).

War voluntarism corresponded with a higher rate of local GAR post establishment, but not significantly so. Republican partisanship is a better predictor than voluntarism. Substantively, a 20 point gain in Republican vote share predicts nearly half a post more per thousand young men, on average. A 10 point shift in local voluntarism corresponds with an extra tenth of a post locally, though short of statistical distinctness ($p = 0.11$).[16] In sum, Republican places made fertile grounds for GAR activism, even after accounting for the prevalence of local veterans.

Electoral Impacts of Local GAR Posts

Next, I test whether GAR post presence related with more local Republican votes. The GAR's history suggests its influence might have been greatest in 1868 with the combination of active partisan electioneering by veterans and a former military commander on the ballot as a Republican. The group's local partisan impact might wane after that. Table 8.3 presents the results predicting that year's Republican presidential vote share relative to Lincoln's 1860 vote share. Whereas the prior analysis assessed total GAR posts per capita across several decades, the key variable here is a raw count of GAR presence in the county in that year.[17] The models include the same suite of predictors as above.

The 1868 estimate marks the only presidential election during the GAR's initial instantiation. There we see the group's presence corresponded with increased Republican vote share by a little more than half a percent for every GAR additional post in the county. The 1870s period marks the time in which the group's numbers were substantially smaller and when veterans were less active in partisan elections. Estimates in that era show some residual influence but dwindle with time. Results are null through the 1880s and 1890s during the GAR's second incarnation, but they become positive and significant again in 1896, just after the group's peak in the early 1890s. The 1868 and 1896 results are the only ones that remain both significant and directionally consistent in models that include a placebo control.[18] In other words, the GAR seems to have boosted Republican vote shares during two presidential elections that coincided with the group's membership peaks.

These GAR tests complete the book's cycle that followed partisan civilians mobilized into partisan combatants who then demobilized after the war to become partisan civilians again, but with a new status – clothed permanently as honored veterans. These results show the partisan life of a singularly important civic group in late nineteenth century America, but they also speak to broader questions about the long shadow of violence in partisan politics – here, veterans of a partisan civil war.

Women's Veteran Organizations

Women worked to organize public recognition and seek reward for the service of combatants and their own wartime service. The Woman's Relief Corps served as the auxiliary to the GAR. That group organized GAR functions, promoted patriotic memory on Decoration Day and with education reforms, and advocated nurse pensions for their difficult service alongside male veterans. Women had their own veterans' groups, representing the thousands of women who served in civilian roles (Schultz 2004). Like their male counterparts, these groups served as social

TABLE 8.3 *GAR posts & Republican vote shares*

	1868 Rep. Pres. Vote Share (Δfrom 1860)	1872 Rep. Pres. Vote Share (Δfrom 1860)	1876 Rep. Pres. Vote Share (Δfrom 1860)	1880 Rep. Pres. Vote Share (Δfrom 1860)	1884 Rep. Pres. Vote Share (Δfrom 1860)
Local GAR Posts (count)	0.007* (0.001)	0.005* (0.001)	0.002* (0.001)	0.002* (0.001)	−0.002 (0.001)
R^2	0.47	0.62	0.70	0.72	0.77
N	674	675	675	675	675

	1888 Rep. Pres. Vote Share (Δfrom 1860)	1892 Rep. Pres. Vote Share (Δfrom 1860)	1896 Rep. Pres. Vote Share (Δfrom 1860)	1900 Rep. Pres. Vote Share (Δfrom 1860)
Local GAR Posts (count)	0.000 (0.001)	0.001 (0.001)	0.002* (0.001)	0.000 (0.001)
R^2	0.78	0.77	0.65	0.72
N	675	675	675	675

Note: Table entries are unstandardized OLS regression coefficients with robust standard errors in parentheses, clustered by state, weighted by 1860 voting-age males. Controls not presented here for concision.
* $p < 0.05$, two-sided t-test.

organizations for members while also organizing efforts seeking public commendation and pensions earned by their service. What began as the Ex-Nurse's Association of the District of Columbia in 1881 eventually grew to become the National Association of Army Nurses of the Civil War by the 1890s (NAANCW), founded by Dorothea Dix. Chapters around the Union formed in 1881, and the group operated national events in conjunction with the Grand Army of the Republic. The NAANCW won pensions for its members in 1892, though most never received any benefits (Schultz 2004).

CONCLUSIONS

Many studies trace the impact of the American Civil War on building the modern American state (and of wars on state building in general; e.g. Bensel 1990; Skocpol 1992). Here I was interested in whether the local Civil War experience – felt through war service and death – shaped local *political culture* long after the war concluded. I find evidence that casualty effects observed in wartime elections persisted for decades after the war. Local casualties eroded Republican vote shares in places that backed Democrats before the war but had little effect on Republican places. That endurance fits well with recent scholarship finding long-term political effects from local traumas (Acharya et al. 2018), and it makes sense given the unparalleled scale of death in the Civil War.

I also found substantial evidence of local partisanship influencing Civil War memorialization, including earlier commemoration of Decoration Day, more extensive local monumentation, and more detailed war service records. Republican places were committed to these memorial activities not just because more Republicans individually led and fought in the war, but also because the war's partisan roots and wartime divides made war memory central to Republican identity.

Finally, I investigated the partisan roots and effects of the Grand Army of the Republic veterans' organization. Here, I found that local partisanship before the war strongly predicted the organizational prevalence of GAR posts in these counties, even after accounting for differences in local war service that were also influenced by party politics. Additionally, I found some hints of GAR influence on local behavior in partisan elections beyond these partisan selection factors, with increased Republican vote share in the 1868 presidential election in which veterans were especially active in electioneering, and again for the with 1896 election near the peak of the group's social and political power.

Conclusion

Lessons from Partisan Warfare

So strong is this propensity of mankind to fall into mutual animosities that where no substantial occasion presents itself, the most frivolous and fanciful distinctions have been sufficient to kindle their unfriendly passions and excite their most violent conflicts.

James Madison
Federalist No. 10
November 22, 1787

Four score and seven years ago our fathers brought forth on this continent, a new nation, conceived in Liberty, and dedicated to the proposition that all men are created equal. Now we are engaged in a great civil war, testing whether that nation, or any nation so conceived and so dedicated, can long endure.

President Abraham Lincoln
Gettysburg, PA
November 19, 1863

In the dark winter of 1860–61, eleven Southern Democratic states rejected the legitimate presidential election of Republican Abraham Lincoln and chose civil war to advance their cause of slavery apart from the United States. They refused to accept any election outcome that didn't grant complete control of federal government to their party. The loyal states joined the war to preserve national integrity – the Union – but also to defend its most sacred institution: democratic elections. Thereafter, the national loyalty of Northern Democrats clashed with their partisanship – past allegiance with Southern Democrats and a deep hatred of "black" Republicans. Northern Democrats began the war ambivalent over those competing motives and ended it in vitriolic war opposition.

With those origins and evolutions, the Civil War was ultimately a *partisan* war, on the largest scale imaginable. Tracing the implications for ordinary partisans in the North has been my focus – in prewar electoral coalitions, partisan news, war service and sacrifice, wartime voting, and postwar memory. Party identities, leaders, and communities motivated and organized the war's mass violence, producing substantial partisan gaps in active war participation at times when party leaders polarized most over the war. That violent experience fed back into the partisan ballots cast during the war, and the war's violence continued to shape voting and other political behaviors long after.

In this concluding chapter, I begin with a brief review of the book's main findings relating partisanship with violence. I continue by considering the book's contributions for Civil War–era political history and the social science of partisanship and public opinion during wartime. Finally, I reflect on the book's themes in light of the uncomfortable resonance nineteenth century politics has with contentious partisanship in our own time, including resurgent efforts to dismiss legitimate elections and the growth in low-level, violent partisan attacks. What can we take from the history of a partisan war that might help support and defend American democracy today?

Findings in Brief

The 1850s revolutionized the U.S. party system. Whigs and Free Soilers crumbled after 1852, and Know-Nothings and Republicans emerged to oppose a largely intact Democratic coalition. By 1860, Republicans and Know-Nothings consolidated into an anti-Democratic party in the North as their opponents fractured by region. Yet, despite this tumult, election evidence in Chapter 2 shows relatively stable voting coalitions throughout the North. That stability does not equal today's partisan persistence, nor match Reconstruction-era stability, but it provides a far stronger base for powerful partisanship during the war than we might otherwise expect in a new party system. With that foundation, I outlined the psychology of partisan identity and made predictions for wartime endurance, resistance, and lethality from a mix of partisan identity, leadership cues, and social influence. Chapter 2 also confirmed the Free Soil origins of the Republican Party and showed the roots of partisan violence in prewar politics too.

Throughout the Civil War, Northern leaders and their party newspapers unified in war support at times and polarized in violent disagreement at other points. Chapter 3's uniquely representative sample of newspapers shows Democrats were ambivalent about the war at the start, in contrast with strong and consistent Republican war support. Republican newspapers sought to limit the threat of partisan war in the North by over-representing Democratic war support. Democrats moved to support the war nearly as much as Republicans in 1862, even as Republican papers strategically painted them as anti-war for electoral gain. Then, following midterm elections, Democrats increasingly moved into outright war opposition, until all Democratic newspapers in the sample opposed the war by the 1864 election. Partisan advocacy for military participation moved in concert with these changing war positions among Democrats, including advocacy for enlistment and the draft, moral disengagement toward rebels, and representations of public support for (or opposition to) the war. I argued that partisan news polarization on the war made similar divides likely in ordinary partisans.

Chapter 4 found partisan war service gaps in soldiers' absentee ballots and local military participation. Republican voters (and communities) joined the ranks at greater rates than Democrats did. Soldiers from Republican places also deserted less and died at higher rates. Crucially, partisan service gaps shrank and then grew in close correspondence with partisan news polarization – plausible evidence of dynamic partisan opinion leadership in war participation, especially in light of public consistent opinion evidence from twentieth and twenty-first century American wars (Berinsky 2009). Local white partisanship boosted black military enlistment as well as white, probably through local leadership. In sum, partisanship was a key factor for mobilizing ordinary people into mass violence.

The last part of the book focused on partisanship in Civil War elections. Chapter 5 identified partisan loyalty and mobilization at the heart of electioneering efforts in partisan newspapers. Democrats sought to erode Republican majorities with demagogic appeals to white supremacy and retrospective voting that cast the Republican administration in an apocalyptic light. Republicans defended themselves by accusing Democrats of disloyalty, shifting blame to rebels, and reframing the dead as heroic martyrs demanding victory. Notably, the ubiquity of the Civil War dead in newspapers – no different for Republican and Democratic papers – stands in stark contrast to U.S. news coverage of twentieth century American wars (Althaus et al. 2012). That unavoidable salience made the potential impact of war casualties on vote choice more likely. Both parties also maintained their coalitions with violent attacks —

rhetorical and literal — on opposing partisans. Suppressing a rebellion led by Southern Democrats brought raw conflict between Northern Democrats and Republicans to the surface. Partisan demonizing, dehumanizing, threats, and calls for violence were highest during wartime election campaigns, consistent with the maximal contention found around modern elections (Harish & Little 2017; Sood & Iyengar 2016). That antagonism threatened to spiral out of control into more systematic acts of violence and even plots for insurrection in the North.

Enormous national casualties seem to have had little influence on wartime partisan voting, as Chapter 6 shows, but *local* casualties shaped partisan votes for president, House, and governor. In highly nationalized and party-synchronized votes, I find no overall decline in Republican vote shares as national casualties accumulated, nor reactions to *recent* mass casualties, contrary to some predictions in political science. However, I find local casualties reduced vote share for Republicans in Democratic bastions while exerting little impact elsewhere. Results are strongest for *recent* local casualties, and presidential dynamics replicate in House and governor votes. The electoral asymmetry in reaction to local casualties suggests strong partisan-motivated reasoning about the dead, consistent with Republican news frames in Chapter 5. Unfortunately, the evidence cannot tell the extent to which voters reacted directly to local deaths or responded to local leaders and neighbors who leveraged the dead in election appeals. Local draft exposure also hurt Republican vote share in Democratic strongholds. In other words, Democratic areas persuaded local swing voters and mobilized more of their partisan base more in places where the war's human costs were greater.

Chapter 7 shows that monumental wartime events had no discernible impact on partisan voting in House and governor elections staggered throughout the war. Those votes serve as a national partisan barometer that indicates substantial partisan stability in vote shares over time. That undermines a great deal of conventional historical wisdom about those elections, including the mythic status of Atlanta in Lincoln's 1864 reelection. Republican newspapers show how Republican voters likely responded – recognizing changes in war progress with consequent emotions, but no change in support for war or for Lincoln and his party. That distinction helps explain why historical accounts describe enormous public volatility, while electoral returns show almost complete stability in party voting patterns. Each party's positions evolved during the war and circumstances changed, but the public's voting behavior was mostly unmoved.

Chapter 8 traces the war's long-term impact on local voting and broader political cultures. Consistent with recent political science research on the enduring effects from localized trauma, I find local casualties depressing Republican vote shares in Democratic bastions for decades after the war ended. I also find state and local war commemoration differed by prewar partisanship and war experiences, with greater remembrance efforts in Republican places and those that suffered most. These include early adoption of Decoration Day, the prevalence of war memorials, and the level of detail entered in each state's soldier records. Republican places were also more likely to organize veterans into political and patriotic activity in the Grand Army of the Republic (GAR). That local activism seems to have benefited Ulysses S. Grant in his 1868 election campaign with more votes in places with more GAR presence, despite the group's official non-partisan stance.

In sum, I found strong, dynamic effects of mass partisanship on the war, its elections, and its aftermath across a wide range of military and political behaviors. And, in turn, the war's mass violence reshaped wartime and postwar partisanship in subtle and profound ways.

IMPLICATIONS FOR CIVIL WAR PARTISANSHIP

It may seem hard to believe anything new could be said about the Civil War, given tens of thousands of books about the conflict. Even so, this book broke new ground with a representative historical portrait of mass partisan ballots and bullets unearthed with innovative methods. The results systematically show more of what drove the public's essential contributions in the nation's most fraught and consequential era.

Historians have debated the nature of Civil War partisanship for decades, with particular attention to whether Northern Democrats helped or hindered the war effort. On one side, Jennifer Weber (2006) points to Democratic war opposition in Congress and in the public, along with partisan hostility including frequent violence and even a few rebellious plots. The other side accepts "no party now" rhetoric on its face as evidence of a non-partisan patriotic effort for the Union (Gallagher 2011; Smith 2006). Of course, some split the difference, arguing that Democratic disruption was rhetorical and not substantive (Neely 2017).

This book provided strong evidence of party polarization in all facets of the war. In fact, partisan divisions *defined* the politics and events of the era. This was not an era of "no party now" in partisan news nor in public military and election behavior. Northern Democrats *did* impede the war effort, by persuading their partisans to contribute less to the war effort and by fielding candidates and a party platform that would have given up the war. My evidence on the role of partisanship in mobilizing military enlistment and how election campaigns exacerbated partisan tensions in the North generally fits Weber's account.[1] I also find substantial *variation* in Democratic rhetoric and military action over time, which could help explain diverging conclusions and evidence cited in the debate. In particular, elite Democratic movement toward war support before 1862 elections and the corresponding reduction in local partisan war participation gaps may be responsible for producing much of the evidence supporting the no-party thesis. These broad conclusions about partisanship — drawn from unusually systematic tests — are my most substantial contribution to Civil War history.

Several particular findings are noteworthy for historical debates, including the public's insensitivity to wartime events, white supremacy in the 1864 Democratic campaign, and nuances in Democratic war views over time. The lack of voter responsiveness to monumental events is strikingly at odds with conventional wisdom in Civil War political histories – and with Lincoln's own anxieties. Some historians have challenged maximal interpretations of wartime events, recognizing, for example, that Republican losses in fall 1862 were mild compared with most midterm elections before or after the war (e.g. McPherson 2002). But every work I've seen that mentions the 1864 election says Atlanta made the difference. I can't claim my evidence is definitive, but I hope it introduces more skepticism into confident but largely unsupported historical claims about 1864 voters. Elections give the only representative view of the public, and Lincoln looked on track for reelection by 1863. We have no telling elections in the key summer 1864 period, but I find it hard to believe Atlanta mattered given (1) the perfectly equal Republican vote shares before and after that summer period, (2) the public's stability throughout the war, and (3) modern studies showing little *voting* movement following most major events.

Chapter 7 challenges Neely's (2017) claims that the 1864 Democratic campaign only minimally engaged with the party's longstanding advocacy for white supremacy. Instead, my relatively small but representative sample of Democratic newspapers identified several clear examples of white supremacy rhetoric in the election campaigns. There is nothing comparable on the Republican side, despite Neely's defensible point that many white Republicans were racists too.

Democratic *ambivalence* at the start of the war, distinct from Republican war support, is clearer here than I've seen in most political histories of the war, which generally start from general Democratic war support. That clarity emerges because our sampling and analytic procedures enable us to specify the likelihood of finding a partisan gap of that size by chance, and a spurious result is quite unlikely here. The worried 1861 plea from Stephen Douglas quoted in Chapter 5 illustrates his concerns about that Democratic ambivalence too. Likewise, the 1864 election newspapers show no remaining Democratic war support, which belies the conventional notion of a consistent body of war Democrats throughout the conflict. The conventional view is better represented by politically *independent* newspapers that tended to back the war while also endorsing Democratic candidates.

The strength of my conclusions comes from methods uncommon in historical work. With more precision and representativeness than most studies, I presented a broad quantitative and qualitative view of partisanship writ large across war rhetoric, mobilization, voting, and memory. These methods are especially good for broad inferences about the public, surpassing conventional historical approaches, even as this work lacked some of the qualitative depth found in the best historical accounts.

BROADER IMPLICATIONS FOR MASS PARTISANSHIP

Political scientists already consider partisan identity to be the strongest force in mass politics (e.g. Iyengar et al. 2019). Nonetheless, I argued here that we *underestimate* the potential power of ordinary partisanship in ways that only become apparent when we move beyond the contextual confines of the United States in the survey era.[2] I used the violent extremes of the Civil War era to test the bounds of mass partisanship. Most important, that context enabled me (1) to identify the endurance of partisan voting across party systems and through events and experiences more tumultuous and painful than most American public opinion studies, and (2) to characterize the latent capacity for party leaders to mobilize mass violence by millions of ordinary voters against partisan opponents who refuse to accept electoral loss. The results suggest a stronger combination of party identities, motivated reasoning, and influence from partisan leaders and communities than past research could possibly show. The political extremes of the Civil War era provide the essential context for testing and identifying the full potential of party attachments.

Partisan Stability in Extraordinary Times

Political scientists know that modern campaign events generally have little influence on vote intention, and partisans cast loyal votes for president roughly 90 percent of the time (e.g. Sides & Vavreck 2013). Major twentieth century political events likewise had little partisan effect (Campbell et al. 1960; Green et al. 2002; Keith et al. 1986). But comparing a strong debate performance to the Emancipation Proclamation or equating marginally increasing unemployment with hundreds of thousands of Americans dead is no comparison at all. Put differently, even the most unusual contexts for testing partisan loyalty and motivated reasoning in past scholarship have been utterly placid compared to the Civil War context. Nonetheless, I found that the same conclusions generally held: partisan votes were extraordinarily stable – even in a relatively new party system – and failed to respond substantially to enormous national casualties, momentous events, and explicit demagogic appeals to white supremacy. Moreover, prewar foundations and wartime effects endure in local political behavior for decades after the war. These are testaments to strong partisan loyalties and the power of motivated reasoning guided by party leaders and communities. Chapter 8's evidence on long-term local effects from local war experiences fits well with recent political science evidence on durable changes in local environments based on traumatic events and extreme practices. Acharya, Blackwell, and Sen's (2018) *Deep Roots* linking the local prevalence of slavery to present-day partisanship and prejudice is the best example of this emerging literature.

Violent American Partisanship

This work helps show our failure to recognize the capacity for violent mass partisanship in the United States when mobilized by party leaders around elections. Public opinion scholarship has moved in recent years to highlight greater levels of partisan animosity in the public. We now know that modern partisans dislike each other, try to avoid each other, see each other as threats to the nation, and even discriminate against each other (e.g. Iyengar et al. 2019). Mason (2018) provides a particularly dark account of the tensions arising from alignments between partisanship and other fractious social identities.

I find evidence suggesting partisan opinion leadership that polarized war *fighting*, not just leadership effects on war attitudes and other subjects (e.g. Berinsky 2009; Karpowitz et al. 2017; Lenz 2012; Zaller 1992). This is literally a willingness among millions of ordinary people to fight and potentially die in a partisan war, following explicit calls by party leaders to join or abstain and taking advantage of the organizational opportunities that leaders provided to do so. My tests can't distinguish elites *leading* public opinion or *reflecting* it. Even so, everything we know from modern studies suggests a public that follows rather than leads on policy, including war. Most of the public isn't capable of independently weighing the policy complexities to make confident choices, and so they defer to party leaders whom they trust.

The Civil War case shows how much further mass partisan animosity can go in the United States. Under extreme legitimizing circumstances, ordinary Americans willingly enact political violence. It's not just a few radical extremists. Scholars studying political violence around the world have done better at recognizing the violent capacity of partisanship and party leaders (e.g. Humphreys & Weinstein 2008). Thus, this work helps expand conceptions of American partisanship and contributes to the growing comparative literature on partisan violence around the globe. In particular, the evidence here reaffirms the crucial importance of elections in heightening the risk for party violence, both before and after the votes are cast and counted (Dunning 2011; Harish & Little 2017; Höglund 2009; Wilkinson 2006).

Public Opinion during Wartime

The casualty tests here favored some theories of war support over others. National casualties matter little in total or in recent bursts. However, *local* casualties – especially recent ones – shaped local voting behavior, but only conditional on local partisanship. Voters responded to local costs of war – local deaths and the draft – in partisan environments that consistently framed those deaths in the harshest terms possible against the incumbent administration. Democratic newspapers did that work by explicitly exhorting readers to cast their votes with the dead in mind. Those efforts probably pulled support from independent voters and from some few wavering, cross-pressured Republicans, but it would have had limited effect on vote choice for the most committed partisans from either side. We also saw some greater voter mobilzation in Democratic places that had suffered more war losses compared to Republican areas. Meanwhile, pro-administration areas used motivated reasoning to sustain their electoral support by reframing the war's costs toward essential moralized goals.

This evidence aligns with Berinsky's (2009) opinion leadership model of twentieth and twenty-first century war opinion, and evidence by others on the partisan contingencies in responses to modern casualties (Karol & Miguel 2007; Kriner & Shen 2007). Other theories positing direct response to national casualties fare poorly. The Civil War public seems electorally unbothered by national casualties, not even through some mediated opinion leadership mechanism. This is true even though news pages were full of accounts of Union dead, in contrast with most modern news coverage of warfare (Althaus et al. 2012).

Partisan Limits

If partisan endurance and reasoning are so powerful, what are their limits? I have tried to emphasize the importance of partisan *environments*, which reinforce individual partisan motives. These are social contexts that complement partisan reasoning in individual psychology. Civil War–era partisan local leaders and neighbors helped keep fellow partisans loyal and encouraged them to interpret the war with frames amenable to party positions. Outside party echo chambers, cross-pressured partisans are more likely to vote for the other side – especially those who aren't especially interested in politics (e.g. Beck et al. 2002; Mutz 2006; Zaller 1992). Likewise, partisan communities sometimes shift over time, often en masse based on other social identities as those groups occasionally realign as coalitions within the party system. Late twentieth century racial realignment is the best example of this process at work (Achen & Bartels 2016; Kuziemko & Washington 2018; Valentino & Sears 2005). Social groups are key to individual partisan endurance or change, with the social group remaining in electoral sync either way.

If partisanship *can* be lethal, why isn't it always? The answer, I think, lies in the legitimization of violence by party leaders and the cloak of legitimacy shrouding organized state violence. A few violent individuals may act without much explicit direction from leaders, but mass violence requires command and organization. The Civil War was unusual for its explicit calls to arms and military organization directed to oppose partisan opponents with massive force. Put differently, party leaders serve as critical regulation valves on violence. In modern American contexts, party leaders have usually worked to suppress potential explosions of anger and violence – like McCain's 2008 concession speech in the Preface (Brader & Marcus 2013). Historically and cross-nationally, leaders sometimes allow or even encourage low to moderate levels of violence while usually inhibiting even larger conflagrations (Grimsted 1998; Potter 1977).[3]

In short, individual ordinary partisans are unlikely to fight unless explicitly called by national and local leaders they trust, perhaps especially when formed into organized state forces, joined by lots of peers, and ostensibly motivated by a laudable goal that goes beyond mere partisanship. Those psychological and social forces involving obedience, conformity, and other forms of moral disengagement make hurting people seem more acceptable. It takes a village, in other words.

* * *

Partisanship already has a bad reputation in the public (Klar & Krupnikov 2016), and this book's evidence of radical partisanship might make it seem worse – extreme loyalty, insensitivity to events on the ground, and mass violence, of course. I think that's the wrong conclusion, or at least it's more complicated than that. Even as Democratic partisanship motivated and organized Southern secession and then bred reluctance to fight within the Union, Republican partisanship helped save the Union, defend democracy, and move the nation closer to realizing founding egalitarian promises. Partisanship can be a force for good as well as evil.

CIVIL WAR PARTISANSHIP IN OUR TIME

This book drew much from modern partisanship to understand the past. What does all this mean for partisan conflict today? Here, I trace partisan lineages, describe historical parallels, and outline some reasons for concern about modern partisan threats to democracy.[4]

Much is different in today's politics and much remains similar. One party still defends the spirit of the Confederate rebellion, including its commitment to racial hierarchy and its antagonism toward democracy. That is little surprise – no national divide has been more persistent than white supremacy in our politics (Hutchings & Valentino 2004). But, in a dispiriting irony, Republicans have replaced Democrats in that role, perpetuating de facto racial disparities across many aspects of social, political, and economic life. That includes continued efforts to reduce turnout among voters of color and others who Republicans rightly presume are unlikely to vote for them. Consequently, Republicans now dominate among more racially prejudiced and white-identified voters, and in the geographies that were once authoritarian enclaves for white Democratic rule (Acharya et al. 2018; Darmofal & Strickler 2019; Jardina 2019; Kuziemko & Washington 2018; Mickey 2015; Schickler 2016; Sides et al. 2018; Valentino & Sears 2005). The growing presence of racial and ethnic minorities in the electorate means Republicans will need to shift their appeals away from white identity politics or ramp up disenfranchisement to win and retain political control. Realignment also means Republicans now benefit from the Constitution's biases that disproportionately empower bigoted white folks in the Senate, the Electoral College, and state governments.

Republicans today make rhetorical appeals to conservatism, the Constitution, and limited government that were once the principled dodges used by Democrats to avoid admitting their true identity-based politics (Baker 1983). Republicans likewise replaced Democrats as the party of toxic masculinity and patriarchal power (Bauer 2018; Edwards 1997; Winter 2010). Even antebellum politics of enslaved people freeing themselves and heading to liberal Republican sanctuaries sounds like the politics surrounding asylum seekers and undocumented immigrants today.[5]

Partisan memory of the Civil War has flipped too, due to the same party shifts in on race. Majorities in both parties sided with the Union over rebels in a 2011 CNN poll, but Republicans were eight percentage points more likely than Democrats to go with the rebellion, despite a Union that was led by the Republican Party's most popular president. Likewise, Republicans were eleven points less likely than Democrats to say they "admire the leaders of the northern states during the Civil War" "a great deal" and twenty-one points more likely to "greatly admire" leaders of the rebellion. Testifying to Lost Cause propaganda, Republicans were twenty-two points likelier than Democrats to say that "slavery was not the main reason why [leaders of the Southern states] seceded from the U.S," with a slight majority of Republicans endorsing that myth. And Republicans are the stoutest defenders of statues that blight Southern squares in honor of the enslaver's rebellion, by forty-four points in 2017 (Ipsos 2017).

Rejecting Elections

Democracy collapsed in 1860 when partisans refused to accept the election, and it took a massive war by the new administration – and arguably another century – to piece it together. In 1860–61, the South didn't claim that the election was invalid – they simply asserted a unilateral right to reject the result. Three days after the popular vote, South Carolina passed a "Resolution to Call the Election of Abraham Lincoln as U.S. President a Hostile Act" and began their secession efforts. The equivalent today might parallel the (in)actions of President Buchanan after Lincoln's election, or they might follow the hypothetical form of an ardent "Fire-Eater" – a pro-slavery radical. Buchanan decried secession but did nothing to stop it, then handed power to Lincoln. A Southern Democrat like Jeff Davis might have refused to step down.

Like secessionists then, Republicans today from Presdient Trump on down now threaten to reject legitimate elections and deny governing rights to their opponents when their party loses. Some even suggest that violence is justified in that case. Today's threats to democracy are asymmetric, as they were in the mid-nineteenth century – and, like then, the party asserting white male Christian supremacy continues to pose the greater threat. Republican efforts to date are far less sweeping than in 1860–61 secession, but they have moved sharply toward that authoritarianism and may soon go farther.

Even before voters cast ballots in 2016, Donald Trump cast doubt on the legitimacy of the presidential election. Most people thought he would lose, and so he sought excuses for his likely failure. Even after he won with an Electoral College majority, he baselessly claimed millions of undocumented immigrants have voted illegally, to explain away his embarrassing popular vote loss by several million votes. In 2018, many prominent Republicans joined Trump in baselessly accusing Democrats of trying to steal close elections. That rhetoric has dangerous effects on the public. A 2017 study by political psychologists Ariel Malka and Yphtach Lelkes found 73 percent of Republicans believed voter fraud was common, and – more troubling – 56 percent said they would support canceling the 2020 election if Republican leaders called for that measure. There is no reason to expect Trump and other Republicans to do anything different if he loses reelection in 2020 (or if he wins reelection and the Republican candidate loses in 2024). The biggest question is whether he would refuse to give up power once his legal challenges were exhausted. A 2019 Ipsos poll reassuringly showed only 11 percent of Republicans (and 7 percent of Democrats) said Trump should stay in office if he loses, but interpretations of "losing" are what matter here. Even if Trump leaves (or is ejected) following an election loss, his hardcore supporters could still cause enormous damage if he and his allies in government and media delegitimize the outcome.

Rejecting an unfavorable presidential election result seems to be the likeliest way in which wider partisan violence could break out in our time, though still far short of all-out war. Vilification and even explicit calls for violence by the president increase the odds. Partisan violence might include assassinations, attacks on ordinary partisans, and even localized armed resistance to federal authority. Reponses by federal, state, and local forces and perhaps armed citizens would decide the result, though peaceful protests including national strikes would matter too. At least some armed government forces may align with each side claiming power. That would make the situation far more dangerous, and it would more closely resemble Civil War–era divides within the U.S. military as secession gathered momentum. In a different form, Republican state officials in Wisconsin, Michigan, North Carolina, and other states followed recent election losses with efforts to strip power from executive and administrative officials before victorious Democrats assumed office. These follow upon partisan gerrymanders and an Electoral College that increasingly empower Republicans even when Democrats win more votes. In short, Republicans are increasingly unwilling to accept their opponents' legitimate election to power, and increasingly win power themselves through undemocratic means.

Some political scientists build models to predict the risk of democratic collapse, and they say chances in the United States today are low. Daniel Treisman's (2018) model counts the Civil War as a non-failure since the Union ultimately won the war, despite a loss of democratic control and mass violence for several years over one-third of the country. I find it hard not to regard that as a democratic failure, and treating it as a success shows the limits of the approach. The 1860 risk was 2–3 percent in that model – very low for what I see as a failure – but still about 100 times higher than the risk today, assuming the model isn't missing key ingredients. Treisman writes, "no democracy has ever failed while its citizens had a per capita income about $22,000 or after surviving 65 years." In other words, we remain a democracy because we've been a democracy. Endurance builds norms, it's true, but the number of democracies that have survived sixty-five years is small – only nine since 1900, including the United States, and twenty-six since 1948 – and so that stat shouldn't reassure us much. The United States lasted seventy-nine years as a democracy (of sorts) before the Civil War unmade it.

Steven Levitsky and Daniel Ziblatt (2018) present a less reassuring view. Democracies are eroding around the globe in recent years. The slide into illiberal democracy undercuts the rule of law, respect for minorities, and free expression; unfairly targets opponents with state powers; and increases corruption and violence. Erosion is more likely in the United States than a complete democratic break, they say, as mutual toleration and forbearance grow scarce. The same early signs of erosion appear here. Levitsky and Ziblatt warned of Trump's clear authoritarianism during his campaign. His party already showed they were willing to move in that direction, and they've gone further since. Fully empowered in federal government, they moved the United States toward illiberal democracy on every dimension and resisted checks on their abuses from the House of Representatives after the 2018 elections elevated Democrats to majority control.

Rejecting fair elections – even delegitimizing rhetoric without resistance by force or obstruction – increases the odds of partisan violence. Democracy fails when partisans only accept the elections they won and threaten violence when they lose.

Modern Partisan Violence

Any growth in partisan violence that *does* occur will not emerge sui generis. Just as scholars have failed to recognize the partisan nature of Civil War mass violence, so too have we failed to appreciate the contentiousness of modern partisanship. The rate of violent political attacks is increasing in recent years, with particular growth in right-wing attacks, though the totals are still relatively low. This includes multiple attacks in the closing days of the 2018 midterm campaigns in response to bigoted and delusional conspiracy theories circulating around the right-wing internet. The massive 2017 melee in Charlottesville, Virginia, between white nationalists with armed militias versus counter-protesters, is another example. Also in 2017 was the shooting attack on the Republican congressional baseball team. The 2016 campaign saw an unusual level of partisan aggression at campaign rallies, including brawls, which would have appeared quite normal – even mild – in the 1850s. And in 2014 and 2016, armed militiamen in Montana and Oregon staged deadly standoffs with federal agencies to avoid paying federal land-use fees they owed. More generally, the Secret Service and FBI investigate hundreds of threats against political leaders each year, along with recurring assassination attempts, for all recent presidents (CBS News 2017; Dade 2011; Payne et al. 2013).

Let me reassure that, contrary to alarmist essays, nothing resembling the Civil War seems likely to occur any time soon. That doesn't void legitimate concerns about a potential rise in smaller-scale political violence, however, which could still kill dozens or hundreds of people while causing terror in millions. Civil War violence was several orders of magnitude larger than the substantial partisan violence that preceded and followed it because *governments* mobilized violence rather than individuals and groups. The near-zero votes for 1860 Republicans in the seceding states have no equal today – the most Democratic state (Hawaii) gave 30 percent of its votes to the Republican, and the Democrat won about a quarter of votes in the most Republican states. That makes it harder for any state to consider mobilizing against an out-party victory. Without legitimation by government, partisans are unlikely to fight in huge numbers. As a result, low-level, relatively disorganized partisan violence by individuals and small groups is far likelier than systematically organized mass violence.

The focus of this book was on ordinary partisans, who tend to follow their party leaders. Political scientist Charles Tilly (2003) shows that choices made by leaders are far more determinative in fueling or extinguishing widespread collective violence than decisions (or intervention efforts) among individuals in the public. Leaders decide whether there will be any organized partisan violence beyond isolated individual attacks. Thus, it matters a lot whether or not a party's leaders split over violence, and what faction ordinary and extremist partisans choose to follow. The president is usually the uncontested leader of their party, and experimental opinion leadership tests confirm that for Trump in particular (Barber & Pope 2019). As in the Civil War, opinion leaders can mobilize aggression with the rhetoric they deploy, including explicit advocacy and supplemental frames (Kalmoe 2014; Kalmoe & Mason 2018).

Even when leader decisions are key, followers must be predisposed to respond to violent calls by leaders, as they were in the Civil War era. This begins with partisan identification but also includes partisan moral disengagement and attitudes supporting violence. Large numbers of partisans today think their opponents are evil, see their own cause as righteous, and dehumanize opponents, though majorities reject these views (Cassese 2019; Kalmoe & Mason 2018). Smaller numbers (5–20 percent) enjoy seeing physical harm befall opposing partisans, wish harm upon them, disproportionately support violent actions by the state against them, and support outright violence by citizens against them – opposing leaders and citizens in similar measure (Kalmoe 2017; Kalmoe & Mason 2018). Violent animus arises in many partisans today even without direct calls for violence by leaders (Kalmoe & Mason 2018, Pew Research Center 1998).

Nonetheless, as was the case before and after the Civil War, prominent party leaders including the president *have* excused and encouraged violence and threats against their opponents. Some right-wing pundits have recently published fantasies about another Civil War, much like Fire-Eaters among 1850s Southern Democrats. Going even further, in 2019, an Alabama newspaper editor called for the Ku Klux Klan – founded just after the Civil War – to return to impose its violent racial-partisan terror on Democrats: "We'll get the hemp ropes out, loop them over a tall limb and hang all of them" (Ingber 2019). In violent attitudes and acts, we now face a darker, more dangerous partisan environment than we have seen in decades.

Maintaining Partisan Peace

For all the talk of "partisan warfare" these days – on cable news, in mass emails, in fiery speeches – it remains mostly metaphorical. Journalists, activists, and politicians play up the inherent conflict in politics in an effort to attract audiences or mobilize campaign activity. Even the literal partisan fights are infrequent compared with routine nineteenth century partisan brawls between party leaders and among the masses (Freeman 2018; Grimsted 1998). Despite millions of Americans holding violent attitudes against their partisan opponents, we do not see partisan warfare today – not even low-level violence equaling Bleeding Kansas, though some clashes like Charlottesville and anti-government standoffs in the West have moved in that direction. Why not? The evidence in this book from a single case can't explain it alone, but, in concert with other evidence, hints of an explanation emerge.

Contentious politics need not produce violence. Political scientist Charles Tilly (2003) notes "most holders of views that justify violence against one sort of human or another never actually abduct, maim, or murder anyone" (p. 8). In other words, violent views are a necessary but not sufficient condition for violent actions. Government strength also matters for the prevalence of unilateral partisan violence (see Tilly 2003, p. 26). The U.S. state was weak before the war, and that likely contributed to the mob and militia violence that helped to fuel animosities and the war itself. In contrast, the U.S. state is strong today, making such anarchy less likely, so long as the state upholds and enforces impartial justice. Tilly describes easy transitions from peaceful coexistence to violence and back again: "The most plausible behavioral accounts of such rapid switching center on the lifting and reimposition of social controls, following the assumption that impulses to attack remain more or less constant" (p. 230). In other words, collective violence is the product of individuals embedded in influential institutional and social contexts – leaders and communities.

Violent attitudes are present today, but the institutional and leadership contexts that were key in enabling *mass* partisan violence in the Civil War have been absent on a national scale for decades. The unsettling implication is that our relatively peaceful status quo is only as durable as the collection of institutions and leaders maintaining it. Peaceful partisanship is not inevitable; it requires maintenance by considerate leaders who carry an interest in avoiding violence at all costs.

Democracy's Double-Edged Sword

Elections are the preeminent instruments of democracy – they determine political control with ballots rather than bullets, as Lincoln asserted and scholars confirm. Parties are essential in organizing competition for legitimate control by coordinating candidate selection, informing voters about their choices, and mobilizing voters to the polls – they even help hold the nation together and prevent mass violence. Even so, partisan campaigns have strong incentives to stoke hatred and fear in their supporters, which must somehow dissipate in the aftermath of an election victory for some and a loss for others. In that way, the democratic *process* itself makes it harder to achieve the loser's consent that is essential for democratic persistence. Campaigns incentivize parties to maximize hostility, predict apocalypse if the other side wins, and threaten violence, as in Civil War elections. The anger generated by partisan leaders and news can drive desirable, nonviolent political action (Valentino et al. 2011), but it is also the emotional fuel of aggression. For democracy to persist, parties and their adherents have to step back from the abyss of partisan violence after every election.

Modern American campaigns now run on for years – longer than any other democracy – which keeps attentive partisan rage at a boil (Sood & Iyengar 2016). Similarly, the recent return of partisan news gives committed activists little incentive to venture outside inflammatory political bubbles that function much like the partisan news environment of the mid-nineteenth century, despite the much larger number of non-partisan news outlets now available (Arceneaux & Johnson 2013; Lelkes et al. 2017; Levendusky 2013). Party leaders no longer directly control partisan news as part of the party organization, but the close ties between the Republican party, Fox News, and other Republican outlets look increasingly similar to that media model.

Beyond individual partisan hate and violence, this book shows that partisan animus is most dangerous when party leaders *organize* violent action with direct calls, plans, and infrastructure for violence against specific targets. Responsible party leaders and strong organizations can hold the worst impulses of their partisans in check, though mid-nineteenth century American history and cross-national examples today show parties can also fuel hostility and direct violence to achieve their aims (e.g. Grimsted 1998; Höglund 2009; LeBas 2006; Wilkinson 2006). Avoiding violence requires leaders to see the long-term benefit of accepting loss today for a chance to win the next time (e.g. Axelrod 1984; Przeworski 1991). That basic electoral structure hasn't changed, but partisan views of acquiescence have deteriorated with extreme social polarization – what Levitsky and Ziblatt (2018) describe as the number one warning sign for democratic decay. Of course, parties and social groups that expect to continue losing elections in the future have *more* incentive to use violence and erode democracy when those tactics are their only hope for holding on to their diminishing political power.

Parties today are far weaker after reformers decentralized their nominating authority and focused efforts nationally rather than locally. That empowers activists who care more about purity than electability, who are less willing to accept a legitimate loss. Political scientist Julia Azari (2016) characterizes the result as weak parties amidst strong partisanship. Party leaders still have levers of power within their organizations (Cohen et al. 2008), at least when they choose to exert themselves, but recent history suggests a voter base driven by negative partisanship and group hostility has more say, and may choose whoever campaigns most aggressively. Party leaders fear alienating that base, which neutralizes their potential power. Ordinary partisans seem to remain loyal to that nominee no matter what, especially when other party leaders are cowed into silence and acquiescence.

Avoiding violence while securing full equality for all citizens requires active effort, not just passive hope. The first step involves recognizing American partisanship as more powerful and more dangerous than we knew. A clear-eyed view of the Civil War shows us the lethal potential of mass partisanship. Democracy literally depends on learning that war's partisan lessons.

* * *

To put down a partisan rebellion, Americans needed the will to sustain the Union with their votes while transforming themselves into agents of death to secure military victory, with hundreds of thousands dying to ensure that end. National salvation required partisan ballots *and* bullets. Prewar partisanship helps to explain who heeded the call to arms, who stayed, and who died; and the experiences of those soldiers at war help explain the political will of their families, friends, and neighbors back home to bear the necessary costs for victory, and how they remembered those sacrifices after. The consequences of the war and its elections have defined our politics ever since.

The Civil War was America's most dangerous, most deadly, and most *partisan* crisis. The essential ingredients for partisan conflict have been present throughout most of American history: strong political identities placed in competition. What changed in the Civil War era was how partisanship aligned with other important social identities, how party leaders fueled the crisis, and then how they mobilized its violence. Nineteenth century political violence underscores the latent threats in partisanship, even in relatively peaceful democratic societies (Tilly 2003). The Civil War also proves the occasional need for partisan *bullets* alongside ballots to defend democracy and the nation's obligations to the equality of its people.

Notes

Acknowledgments

[1] Nothing unusual, that is, beyond longer lines in black Democratic precincts, voter ID laws, and felon disenfranchisement in a state with a long history of disproportionate law enforcement against black Louisianans and the second-highest incarceration rate – which means voter disenfranchisement – in the country.

[2] Daniel Posner's (2004) research in Zambia and Malawi perfectly captures this dynamic – how partisan electoral competition that cleaves along ethnic and other group lines is particularly dangerous, whereas parties with cross-cutting group identities tend to produce much less dangerous politics.

[3] Don advised John Zaller to write the final chapter of *Nature and Origins of Mass Opinion* at a cabin in the woods with a bottle of whiskey on a weekend getaway. That turned out well for John, and so I took up Dr. Kinder's prescription for writing the whole book.

[4] Other Michigan faculty and friends not mentioned above or below: Jenna Bednar, Mika Lavaque-Manty, Brooke Allen, Richard Anderson, Antoine Banks, Matias Bargsted, Andrea Benjamin, Janna Bray, Logan Casey, Jenn Chudy, Dave Cottrell, Sarah Croco, Allison Dale-Riddle, Papia Debroy, Menna Demessie, Carolina DeMiguel, Charles Doriean, Kate Gallagher-Robbins, Ella Gao, Ben Goldman, Abe Gong, Cassie Grafström, Eric Groenendyk, Josh Gubler, Krysha Heavner, Shana Hodgson, Mihwa Hong, Alex Jakle, Ashley Jardina, Hakeem Jefferson, Andrea Jones-Rooy, Kristyn Karl, Nam Kyu Kim, Lisa Koch, Pam McCann, Erin McGovern, Bill MacMillan, Jen Miller-Gonzalez, Neill Mohammad, Pat O'Mahen, Davin Phoenix, Molly Reynolds, Michael Robbins, Tim Ryan, Katie Simmons, David Smith, Derek Stafford, LaFleur Stephens, Liz Suhay, Kharis Templeman, Kathleen Tipler, Michio Umeda, Johannes Urpelainen, Keith Veale, Alex Von Hagen Jamar, Brooklyn Walker, and Alton Worthington. Yanna Krupnikov and Adam Levine were my great grad mentors who continue to inspire. David Magleby was generous in his mentorship and friendship from our first meeting onward – Dan's MPSA birthday party at Giordano's, which became a regular happening. Thanks to

Brendan Nyhan for regularly sharing my early work on political violence in his public-facing Twitter commentary.

5 We camped for a weekend in 105-degree heat for the first big 150th at Manassas. Following a terrific Tennessee hailstorm near Shiloh the next spring, we spent the night in camp listening as a period band played wedding dances for reenactor newlyweds in the distance, with lighting flashing silently far beyond. We recreated the pontoon boat river crossing at Fredericksburg and fought our way through the historic town up to disaster on the heights. In the garb of the 2nd Wisconsin at Antietam, we advanced at dawn through the battlefield's foggy cornfields 150 years to the moment they had before us, in total silence but for our footsteps, and we later crested the rise leading up to the Sunken Road under the banner of the Irish Brigade. And I'll never forget camping on the Gettysburg battlefield near the huge Pennsylvania monument, walking in moonlight and mist in the middle of the night to the site of the 1st Minnesota's desperate charge.

6 A while back, Charles Franklin observed on Twitter that the light and charming holiday film *White Christmas* (1954) includes dialogue about how Vermonters would stone a Democrat to death if they happened to encounter one, at a time when New England was homogeneously Republican (71 percent for Ike in 1952) and had not yet realigned away from its Civil War–era partisanship. That animosity doesn't fit our memory of placid mid-twentieth century party politics, when political scientists warned that the two parties were so agreeable and indistinct that they threatened democratic choice.

7 As it turns out, I have an older connection to Louisiana as well: my great-great-grandfather Ole Rocksvold fought his way through Louisiana in 1864 as a Union soldier during the ill-fated Red River Campaign. He was lightly wounded in the hip at Pleasant Hill, about a three-hour drive from Baton Rouge today. My family has a letter he wrote from the bluffs of Grand Ecore to his fiancée, translated from Norwegian, detailing the personalized violence of that battle.

8 Mom wrote a great biography of Ole's life, including his Civil War service, called *Letters from Ole Rocksvold*, drawing heavily on wartime and postwar letters he wrote to friends and family.

Preface

1 In 1865, rebel soldiers at Appomattox ceremoniously stacked their arms before the assembled U.S. Army. Like McCain's promise to the president-elect, Confederate soldiers swore a loyalty oath to the United States – including an explicit pledge to respect abolition. In exchange, the United States pardoned their treason and promised protection under its laws.

2 The digital versions of concessions have taken a modified form on social media in recent years for losing congressional candidates. Similar to the forms and conventions of the televised speech, they still declare the result, affirm the campaign, thank supporters, and acknowledge their own changing role, but they are less likely to call for unity or make tributes to democracy online – both of which are important for reconciling their supporters to the result (Mirer & Bode 2015).

3 Nixon's party pursued election recounts and investigations after his concession, though those legal efforts came to nothing as courts dismissed the cases and reviews. More recent examinations find no evidence of fraud large enough to sway the election (e.g. Kallina 1985).

4 Al Gore quoted this Douglas line in his 2000 concession speech.

Chapter 1

1 Lincoln was certainly right to condemn potential post-election violence by Democrats, who sought to extend the evils of slavery under legal pretense. His rightness about extra-constitutional violence by John Brown – or Nat Turner and others who violently attacked slavers and slavery – is doubtful. Lincoln was a consistent moderate among Republicans, detesting slavery but only calling for its limit rather than its extinction before the war, given Supreme Court protections of the practice. Most Republicans took the same tack, though some referred to a "higher law" of justice – in religious terms – that might supersede the Constitution. Extra-constitutional violence against supreme injustice is arguably just, especially in a political system lacking democratic means to address it – enslavement and disenfranchisement of African Americans (and women, for that matter). Violence loses any rationale with full enfranchisement alongside fair elections and protected rights. Authoritarian despotism and disenfranchisement *can* justify violence, even when unfair elections are held, though peaceful means are preferable. But the *level* of authoritarianism at which violence is just is unclear.

2 Of course, the United States wasn't a full democracy in the mid-nineteenth century. Well over half of adults– women and people of color – fell outside the "public" and were unable to vote. Most African Americans were enslaved. The stability that peaceful elections usually produced did not serve the interests of these non-publics.

3 The Census Bureau projects the 2020 U.S. population at 333 million, versus 31 million in 1860 – 10.7 times smaller. In 1940, it was 132 million, 4.3 times larger than 1860. The military size today would be 24 million on the U.S. side alone.

4 These via the 14th Amendment (1868), Yosemite's federal protection (1864), and land-grant colleges (1862 Morrill Act).

5 Scholars are also now recognizing the ineffectiveness of folk wisdom on bridging social and political divides, like Wells and colleagues (2017) and Walsh (2007), who find major limits in talk-it-out prescriptions for resolving conflict.

6 Aldrich, Jillson, and Wilson (2002) note that the Framers *did* recognize some of the first signs of parties under the Articles of Confederation–the nation's first, failed constitution – and that the new Constitution responded in part to those insights.

7 For an excellent review, see Smith (2014). For another contentious view of Civil War parties, see Orr (2006).

8 As *The American Voter* (Campbell et al. 1960) puts it, "The emergence of the Republican Party and its subsequent domination of national politics were the direct outgrowth of the great debate over slavery and the ultimate issue of the Civil War" (p. 534).

9 *Congressional Globe*, Feb. 21, 1863, p. 1163.

10 Some notable social science works take a similar historical approach: Costa and Kahn's (2009) *Heroes and Cowards* on the Civil War, Berinsky's (2009) *In Time of War* on twentieth century wartime public opinion, Acharya, Blackwell, and Sen's (2018) *Deep Roots* on slavery's impact on white Southern partisanship since the Civil War, Taeku Lee's (2002) study of Civil Rights letters, Corder and Wolbrecht's (2016) *Counting Women's Ballots* on the electoral impact of women's suffrage, and Carpenter and Moore's (2014) work on the particular efficacy of women circulating antebellum abolition petitions.

11 Quantification is inherently reductive, stripping richness from lived experiences and boxing it in simple categories. But those statistics, despite their limits, give a more representative view of political and military behaviors of ordinary people when characterizing the whole population or probabilistically sampling from it.

12 Historians and nineteenth century leaders used some of these materials. In fact, although quantitative historical analysis may be new to some, the "New Political History" of the 1960s and 1970s used statistics to assess mass behavior. My attention to socialization and language fits the "cultural turn" in the field (e.g. Baker 1983; Edwards 1997; Frank 1998).

13 The *Missouri Republican* (MO-D, July 23, 1863) describes this inferential challenge in criticizing anti-war Democrat Clement Vallandigham's dire reports on resolute Southern public opinion: "It is possible that in his rather hasty transit through the Confederate States Mr. Vallandigham saw no person not desperately resolved to hold out to the last. ... But ... [he] had no opportunity of associating with the Southern people. He was constantly in the company of those most deeply committed to the cause of rebellion. ... Mr. Vallandigham was not in a position, and was not the person, to see anything of Southern Unionism." Of course, the *Republican* had little better basis for its claim of a weary South.

14 A quota sample can provide decent inferences by aligning attributes of the sample with the population, but the method selects people with purpose rather than randomly, which is a step in the right direction but less than ideal. McPherson (1997) uses a quota sample of soldiers' letters and diaries to make better inferences than other investigators. Some scholars have used a random sample of Civil War military units to make inferences about soldiers' experiences (see e.g. Costa & Kahn 2008).

15 Soldier data from seven other Union states was inadequate on where the soldiers were from for my tests.

16 Today's methods for polling, experiments, communication exposure measures, and network analysis enable much more discerning mechanism tests for disentangling the causes and consequences of partisanship.

17 Of course, partisan patterns are not entirely constant across time, as Hetherington (2001) notes in the latter half of the twentieth century, and as Bradley Spahn (2019) shows with California voter registration during the first half of the twentieth century. Vote choice today and in recent years is also more rigidly partisan than it was in the mid-twentieth century (Campbell et al. 1960; Lewis-Beck et al. 2008).

18 In 1860, free black men could vote in Maine, New Hampshire, Vermont, Rhode Island, and Massachusetts, and in New York among those who owned

at least $250 worth of property. In 1870, the 15th Amendment recognized the legal right of all black men to vote. Though thwarted in the South for a century, suffrage was generally available to black men in the North. http://archive.fairvote.org/righttovote/timeline.htm

Chapter 2

1 This section's summary is drawn especially from works by McPherson (1988), Potter (1977), and Wilentz (2005).

2 All party platforms from the UCSB American Presidency Project.

3 The Southern Democratic platform contained a single non-slavery plank, favoring a transcontinental railroad.

4 Lincoln's ballot absence in the South reduced his popular vote by a small margin but not his Electoral College votes.

5 This nineteenth century dynamic of violent white grievance and loss of white power has echoes in the backlash among prejudiced whites today as the country diversifies and whites lose their stranglehold on power (e.g. Jardina 2019).

6 Quoted in Ken Burns' *The Civil War* documentary, Episode 1.

7 Holt (1978) says these states differ much from the first batch of secessionists, but the distinction between immediate rejection of the election and rejection when the president chooses to exercise his national authority is not much.

8 Secessionists were not *all* Southern Democrats, of course. Some Southern Whigs rebelled too, though Democrats predominated. The key point is that they rejected *Republican* electoral victory. Secessionists could be styled anti-Republicans in my argument, if that is more palatable. Many Northerners viewed secessionists as Democrats, however.

9 Quoted in Foner (2018).

10 From an 1840 Whig Party newspaper called the *Old Soldier*, quoted in Holzer (2014, p. 44); from 1858, quoted in Holzer (2014, p. 186): "Against the slavery-extension policy of the mis-named Democratic party, the *Journal* will make increasing and unrelenting warfare." 1859 letter from Republican editor to Lincoln, quoted in Holzer (2014, p. 204).

11 Quoted in Holzer (2014, p. 152).

12 www.whig.com/story/12514414/political-rally-that-turned-into-riot-being-celebrated#//

13 Historian Eric Hobsbawn concurs on a generally non-ideological public: "Official ideologies of states and movements are not guides to what is in the minds of even the most loyal citizens and supporters" (quoted in Lawson 2002, p. 13).

14 Holt (1978) also shares this group-centric view of partisanship. Bensel (2004) describes most nineteenth century voters as loyal partisans, though with a more transactional and localized view of identification: "men came to think of themselves as Democrats because they were given things by men who worked for the Democratic party" (p. ix).

15 Quoted in Astor (2011).

16 Drew Gilpin Faust (2008) illustrates the utility of moral disengagement in combat, quoting a *New York Tribune* reporter at the Battle of Shiloh: "'Men lost their semblance of humanity and the spirit of the demon shone in their faces. There was but one desire, and that was to destroy'" (p. 36).

17 Likewise, reactions against disliked leaders push opposing partisans in the opposite direction. For example, Feldman, Huddy, and Marcus (2015) find that ordinary Democrats opposed the 2003 Iraq War led by a Republican president – especially those well informed by print journalism – despite a lack of unified Democratic leadership on the issue.

18 Gerring notes ideological and rhetorical continuities bridging Whigs and Republicans, and literally deems them "Whig-Republicans." As I note below, the immediate connection is stronger between Free Soil–Republicans than Whigs, but the result is equivalent by the end of the war. Mayhew argues most party change is incremental rather than abrupt.

19 For reasons unknown to me, ICPSR election data do not include presidential votes for Maryland counties in 1848. Iowa had a third of the counties that it would eventually have, and northern counties in Wisconsin and Michigan were omnibuses until their later subdivision. A few of those counties split between the two elections. Other states saw minor shifts in a few county boundaries. Such changes would *reduce* stability estimates, making estimates here lower bounds of continuity.

20 Vote shares are the party's raw vote divided by all votes cast in the county (or state). I test continuity in vote shares with a simple correlation, which can range continuously on a scale from −1.0 to +1.0. The latter indicates perfect correspondence in vote shares from one year to the next. If every place cast identical party percentages in both years, the correlation is +1.0. But +1.0 also arises if party votes in every place shifted up or down by the same percentage with rising or falling national tides. Thus, it measures rank and relative position for each party across the localities. A correlation of −1.0 would mean a perfect inversion of vote shares, and a correlation of 0.0 would mean no systematic relationship between votes from one year to the next. Large counties are proportionally more important for elections, so rather than count big and small counties equally, I weight them by the number of votes cast in the later year. That gives more analytic leverage to places with thousands of voters over those with hundreds. Results are roughly similar without.

21 In free states, correlations are +0.83 (Whigs), +0.68 (Free Soil), and +0.64 (Democrats).

22 State-level tests – that include all nineteen states – are unweighted.

23 A Republican–Know-Nothing coalition would have beaten Buchanan in popular votes by 10 points but still lost the Electoral College by 8 points despite adding California (4), Illinois (11), and New Jersey (7) to the Republican total.

24 California and Oregon politics divided much like the loyal slave states. Massachusetts was the only outlier, giving 13 percent of its votes to Bell, due to a Massachusetts native son as vice presidential candidate (Everett). His next best performance in the free contiguous states was Ohio at 3 percent. Connecticut

was the outlier among these states for Breckinridge votes, at 19 percent. His next best was only 6 percent in Maine. Democrats would have lost the popular vote in 1860 even if united, unless Constitutional Union voters had joined them as well. United Democrats would have won California (4), Oregon (3) – not enough to overcome Lincoln's large Electoral College victory.

25 Many slave states excluded Free Soil and Republican candidates from the ballot. Where they did appear, they won few votes. Thus, continuity in those places primarily reflects votes for the other anti-Democratic party in each year.

26 From an 1852 baseline: Free-Soil-to-Republican votes correlate well (+0.57), as do Whig-to-Know-Nothing votes (+0.36), with negative correlations for Republicans and Know-Nothings when reversing predecessor parties. At the state level, Free-Soil-Republicans (+0.79), and Whigs-Know-Nothings (+0.55) showed similar continuity.

27 Eric Foner (1970/1995) suggests about one-quarter of the Republican coalition came from recent Democratic departures. Earle (2004) shows that the Free Soil Party in the 1840s had strong roots in radical Jacksonian Democracy, of an anti-slavery variety, with social and economic components. Most of the third party's votes in the 1840s came from former Democrats. Their crowning achievements, realized a decade later, were emancipation and the Homestead Act.

28 Identical patterns replicate at the town level in Massachusetts in results not shown here. Massachusetts is the only state for which I have town-level data; otherwise, town-level tests might be best throughout the book. I utilize this Massachusetts data wherever possible as a third level to test partisan war dynamics.

29 The 1850s saw an especially high level of migration and immigration compared with the wartime years. Likewise, the 1860–1864 continuity is attenuated some by disproportionately Republican voters away at war missing from their counties. County totals recorded some of their votes as absentee, for the first time in history, while others separately counted a soldier's vote category. Democratic states prevented them from voting absentee to disenfranchise disproportionately Republican soldiers. The Army furloughed some of these soldiers to vote at home, while others had no chance to vote. Of course, disproportionate Republican war mortality would also disrupt vote shares.

30 In 2000 and again in 2004, the American National Election Study (ANES) interviewed the same representative sample of voters. Ninety percent of panel voters chose the same party (r = 0.81), and partisan identity produced loyalty rates over 90 percent (rs ~ 0.78). Exit polls using different sampling methods show the same. Likewise, 89 percent of Democrats and Republicans held the same party identification over these four years (r = 0.84). Of course, campaign messages and social contexts reinforce individual partisan dynamics, just as I theorize for the nineteenth century. In other words, partisanship's effects arise from interactions with social context, not intrinsically in isolation. The ANES also fielded a similar panel study four decades earlier, between 1956 and 1960. Providing some contrast, 78 percent of voters in this panel reported choosing the same party's candidate (r = 0.57). About 77 percent of partisans were loyal to their party's candidate in both years (Pearson's rs ~ 0.69), and

partisan identity was stable for 84 percent of Democrats and Republicans (r = 0.80). These estimates still show durable and powerful partisanship, but they are somewhat lower than the same tests between 2000 and 2004. That may be due to greater party polarization and the role of Southern Democrats as a sort of third party between Republicans and Northern Democrats.

Partisan votes are strongly driven by party identity but, as Green and colleagues (2002) note, they are not the same – "voting is an inadequate measure of self-conception" (p. 17). This is especially important to remember in this book, where the only available measure of mass partisanship is partisan votes. Much of the nineteenth century partisan stability across localities is certainly a product of partisan identities, but the degree is impossible to determine for lack of a direct test.

Chapter 3

1 U.S. government censorship and mob violence occasionally influenced news, mostly in Border States. Democratic newspapers generally published without interference in 1862 and 1864 (Holzer 2014). The government briefly shuttered pro-secession and anti-draft papers in the other years and jailed or deported their editors. U.S. military authorities did this, often without (but sometimes with) the implicit assent of federal officials, including the president. Usually print disruptions were brief – a day or two. One can imagine it had a chilling effect on some content (though censorship likely radicalized others). Likewise, several instances of mob violence against newspapers of both parties probably had some chilling effect on the expression of the most radical partisan views (Holzer 2014; Towne 2005; Weber 2006). Legal and mob efforts to censor news coverage would have diminished differences between Democratic and Republican newspapers.

2 We employed two independent coders who did not know the book's hypotheses nor the partisanship of the papers they coded (as identified by Rowell). Between them, they split the entire corpus of issues. To test reliability, a third coder double-coded 30 percent of the newspaper dates. This check produced acceptable reliability for the codes (see Online Appendix). War support was most reliable at $r = 0.81$, views of the war's progress and party support were at $r = 0.76$, slavery views were $r = 0.59$, linking votes to war ($r = 0.78$), recent casualties ($r = 0.58$), local casualties ($r = 0.68$), framing the dead ($r = 0.79$), dead in voting ($r = 0.71$). Although some reliabilities are on the low side, the coding for overall war positions were highly reliable. To the extent that some supplemental codes have lower reliability, this would reduce the likelihood of finding significant partisan differences. That arguably makes the tests more conservative.

3 Estimates for party war support hardly change with weighting – unweighting changes them by under 5 percent of the scale.

4 War topics included mentions of battles, troops, enlistment, casualties, etc. Politics included party mentions, elections, slavery, or the draft, focused on Union politics only (not Confederate). Often, the two fused.

5 The difference in war views between Republican and Democratic papers: April 1861 ($b = 0.62$, $s.e. = 0.20$, $p < 0.001$), July 1861 ($b = 0.21$, $s.e. = 0.10$, $p = 0.05$), statistically indistinct in 1862 and midterm issues, July 1863 ($b = 0.58$, $s.e. = 0.24$, $p < 0.05$), July 1864 ($b = 0.87$, $s.e. = 0.26$, $p < 0.01$), and November 1864 ($b = 1.42$, $s.e. = 0.14$, $p < 0.001$).

6 The scales for the two panels in Figure 3.2 differ because the Democratic code ranges from negative to positive, whereas the Republican code measures only whether Republican war support was mentioned or not, given that Republican papers never opposed the war outright.

7 Despite few pages making "manly duty" the main appeal, we found many cases of masculinity at work. The *Berkshire County Eagle* (MA-R, July 1862) described the kind of man who would not enlist: "If he has lost all self-respect.- ... If he thinks it better to remain in the city and live on *foi gras*, than to go out on the battle-field and perhaps die by a fall on the grass. ... If he is a luggard, and a muff, and a COWARD." The *Boston Evening Traveller* (MA-R, July 1862) reported, "Roxbury would fill up her quota promptly and manfully." Likewise, the *Louisville Journal* (KY-D, Aug 1863) warned, "By refusing to fight the rebellion ... you surrender to it, and lose your manhood."

8 The independent papers we assessed looked much more like Republican ones in their war support, even as those papers mostly endorsed Democratic candidates.

Chapter 4

1 Quoted in Silbey (1977), p. 174.

2 Even after initial battles deadened soldiers' thirst for combat, newspapers continued to print noble fictions about war and the troops' eagerness to fight, distorting the views of war participation for potential new recruits (McPherson 1997).

3 Historical and modern studies provide scant evidence of coherent political belief systems for most people (see Chapter 2). Instead, social identities and group attitudes – including partisanship – more powerfully influence mass politics.

4 The states that made no allowance for absentee soldier votes were IL, IN, NJ, DE, MD, OR, and MA.

5 McPherson posits a twenty-point increase in soldier votes for Republicans by the war's end compared with estimates of their prewar partisanship. That seems to assume that soldiers matched their communities at the start. I find that unlikely. If accurate, by the war's end, nearly half of those prewar Democrats may have voted for Lincoln in 1864 to bring the total soldier vote share for Republicans up between 76 percent and 79 percent, depending on whether using estimates for all states or just for free-contiguous states, weighted by total white troops supplied for the Union. Statistics from Dyer's troop furnishings and Benton's *Voting in the Field* (1915). About 20 percent of eligible soldier voters abstained. They may have held more Democratic leanings (White 2014), but that non-participation rate is similar for civilians, and so it adds no evidence of *unusual* pressure.

6 Dyer disaggregated "colored troops" and "white troops," but he presented sailor and marine counts not separated by race.

7 Of course, teenagers who came of age during the war are uncounted, as are wartime immigrants who fought. Conversely, men who were forty-five in 1860 were ineligible and those a few years younger became ineligible during the war. Thus, military-age males are a rough estimate of eligibility, but those close approximations are unlikely to bias *party* comparisons much.

8 For more information about the soldier data, see: www.civilwardata.com/moreinfo.html

9 The fifteen states with sufficient soldier data to facilitate the book's main tests are CA, CT, IL, IN, IA, KY, ME, MA, MI, MN, NH, NY, RI, VT, and WI.

10 Northeastern states are near 100 percent complete for identifying the prewar residence of combatants. Non-coding in the Midwest was mostly due to town names duplicated in multiple counties. This only poses a systematic threat for partisan tests if counties with duplicate town names systematically differed in partisanship from places without – not just a different level of Republican vote share, but a different *function* relating partisanship and fighting compared with similar counties with entirely unique town names. Note that the *county* is not dropped in the analysis, but soldiers from those towns are not credited to the county's totals. For robustness, I conducted separate tests among states with nearly all their soldiers assigned to counties to ensure undercounts do not bias the estimates. The results there are similar.

11 The estimate for free contiguous states is smaller but remains substantial and significant. The diminution is due to excluding California, which cast the second fewest votes for Republicans among these states but was an extreme outlier in its white voluntarism levels (<4 percent here, versus 21 percent for KY next lowest).

12 States with more than 90 percent of soldiers geo-coded are CT, ME, MA, MN, NH, RI, VT, NY, and MI. The next highest coded rates are CA at 83 percent and IL at 81 percent. Setting an 80 percent threshold yields similar results to those 11 states ($b = 0.34$, *s.e.* = 0.10), excluding KY, WI, IA, and IN.

13 Liturgical denominations (Catholics and Episcopalians) contributed larger shares of white men to fight, all else equal. Pietistic denominations were unrelated. Free-contiguous states have substantively similar but non-significant estimates.

14 See Online Appendix for additional ecological analysis details. Four additional datasets provide limited supplemental tests (see Online Appendix): An 1862 Indiana conscription report that lists county volunteers through September produces null results, which is the same as ACWRD county data for Indiana through the same date. A full-war Illinois adjutant report that lists all county combatants (including draftees) produces null results equal to the full-war ACWRD county data for Illinois. A town-level test of Massachusetts voluntarism, desertion, and mortality produces null results, compared with New England–wide ACWRD estimates with substantially larger point estimates (significant for desertion and death). A town-level test of Iowa voluntarism, desertion, and mortality produces a voluntarism estimate of equal substantive size to the national county results but falls short of statistical

significance. The Iowa desertion estimate is zero. The Iowa soldier mortality tests is about half the national ACWRD estimate and non-significant.

15 The difference between the 1862 nadir and the 1864 maximum in partisan voluntarism estimates is statistically distinct (p = 0.08), but the 1861 and 1863 estimates between them are not distinguishable from the others.

16 In related analysis, Costa and Kahn (2008) show Union deserters were more likely to change their names and more likely to move farther away after the war than similar soldiers who initially left their units but returned. Name-changing and moving strategies reduced the social costs of desertion in some ways, but the uprooting and identity-changing process was itself a large cost.

17 Any gap exposed weak flanks that could destroy the whole line if hit by the enemy. So, for instance, when Union General Winfield Hancock saw several Confederate regiments marching toward a gap in his line on the second day of Gettysburg, he ordered the 1st Minnesota to charge them despite being outnumbered five to one. It was suicide, they knew, but they complied. Eighty-two percent of those Minnesota soldiers were killed, wounded, or captured in just a few minutes, but they bought the time needed to bring up reinforcements to fill the gap and prevent disaster for the whole Union Army. Minnesota was a strong Republican state, second only to Vermont in its support for Lincoln in 1860 at 63 percent.

18 www.gilderlehrman.org/sites/default/files/inline-pdfs/Elizabeth%20Robert son_0.pdf

19 Fehrenbacher (1989), p. 499

20 U.S. National Archives (2017), "Black Soldiers in the U.S. Military during the Civil War." www.archives.gov/education/lessons/blacks-civil-war

21 U.S. National Archives (2017), "Black Soldiers in the U.S. Military during the Civil War." www.archives.gov/education/lessons/blacks-civil-war

22 Quoted in Berlin et al. (1998), pp. 131–132.

23 Quoted in Berlin et al. (1998), p. 153.

24 National Archives poster. www.archives.gov/files/education/lessons/blacks-civil-war/images/recruitment-broadside.gif

25 U.S. National Archives (2017), "Black Soldiers in the U.S. Military during the Civil War." www.archives.gov/education/lessons/blacks-civil-war

26 https://archive.org/stream/inhonorofnationaoonati/inhonorofnationaoonati_djvu.txt

27 The section title is a quote from a letter by USSC/WCAR nurse Dr. Elizabeth Blackwell, in reference to the organization's difficulty in getting administrators to accept women as nurses through the group. www.gilderlehrman.org/sites/default/files/inline-pdfs/Elizabeth%20Robertson_0.pdf

28 Women in leadership roles during the war are best known, though not nearly as much as their male counterparts. Dorothea Dix, Clara Barton, and Mary Ann Bickerdyke revolutionized care in U.S. military hospitals to provide organized, medically sound treatment for hundreds of thousands of injured and sick Union soldiers. Harriet Tubman, who freed herself from slavery as a young woman, served as a Union spy in South Carolina, passing along essential intelligence to U.S. forces. Women's rights pioneers Elizabeth Cady Stanton and Susan B. Anthony played key roles in organizing petitions to

Congress supporting the 13th Amendment to abolish slavery, continuing women's decades of successful abolition organizing and petition-gathering (Carpenter & Moore 2014). Harriet Beecher Stowe played a key communication role in galvanizing opposition to slavery before the war with her 1852 novel *Uncle Tom's Cabin*, which sold more copies than any other nineteenth century book, second only to the Bible.

Chapter 5

1 *Congressional Globe*, Feb. 21, 1863, p. 1163. Summarized in *Cheshire Republican* (NH-D), March 4, 1863.

2 Chapter 3 describes our newspaper content methods (see also Online Appendix). All parenthetical statistical reports are OLS coefficients, comparing Republicans to a Democratic baseline, weighted by regional population. Systematic tests and most quotes are from election dates, with some illustrations from other dates. Michael Dubin's (1998; 2003) House and gubernatorial election compendia provided each state's election dates for each type of vote. I use these dates for the newspaper analysis and for the casualty tests in subsequent chapters.

3 Other factors like policy views and values play a surprisingly small role (e.g. Achen & Bartels 2016; Kinder & Kalmoe 2017; Neely 2017). Consistent with modern views, historian Neely writes Civil War partisans were "moderates of only vague ideological identification" (p. 114).

4 The *New York Herald* (NY-I, July 1864) gave a generous but naïve view of the public: "in revolutionary times like the present, ... they read, think and decide for themselves, and trust to no politicians in resolving upon their political action."

5 The *Cincinnati Enquirer* (OH-D, Nov 1864) printed a soldier's letter worrying soldier ballots wouldn't count: "My regiment suffered some, but, by good luck, the poor fellows who were killed and captured had already voted, and most of them for McClellan. He got more than four votes to Lincoln's one. I hope our votes will be counted. If this army is cheated by the Government, you will see h—. No one here knows our total loss except at headquarters. They are afraid it will leak out and hurt Lincoln."

6 The independent *Baltimore Sun* supported Republicans in midterms and 1864. Two of the four remaining independent papers consistently backed Democrats. One chose Democrats in 1862 and neutrality in 1864; another did the reverse.

7 Many mid-nineteenth century people with anti-slavery views held them because they believed slavery morally damaged slaveholders, more so than sympathy for the enslaved, which many also had. Some leading Republican ideas for a post-slavery society involved deporting black Americans, presuming a multi-racial society was impossible (Foner 2011).

8 Over-attentive to the specific terms "white supremacy" and "miscegenation," Neely finds them in limited use.

9 Four independent papers endorsed the 13th Amendment, but the *Baltimore Sun* in slave-state Maryland objected to any emancipation.

10 The *Davenport Democrat* (IA-D, Nov 1864) alleged Lincoln used the Army "not to subdue armed rebellion, but to secure his partisan ends" – namely, emancipation.

11 The *Enquirer* printed a Richmond news column that day: "This war has not failed to teach the negro the lesson that his interest and those of his master are identical; that his only friend is the master."

12 The pro-war *Missouri Republican* (MO-D, July 1861) initially defended slavery, reassured by signs they interpreted as loyalty among enslaved people: "There is no evidence that the mass of the negroes down South are not well contented with their condition as before the war, and no more inclined to leave their masters for the doubtful hospitalities of the abolitionists." But by July 1863, they had executed a startling about-face, while insisting on separate territories for each race: "regarding slavery as an unqualified evil to our State and people, we cordially approve the policy of emancipation." They also wrote: "If the negroes are to be liberated at no distant time, measures must be taken to humanize them" with education and marriage.

13 The *Cincinnati Enquirer* (OH-D, Nov 1864) listed some of the war-related Democratic complaints: "the abolitionists have the political power of the country in their hands; that they have overridden the Constitution, bridled the Supreme Court, and made and altered laws according to the counsel of their own will; that they have, in many cases, laid violent hands upon those who differed with them in opinion, or questioned their infallibility; and that the finances of the country are very nearly in a state of bankruptcy, and large tracts of its soil deluged with the blood of its citizens."

14 Even so, as young men first rushed to enlist, the *New York Evening Post* (NY-R, April 1861) recalled grim knowledge gleaned from wars past: "Remember, more men die from sickness in a campaign than do by the bullet."

15 Although the unit here is pages rather than articles, it is clear that casualty coverage was much greater in the Civil War.

16 Republican news *named* the dead more than Democrats for midterms, but not significantly so (65 percent vs. 41 percent of death mentions), and November 1864 saw no difference (both ~54 percent). This also contrasts with Althaus et al. (2014), which found that naming the U.S. dead was rare in modern American wars (35 percent of casualty mentions, of 10–20 percent = ~4 percent). Recent national casualty counts did not differ by party in either election cycle, mentioned on roughly half the pages with casualty mentions, nor did recent local counts, appearing on roughly 12 percent of pages with casualty mentions in both cycles.

17 Modern U.S. war news took a similar tack in frequently comparing allied and enemy losses (Althaus et al. 2014).

18 Timothy Orr's (2006) essay on draft resistance in Pennsylvania presents a similarly contentious view, which partly aligned with anti-war Democratic partisanship.

19 The *La Crosse Democrat* (WI-D, April 1861) cited rebel hopes for active aid from Democrats against their common Republican enemy: "the South expects us democrats of the north, who are too loyal to dishonor our glorious flag as they have done, to aid them in their treason! God forbid that in the north there

should be found a man so base. .... the north will unite to punish insults and teach traitors a lesson, and settle political differences hereafter."

20 The *Tribune* made clear to anti-war Democrats that voting itself could be deadly: "[t]he names of all who approach the ballot-box, not already enrolled, will be immediately added to the list of those liable to be drafted ... many a guerilla who proposed to a sneaking shot at our army in the rear, will find himself by-and-by under rebel fire from the front." Those dodging the draft could not vote without fear that officials would send them into the ranks, as required by law.

21 White women were among the arsonists who torched the children's home, the instigators, the brick throwers, and the group that tortured a U.S. Army officer to death, though women were not in the majority (Giesberg 2009, pp. 127–128).

22 In Lancaster, PA, over one hundred armed women mobbed a courthouse to stop the draft. Historian Judith Giesberg (2009) writes, "draft riots often became gender-integrated expressions," with partisan women as frequent instigators in anti-draft and anti-enlistment violence, to punish and humiliate men supporting and leading the war (p. 130).

23 Partisan news has strong effects on same-party expectations of party electoral prospects (Searles et al. 2018). In what would be the biggest media effect in U.S. history, naïve electoral optimism in Democratic newspapers might have inadvertently prevented a Northern rebellion.

24 Democrats tried quasi-legal political subversion to impede the war as well. When Illinois Democrats won majority control of the state legislature in 1862, they tried to strip power from the state's Republican governor and end Illinois's military participation in the war. The measures failed in a statewide referendum, and the governor countered by suspending the legislature for the rest of the war, entirely neutralizing it as a political force (Neely 2002).

25 Holt (1978) suggests this may contrast with prewar news that was predominantly local- and state-focused.

Chapter 6

1 On the other hand, the death toll could have been much worse. Both sides constrained their violence against white combatants based on international rules of killing and restraint. By comparison, civil wars from the same era in Mexico and China had far larger death tolls in number and per capita (Sheehan-Dean 2018).

2 Many veterans suffered psychological scars with symptoms known in later wars as post-traumatic stress disorder, from witnessing and participating in mass killing (Dean 1999). Still others had physical maladies from minor wounds that never quite healed, and a greater susceptibility to illness caused by exposure to the heat and cold of soldiering.

3 These were Gettysburg, Seven Days, Chickamauga, Chancellorsville, Wilderness, Antietam, Second Bull Run, Shiloh, Fredericksburg, Cold Harbor, Stones River, Spotsylvania, Port Hudson, and Second Petersburg. The mid-nineteenth

century had higher overall mortality rates, but a soldier was five times likelier to die than a young man outside military service (Faust 2008, p. xiii).

4 Printed in the *Missouri Republican* (MO-D, July 1863).

5 Quoted in McPherson (2002), p. 91.

6 Quoted in "Dividing and Weakening" the North: Virginia, June 1863, Robert E. Lee to Jefferson Davis. www.gilderlehrman.org/sites/all/themes/gli/panels/ civilwar150/Lee%20to%20Davis%20(June%201863).pdf

7 The Online Appendix shows the same result with all Union states, though slave state and western elections show extreme volatility, in sharp contrast with the rest of the states. The solid horizontal line at 0 equals Lincoln's 1864 vote share in that state, so deviations from it show the difference between the Republican candidate's vote share and Lincoln's eventual votes. Thus, it is a conservative test for claiming minimal partisan movement.

8 A flexible fit line needs to be flexible enough to show short-term shifts. The bandwidth here is set to 0.1, which allows enough sensitivity to see shifts even toward outliers.

9 Notice here that the counties were almost always lopsided by party: only about 25 percent of counties had vote shares in which one party was within ten points of the other.

10 Evidence from the 2004 U.S. presidential election exemplifies this polarizing war pattern in a modern context: state-level deaths reduced votes for the incumbent president, but only in states that had a Democratic plurality four years earlier (Karol & Miguel 2007). The reinterpretation of the dead as martyrs demanding resolve to finish their work could even *increase* Republican vote share in the strongest Republican areas, yielding positive casualty effects on the incumbent party's electoral support, as some scholars have found in modern contexts (e.g. Loewen & Rubenson 2012).

11 The Civil War Sites Advisory Commission lists thirteen decisive 1862 battles, of which the Union won seven (54 percent) and Confederates won three (23 percent), with three outcomes that were mixed. The period after November 1862 elections through 1863 had eight decisive battles, of which four were Union victories (50 percent), three were Confederate victories (38 percent), and one was mixed. I count the "A" category for strategic importance as "decisive." Union armies in the West fared better than in the East in 1862, and 1863 was a better year for eastern armies than 1862. Easterners focused more on the success of the Army of the Potomac. However, the broader generalization that 1863 was better than 1862 cannot hold.

12 The state-level correlation between war participation and deaths is large ($r = 0.77$), which makes it hard to disentangle the two, especially with only twenty-two observations. Even so, the figure closely resembles Karol and Miguel's (2007) visualization of the change in President Bush's vote share as a function of Iraq War casualties, both at the state level (Fig. 1). Like the Karol-Miguel result, lower casualty rates seem to *increase* the president's vote share versus no change at the high end of human costs. This despite U.S. deaths many orders of magnitude larger than in Iraq.

13 The measure combines white and black casualties. The Online Appendix presents evidence of similar responsiveness to all local casualties. Past studies

differ on death measures (raw count, logged count, proportion of population), "recent" operationalization (ranging from one week to one year), and "local" data (state, county, mile radius, media market). Here, I find raw counts of deaths and logged counts of deaths provide similar results, despite low correlations between them.

14 Placebo tests provide assurance that results attributed to local dead are not due to some other factor. One such test uses the same model to predict the change in Republican votes between 1856 and 1860. War deaths should have no impact on prewar voting, but instead I find a red flag: war dead predict significantly higher Republican vote shares in 1856 (over 1860). Why that is, is not clear, but the pattern seems to be a secular trend in Republican vote shares from 1856 through 1864. Rather than search for an un-modeled correlate of deaths and votes, I simply add the 1856–1860 change as a statistical control in the main models as a blunt alternative to resolve concerns. The changes barely correlate, however. Adding 1856 votes drops Minnesota and a smattering of minimally populated midwestern counties missing in that year. The revised Table 6.1 models indicate slightly *larger* estimates for deaths. Despite the placebo test concern, simple adjustments rule out that alternative explanation and show robust estimates.

15 The Online Appendix describes a range of robustness checks, including a model with continuous measures of prewar county partisanship, an alternative model interacting local voluntarism with prewar partisanship, various state exclusions, and a town-level substantive replication in Massachusetts.

16 For example, Blattman (2009) finds more voting by people forced to fight in modern Uganda, due to political activation and trauma.

Chapter 7

1 Quoted in Donald (1995), p. 529.

2 Roy P. Basler (ed.), *The Collected Works of Abraham Lincoln*, Volume VII, "Letter to Albert G. Hodges" (April 4, 1864) (Abraham Lincoln Association, 1953), p. 281.

3 Quoted in Burlingame & Ettlinger (1999), p. 135.

4 Horace Greeley, the Republican editor of the *New York Tribune*, famously editorialized against Lincoln in early 1864 and worked with Lincoln's secretary of treasury to nominate another presidential candidate – Secretary Chase himself.

5 For example, Sides and Vavreck (2013) found the press citing sixty-eight events in the 2012 presidential election as "game-changers." None of them actually moved polls in a meaningful way. That news makes for a good read, but it's fiction.

6 The *Boston Journal* (MA-R, Nov 1864) was sure that recent victories would influence public opinion. They accused a rival Democratic newspaper of not reporting the capture of the *Florida*, a rebel warship: "Did they believe that the story was got up by the Administration? Or were they afraid of the effect of cheering news upon their cause at the polls?"

7 Rhode Island voted for House and governor at this time, excluded here because Democrats did not contest those elections.

8 Alternatively, midterm cycles may be unreliable amidst maximal national tumult, as Rob Mickey suggested to me (pers. comm., October 16, 2018). In any case, it wasn't a bad year for Republicans compared with most incumbent parties in this era.

9 www.nps.gov/civilwar/facts.htm

10 www.nps.gov/vick/learn/education/educators-guide-the-river-and-the-campaign.htm

11 The 38th Congress was far less productive than its predecessor in terms of major legislation, likely due to Republican plurality control in place of a solid majority. Nonetheless, in the spring of 1864, it passed legislation revising federal coins to include the phrase "In God We Trust" and it set aside land in Yosemite Valley and Mariposa Grove, the first such federal land preserved in this way for its natural beauty.

12 Lincoln asked, "Must I shoot a simple-minded soldier-boy who deserts, while I must not touch a hair of the wily agitator who induces him to desert?" www .nytimes.com/1863/06/15/archives/the-president-on-arbitrary-arrests-presi dent-lincoln-in-reply-to.html

13 Some historians doubt McClellan would have enacted his party's stated platform if elected president, which would mitigate some of the impact. Nevertheless, Lincoln was convinced his loss would give only until March of the next year for winning the war before the incoming administration ended it.

14 The *New York Tribune* reported Atlanta's capture on September 3, when Sherman telegraphed the news, so Vermont and Maine probably had the news by Election Day a few days later. In any case, their votes and those that followed later in 1864 show similar levels of Republican support seen before Atlanta, including 1863 elections.

15 Republican papers were no likelier to mention recent fighting than others were, and they were no likelier to frame a battle as a U.S. victory. That suggests some level of partisan agreement about facts on the ground as the war progressed.

16 Naturally, pro-Republican expressions were higher in Republican papers for election dates than these other dates.

Chapter 8

1 Quoted in Dearing (1952), p. 149.

2 Quoted in Dearing (1952), p. 165.

3 Quoted in the *Baltimore Sun*, July 1861.

4 Shom Mazumder (2018) finds present-day electoral effects from mid-twentieth century Civil Rights activism.

5 Partisan alignments can cycle in and out of phase, however. Remarkably, Darmofal and Strickler (2019) find 1828 vote returns predicted county-level votes for Trump and Clinton in 2016 better than vote returns for Ford and Carter in 1976. Of course, that may also express lingering Democratic support of white Southerners for Georgian Carter.

246 Notes to Pages 192–217

6 Results are consistent for models with all states but show more muted polarization in free contiguous states.

7 For these tests, I combine votes in two-year increments (e.g. 1869 and 1870) to preserve larger numbers of observations. If anything, this combination should understate casualty effects in presidential election years by diluting them with off-cycle votes from the prior year.

8 www.pbs.org/national-memorial-day-concert/memorial-day/history/

9 Carroll D. Wright (1896), p. 13.

10 Those states are CT, ME, MI, NH, NJ, NY, PA, RI, and VT. (W. H. De Puy, *The People's Cyclopedia of Universal Knowledge* [New York: Phillips & Hunt, 1879], p. 2082.)

11 Weighted by state population in 1860, the gap is 15 percentage points, from 41 percent to 56 percent. The gap is minimal and non-significant when limited to free contiguous states, which averaged 58 percent for Lincoln (range 48–76 percent) compared to 18 percent in slave or western states (range 1–36 percent). The gap disappears when using Lincoln's 1864 vote share, so the difference reflects prewar partisan gaps rather than late-war partisanship.

12 Totals as of 2018. I ignore rebel memorials or historical markers in these Union states, including those marking paths of rebel invasions, raids, and burial sites. Almost all include year, and none went up in the nineteenth century.

13 Results are similar with all monuments and with pre-1900 monuments (and whether or not undated monuments are included), but the 1930 cutoff seems most valid for memorialization in particular.

14 https://catalog.hathitrust.org/Record/008885322

15 http://suvcw.org/garrecords/

16 The Online Appendix describes similar results for models predicting the prevalence of posts in each presidential year.

17 Posts per capita reflect joining behavior, whereas population matters less for the potential impact of GAR.

18 The placebo control is the county-level 1864–1860 change in presidential vote share.

Conclusion

1 My findings are adjacent to Holt's (1978) thesis that party competition within states stabilized the Second Party System, while the less competitive Third Party System fueled conflict. I think he overstates the competition contrast, but I focus on changes between campaign season and other times rather than competition shifts that occur over several years. In particular, party competitiveness is endogenous with extremism in a district or state. Places that lacked robust two-party competition were already inhospitable to alternatives by definition.

2 This book joins several other recent works that probe the past for broader behavioral science insights (e.g. Acharya et al. 2018; Achen & Bartels 2016; Berinsky 2009; Corder & Wolbrecht 2016).

3 Michael Holt (1978) suggests local and state partisan competitiveness also serves to hold partisan extremes at bay.

4 Describing the partisan past is far easier than predicting its future, so any inferences are necessarily more speculative. History doesn't repeat, but broad social and political patterns recur, and that recognition forms the basis of social science.

5 The parties have flipped in other ways too. For example, mid-nineteenth century Republicans were the party of environmental protection and public education, and they supported the beginnings of the welfare state, all areas where Democrats now hold court. Democrats previously opposed taxes and defended the patriarchy most ardently, compared with the more benevolent sexism of Republicans, who encouraged husbands to embrace the moral influence of their wives (Edwards 1997). Republicans remain the party favoring industrial interests and opposing immigrants who aren't white Protestants.

References

Abramowitz, Alan I., and Steven Webster. 2018. Negative partisanship: why Americans dislike parties but behave like rabid partisans. *Advances in Political Psychology*, 39(1), 119–135.

Acharya, Avidit, Matthew Blackwell, and Maya Sen. 2018. *Deep Roots*. Princeton, NJ: Princeton University Press.

Achen, Christopher H., and Larry M. Bartels. 2016. *Democracy for Realists*. Princeton, NJ: Princeton University Press.

Ahler, Douglas, J., and Guarav Sood. 2018. The parties in our heads: Misperceptions about party composition and their consequences. *Journal of Politics*, 80(3), 964–981.

Albertson, Bethany, and Shana Kushner Gadarian. 2015. *Anxious Politics*. New York: Cambridge University Press.

Aldrich, John H. 1995. *Why Parties? The Origin and Transformation of Political Parties in America*. Chicago: University of Chicago Press.

Aldrich, John H., Calvin Jillson, and Rick K. Wilson. 2002. Why Congress: what the failure of the Continental and the survival of the federal Congress tell us about the New Institutionalism. In *Party, Process, and Political Change in Congress*, ed. D. Brady and M. D. McCubbins. Palo Alto, CA: Stanford University Press.

Alexander, Thomas B. 1981. The Civil War as institutional fulfillment. *Journal of Southern History*, 47(1), 3–32.

Althaus, Scott L., Brittany H. Bramlett, and James G. Gimpel. 2012. When war hits home: the geography of military losses and support for war in time and space. *Journal of Conflict Resolution*, 56(3), 382–412.

Althaus, Scott L., and Kevin Coe. 2011. Priming patriots: social identity processes and the dynamics of public support for war. *Public Opinion Quarterly*, 75(1), 65–88.

Althaus, Scott L., Nathaniel Swigger, Svitlana Chernykh, David J. Hendry, Sergio, C. Wals, and Christopher Tiwald. 2014. Uplifting manhood to wonderful heights? News coverage of the human costs of military conflict from World War I to Gulf War Two. *Political Communication, 31,* 193–217.

Anderson, Christopher J., Andre Blais, Shaun Bowler, Todd, Donovan, and Ola Listhaug. 2005. *Loser's Consent.* New York: Oxford University Press.

Anderson, Craig A., and Brad J. Bushman. 2002. Human aggression. *Annual Review of Psychology, 53,* 27–51.

Ansolabehere, Stephen, and Shanto Iyengar. 1995. *Going Negative.* New York: Free Press.

Arceneaux, Kevin, and David Nickerson. 2009. Who is mobilized to vote? A re-analysis of 11 field experiments. *American Journal of Political Science,* 53(1), 1–16.

Arceneaux, Kevin, and Martin Johnson. 2013. *Changing Minds or Changing Channels?* Chicago: University of Chicago Press.

Astor, Aaron. October 9, 2011. The party spirit on trial. *New York Times.* https://opinionator.blogs.nytimes.com/2011/10/09/the-party-spirit-on-trial/

Axelrod, Robert. 1984. *Evolution of Cooperation.* New York: Basic Books.

Azari, Julia. November 3, 2016. Weak parties and strong partisanship are a bad combination. *Vox.* www.vox.com/mischiefs-of-faction/2016/11/3/13512362/weak-parties-strong-partisanship-bad-combination

Baker, Jean H. 1983. *Affairs of Party.* Ithaca, NY: Cornell University Press.

Bandura, Albert, Claudio Barbaranelli, Gian Vittorio Caprara, and Concetta Pastorelli. 1996. Mechanisms of moral disengagement in the exercise of moral agency. *Journal of Personality & Social Psychology, 71,* 364–374.

Banks, Antoine. 2016. *Anger and Racial Politics.* New York: Cambridge University Press.

Barber, Michael, and Jeremy C. Pope. 2019. Does party trump ideology? Disentangling party and ideology in America. *American Political Science Review, 113*(1), 38–54.

Bargh, John A., and Tanya Chartrand. 1999. The unbearable automaticity of being. *American Psychologist, 54*(7), 462–479.

Bar-Tal, Daniel, Lily Chrnyak-Hai, Noa Schori, and Ayelet Gundar. 2009. A sense of self-perceived collective victimhood in intractable conflicts. *International Review of the Red Cross, 91*(874), 229–258.

Bartels, Larry M. 2002. Beyond the running tally: partisan bias in political perceptions. *Political Behavior, 24*(2), 117–150.

Bauer, Nichole M. 2018. Untangling the relationship between partisanship, gender stereotypes, and support for female candidates. *Journal of Women, Politics & Policy, 39*(1), 1–25.

Bearss, Ed. 1986. *The Civil War*; Interview by Ken Burns, Florentine Films, American Archive of Public Broadcasting (WGBH and the Library of Congress), Boston, MA and Washington, DC, http://americanarchive.org/catalog/cpb-aacip_509-pk06w9749m

Beck, Paul A., Russell J. Dalton, Steven Greene, and Robert Huckfeldt. 2002. The social calculus of voting: interpersonal, media, and organizational influences on presidential choices. *American Political Science Review, 96*(1), 57–73.

Bensel, Richard F. 1990. *Yankee Leviathan.* New York: Cambridge University Press.

2004. *The American Ballot Box in the Mid-Nineteenth Century*. New York: Cambridge University Press.

Benton, Josiah H. 1915. *Voting in the Field*. Boston: printed by the author.

Berinsky, Adam J. 2009. *In Time of War*. Chicago: University of Chicago Press.

Berlin, Ira, Joseph P. Reidy, and Leslie S. Rowland. 1998. *Freedom's Soldiers*. New York: Cambridge University Press.

Blackmon, Douglas A. 2008. *Slavery by Another Name*. New York: Doubleday.

Blattman, Christopher. 2009. Comparative violence. From violence to voting: war and political participation in Uganda. *American Political Science Review*, *103*(2), 231–247.

Blight, David W. 2001. *Race and Reunion*. Cambridge, MA: Harvard University Press.

Bond, Robert M., Christopher J. Fariss, Jason J. Jones, Adam D. I. Kramer, Cameron Marlow, Jaime E. Settle, and James H. Fowler. 2012. A 61-million-person experiment in social influence and political mobilization. *Nature*, *489*(7415).

Box-Steffensmeier, Janet, Suzanna De Boef, and Tse-min Lin. 2004. The dynamics of the partisan gender gap. *American Political Science Review*, *98*(3), 515–528.

Boydstun, Amber E., Rebecca A. Glazier, and Matthew T. Pietryka. 2013. Playing to the crowd: agenda control in presidential debates. *Political Communication*, *30*(2), 254–277.

Brader, Ted, and George E. Marcus. 2013. Emotion and political psychology. In *The Oxford Handbook of Political Psychology*, ed. L. Huddy, D. O. Sears, and J. S. Levy. New York: Oxford University Press.

Brader, Ted, and Joshua A. Tucker. 2001. The emergence of mass partisanship in Russia, 1993–1996. *American Journal of Political Science*, *45*(1), 69–83.
  2008. Pathways to partisanship: evidence from Russia. *Post-Soviet Affairs*, *24*(3), 1–38.

Brader, Ted, and Nicholas A. Valentino. 2007. Identities, interests, and emotions: symbolic versus material wellsprings of fear, anger, and enthusiasm. In *The Affect Effect: The Dynamics of Emotion in Political Thinking and Behavior*, ed. W. Russell Neuman, George E. Marcus, Ann N. Crigler, and Michael MacKuen. Chicago: University of Chicago Press, pp. 180–201.

Bratton, Michael. 2008. Vote buying and violence in Nigerian election campaigns. *Electoral Studies*, *27*(4), 621–632.

Broockman, David, and Joshua Kalla. 2016. Durably reducing transphobia: a field experiment on door-to-door canvassing. *Science*, *352*(6282), 220–224.

Burlingame, Michael, and John R. Turner Ettlinger, eds. 1999. *Inside Lincoln's White House: The Complete Civil War Diary of John Hay*. Carbondale: Southern Illinois University Press.

Burnham, Walter D. 1955. *Presidential Ballots, 1836–1892*. Baltimore: The Johns Hopkins Press.

Burns, Nancy, Kay Schlozman, and Sidney Verba. 2001. *The Private Roots of Public Action*. Cambridge, MA: Harvard University Press.

Cain, B., J. Ferejohn, and Morris Fiorina. 1987. *The Personal Vote: Constituency Service and Electoral Independence*. Cambridge, MA: Harvard University Press.

Campbell, Angus, Philip E. Converse, Warren Miller, and Donald Stokes. 1960. *The American Voter*. Chicago: University of Chicago Press.

Campbell, Rosie, and Philip Crowley. 2014. What voters want: reactions to candidate characteristics in a survey experiment. *Political Studies*, 62, 745–765.

Carmines, Edward G., and James A. Stimson. 1989. *Issue Evolution*. Princeton, NJ: Princeton University Press.

Carpenter, Daniel, and Colin D. Moore. 2014. When canvassers became activists. *American Political Science Review*, 108(3), 479–498.

Carson, Jamie L., Jeffrey A. Jenkins, David W. Rohde, and Mark A. Souva. 2001. The impact of national tides and district-level effects on electoral outcomes: the U.S. congressional elections of 1862–1863. *American Journal of Political Science*, 45(4), 887–898.

Cassese, Erin C. 2019. Partisan dehumanization in American politics. *Political Behavior*, First Online.

Cassese, Erin C., and Mirya Holman. 2019. Playing the woman card: ambivalent sexism in the 2016 U.S. presidential race. *Political Psychology*, 40(1), 55–74.

CBS News. June 1, 2017. Several threats made against Trump per day: Secret Service director. *CBS News*. www.cbsnews.com/news/several-threats-made-against-president-trump-secret-service-director-randolph-alles/

Chen, M. Keith, and Ryne Rohla. 2018. The effect of partisanship and political advertising on close family ties. *Science*, 360(6392), 1020–1024.

Cho, Wendy, Tam, James G. Gimpel, and Iris S. Hui. 2013. Voter migration and the geographical sorting of the American electorate. *Annals of the Association of American Geographers*, 103, 856–870.

Chong, Dennis, and James N. Druckman. 2013. Counterframing effects. *Journal of Politics*, 75(1), 1–16.

CNN Opinion Research. Aprril 12, 2011. CNN opinion research poll. http://i2.cdn.turner.com/cnn/2011/images/04/11/rel6b.pdf

Cohen, Marty, David Karol, Hans Noel, and John Zaller. 2008. *The Party Decides*. Chicago: University of Chicago Press.

Collier, Paul, and Anke Hoeffler. 2004. Greed & grievance civil wars. *Oxford Economic Papers*, 56, 563–595.

Collier, Paul, and Pedro C. Vicente. 2014. Votes and violence: evidence from a field experiment in Nigeria. *Economic Journal*, 124, F327–F355.

Connors, Elizabeth C. 2019. The social dimension of political values. *Political Behavior*. First View.

Converse, Philip E. 1964. The nature of belief systems in mass publics. In *Ideology & Discontent*, ed. David E. Apter. New York: Free Press of Glencoe.

1969. Of time and partisan stability. *Comparative Political Studies*, 2(2), 139–171.

2000. Assessing the capacity of mass electorates. *Annual Review of Political Science*, 3, 331–353.

Converse, Philip E., and Roy Pierce. 1985. Measuring partisanship. *Political Methodology*, 11, 3–4, 143–166.

Corcoran, Paul E. 1994. Presidential concession speeches: the rhetoric of defeat. *Political Communication*, 11, 109–131.

Corder, Kevin, and Christina Wolbrecht. 2016. *Counting Women's Ballots*. New York: Cambridge University Press.

Costa, Dora L., and Matthew E. Kahn. 2008. *Heroes and Cowards*. Princeton, NJ: Princeton University Press.

Cramer, Katherine J. 2016. *The Politics of Resentment*. Chicago: University of Chicago Press.

Cubbison, William, and Ismail K. White. 2016. Saved from a second slavery: black voter registration in Louisiana from Reconstruction to the Voting Rights Act. Working Paper. http://docs.wixstatic.com/ugd/3a8coa_0991c16bf3864af991fd67ddc44978c6.pdf

Dade, Corey. January 9, 2011. Shooting fallout: political rhetoric takes the heat. *NPR*. www.npr.org/2011/01/10/132784957/shooting-fallout-political-rhetoric-takes-the-heat

Dahl, Robert A. 1956. *A Preface to Democratic Theory*. Chicago: University of Chicago Press.

Darmofal, David, and Ryan Strickler. 2019. *Demography, Politics, and Partisan Polarization in the United States, 1828–2016*. Dordrecht: Springer.

Darr, Joshua P., and Matthew S. Levendusky. 2014. Relying on the ground game: the placement and effect of campaign field offices. *American Politics Research*, 42(3), 529–548. doi:10.1177/1532673X13500520

Dawson, Michael. 1992. *Behind the Mule*. Princeton, NJ: Princeton University Press.

Dean, Eric T., Jr. 1999. *Shook over Hell*. Cambridge, MA: Harvard University Press.

Dearing, Mary R. 1952. *Veterans in Politics*. Greenwood Press.

Dicken-Garcia, H. 1998. The popular press, 1833–1865. In *The Age of Mass Communication*, ed. W. D. Sloan. Northport: Vision Press.

Donald, David. 1995. *Lincoln*. New York: Simon & Schuster.

Donovan, Kathleen, Paul M. Kellstedt, Ellen M. Kay, and Matthew J. Lebo. 2019. Motivated reasoning, public opinion, and presidential approval. *Political Behavior*. First View.

Druckman, James N., Erik Peterson, and Rune Slothuus. 2013. How elite partisan polarization affects public opinion formation. *American Political Science Review*, 107(1), 57–79.

Druckman, James N., and Kjersten R. Nelson. 2003. Framing and deliberation: how citizens' conversations limit elite influence. *American Journal of Political Science*, 47(4), 729–745.

Druckman, James N., Matthew S. Levendusky, and Audrey McLain. 2018. No need to watch: how the effects of partisan media can spread via interpersonal discussions. *American Journal of Political Science* 62 (1), 99–112.

Dubin, Michael J. 1998. *United States Congressional Elections, 1788–1997*. 2003. *United States Gubernatorial Elections, 1776–1860*.

Du Bois, W. E. B. 1935. *Black Reconstruction in America*. New York: Harcourt, Brace and Company.

Dudley, William S. 1981. *Going South: U.S. Navy Officer Resignations & Dismissals on the Eve of the Civil War*. Washington, DC: Naval Historical Foundation.

Dunning, Thad. 2011. Fighting and voting: violent conflict and electoral politics. *Journal of Conflict Resolution*, 55(3), 327–339.

Duverger, Maurice. 1963. *Political Parties: Their Organization and Activity in the Modern State*. New York: Wiley

Dyer, Frederick. 1908. *Compendium of the War of the Rebellion*. Des Moines, IA: Dyer Publishing Company.

Earle, Jonathan H. 2004. *Jacksonian Anti-slavery & the Politics of Free Soil, 1824–1854*. Chapel Hill: University of North Carolina Press.

Edwards, Rebecca. 1997. *Angels in the Machinery*. New York: Oxford University Press.

Erikson, Robert S., and Christopher Wlezien 2012. *Timeline of Presidential Voting*. Chicago: University of Chicago Press.

Fair, C. Christine, Neil Malhotra, and Jacob N. Shapiro. 2014. Democratic values and support for militant politics: evidence from a national survey of Pakistan. *Journal of Conflict Resolution*, 58(5), 743–770.

Faust, Drew Gilpin. 2008. *This Republic of Suffering*. New York: Knopf.
November 15, 2013. 150 years after the Gettysburg Address, is government by the people in trouble? *Washington Post*. www.washingtonpost.com/opin ions/150-years-after-the-gettysburg-address-is-government-by-the-people-in-trouble/2013/11/15/b37841f0-4bdf-11e3-be6b-d3d28122e6d4_story.html

Fearon, James D., and David D. Laitin. 2003. Ethnicity, insurgency, and civil war. *American Political Science Review*, 97(1), 75–90.

Fehrenbacher, Don E. 1989. *Lincoln, Speeches & Writings*, Vol. 2. New York: Penguin.

Feldman, Stanley, Leonie Huddy, and George E. Marcus. 2015. *Going to War in Iraq: When Citizens and the Press Matter*. Chicago: University of Chicago Press.

Finifter, Ada. 1974. The friendship group as a protective environment for political deviants. *American Political Science Review*, 68(2), 607–625.

Fiorina, Morris P. 1981. *Retrospective Voting in American National Elections*. New Haven, CT: Yale University Press.

Fisher, Noel C. 1997. *War at Every Door: Partisan Politics & Guerilla Violence in East Tennessee, 1860–1869*. Chapel Hill: University of North Carolina Press.

Foner, Eric. 1988. *Reconstruction: America's Unfinished Revolution, 1863–1877*. New York: HarperCollins.
1995 [1970]. *Free Soil, Free Labor, Free Men: The Ideology of the Republican Party Before the Civil War*. New York: Oxford University Press.
2011. *The Fiery Trial: Abraham Lincoln and American Slavery*. New York: Norton.
November 22, 2018. The great national circus, review of The Field of Blood by Joanne Freeman. *London Review of Books*.

Frank, Joseph A. 1998. *With Ballot and Bayonet*. Athens: University of Georgia Press.

Freeder, Sean, Gabriel S. Lenz, and Shad Turney. 2019. The importance of knowing "what goes with what": reinterpreting the evidence on policy attitude stability. *Journal of Politics*, 81(1), 274–290.

Freeman, Joanne. 2018. *Field of Blood*. New York: Macmillan.

Gallagher, Gary. 2011. *The Union War*. Cambridge, MA: Harvard University Press.

Gartner, Scott S. 2008. The multiple effects of casualties on public support for war: an experimental approach. *American Political Science Review*, 102(1), 95–106.

Gartner, Scott S., and Gary M. Segura. 1998. War, casualties, and public opinion. *Journal of Conflict Resolution*, 42, 278–300.

Gartner, Scott S., Gary M. Segura, and Bethany A. Barrett. 2004. War casualties, policy positions and the fate of legislators. *Political Research Quarterly*, 53(3), 467–477.

Gartner, Scott S., Gary M. Segura, and Michael Wilkening. 1997. All politics are local: local losses and individual attitudes toward the Vietnam War. *Journal of Conflict Resolution*, 41(5), 669–694.

Gates, Henry Louis, Jr. 2019. *Stony the Road: Reconstruction, White Supremacy, and the Rise of Jim Crow*. New York: Penguin Press.

Gay, Claudine. 2004. Putting race in context: identifying the environmental determinants of black racial attitudes. *American Political Science Review*, 98(4), 547–562.

Gelman, Andrew, and Gary King. 1993. Why are American presidential election campaign polls so variable when votes are so predictable? *British Journal of Political Science*, 23(4), 409–451.

Gelpi, Christopher, Peter D. Feaver, and Jason Reifler. 2006. Success matters: casualty sensitivity and the war in Iraq. *International Security*, 30(3), 7–46.

Gerber, Alan S., and Donald P. Green. 2000. The effects of canvassing, telephone calls, and direct mail on voter turnout: a field experiment. *American Political Science Review*, 94(3), 653–663.

Gerber, Alan S., James G. Gimpel, Donald P. Green, & Daron R. Shaw. 2011. How large and long-lasting are the persuasive effects of televised campaign ads? Results from a randomized field experiment. *American Political Science Review*, 105(1), 135–150.

Gerring, John. 1998. *Party Ideologies in America, 1828–1996*. New York: Cambridge University Press.

Giesberg, Judith. 2009. *Army at Home*. Chapel Hill: University of North Carolina Press.

Ginges J., S. Atran, D. Medin, and K. Shikaki. 2007. Sacred bounds on rational resolution of violent political conflict. *Proceedings of the National Academy of Sciences*, 104(18), 7357–7360.

Goodwin, Doris Kearns. 2005. *Team of Rivals*. New York: Simon & Schuster.

Goren, Paul. 2005. Party identification and core political values. *American Journal of Political Science*, 49(4), 881–896.

Graham, Hugh D., and Ted R. Gurr. 1979. *Violence in America: Historical and Comparative Perspectives*, 2nd ed. Beverly Hills: Sage Press.

Green, Donald, Bradley Palmquist, and Eric Schickler. 2002. *Partisan Hearts and Minds*. New Haven, CT: Yale University Press.

Greene, Steven. 2004. Social identity theory and political identification. *Social Science Quarterly*, 85 (1), 138–153.

Grimsted, David. 1998. *American Mobbing, 1828–1861: Toward Civil War.* New York: Oxford University Press.

Grinspan, Jon. 2009. "Young men for war": the Wide Awakes and Lincoln's 1860 presidential campaign. *Journal of American History*, 96, 357–378.

Groenendyk, Eric W. 2013. *Competing Motives in the Partisan Mind.* New York: Oxford University Press.

Grose, Christian R., and Bruce I. Oppenheimer. 2007. The Iraq War, partisanship, and candidate attributes: variation in partisan swing in the 2006 U. S. House elections. *Legislative Studies Quarterly*, 32(4), 531–557.

Gubler, Joshua R., and Joel Sawat Selway. 2012. Horizontal inequality, cross-cutting cleavages, and Civil War. *Journal of Conflict Resolution*, 56(2), 206–232.

Guess, Andrew, and Alexander Coppock. 2018. Does counter-attitudinal information cause backlash? Results from three large survey experiments. *British Journal of Political Science*, 1–19. First View.

Hacker, J. David. 2011. A Census-based count of the Civil War dead. *Civil War History*, 57(4), 307–348.

Hafner-Burton, Emilie M., Susan D. Hyde, and Ryan S. Jablonski. 2014. When do governments resort to election violence? *British Journal of Political Science*, 44(1), 149–179.

Harish, S. P., and Andrew T. Little. 2017. The political violence cycle. *American Political Science Review*, 111(2), 237–255.

Halperin, Eran, Alexandra G. Russell, Kali H. Trzesniewski, James J. Gross, and Carol S. Dweck. 2011. Promoting the Middle East peace process by changing beliefs about group malleability. *Science*, 333(6050), 1767–1769.

Hetherington, Marc J. 2001. Resurgent mass partisanship: the role of elite polarization. *American Political Science Review*, 95(3), 619–613.

Hewstone, Miles, Mark Rubin, and Hazel Willis. 2002. Intergroup bias. *Annual Review of Psychology*, 53, 575–604.

Hillygus, Sunshine D. 2005. Campaign effects and the dynamics of turnout intention in election 2000. *Journal of Politics*, 67(1), 50–68.

Hochschild, Jennifer. 2001. Where you stand depends on what you see: connections among values, perceptions of facts, and political prescriptions. In *Citizens and Politics*, ed. James H. Kuklinski. New York: Cambridge University Press, pp. 313–340.

Höglund, Kristine. 2009. Electoral violence in conflict-ridden societies: concepts, causes, and consequences. *Terrorism and Political Violence*, 21(3), 412–427.

Holt, Michael F. 1978. *The Political Crisis of the 1850s.* New York: Norton.

Holzer, Harold. 2014. *Lincoln and the Press.* New York: Simon & Schuster.

Hopkins, Daniel J. 2018. *The Increasingly United States: How and Why American Political Behavior Nationalized.* Chicago: University of Chicago Press.

Horowitz, Donald L. 1985. *Ethnic Groups in Conflict.* Berkeley: University of California Press.

Horowitz, Michael C., and Matthew S. Levendusky. 2011. Drafting support for war: conscription and mass support for warfare. *Journal of Politics*, 73(2), 524–534.

Huber, Gregory A., and Kevin Arceneaux. 2009. Identifying the persuasive effects of presidential advertising. *American Journal of Political Science*, 51(4), 957–977.

Huckfeldt, Robert, Paul E. Johnson, and John Sprague. 2006. *Political Disagreement*. New York: Cambridge University Press.

Huddy, Leonie. 2001. From social to political identity: a critical examination of social identity theory. *Political Psychology*, 22, 127–156.

Huddy, Leonie, Alexa Bankert, and Caitlin Davies. 2018. Expressive versus instrumental partisanship in multiparty European systems. *Political Psychology*, 22, 127–156.

Huddy, Leonie, Lilliana Mason, and Lene Aaroe. 2015. Expressive partisanship: campaign involvement, political emotion, and partisan identity. *American Political Science Review*, 109(2), 1–17.

Huddy, Leonie, Stanley Feldman, and Erin Cassese. 2007. On the distinct political effects of anxiety and anger. In *The Affect Effect: Dynamics of Emotion in Political Thinking and Behavior*, ed. W. Russell Neuman, George E. Marcus, Michael MacKuen, and Ann Crigler. Chicago: University of Chicago Press, pp. 202–230.

Humphreys, McCartan, and Jeremy M. Weinstein. 2008. Who fights? The determinants of participation in civil war. *American Journal of Political Science*, 52(2), 436–455.

Hutchings, Vincent H., and Nicholas A. Valentino. 2004. The centrality of race in American politics. *Annual Review of Political Science*, 7, 383–408.

Ingber, Sasha. February 19, 2019. Publisher of an Alabama newspaper calls for the KKK to "clean out" Washington. *NPR*. www.npr.org/2019/02/19/695903336/publisher-of-an-alabama-newspaper-calls-for-the-kkk-to-clean-out-washington

Imai, Kosuke, and Gary King. 2004. Did illegal overseas absentee ballots decide the 2000 U.S. presidential election? *Perspectives on Politics*, 2, 537–549.

Ipsos. August 22, 2017. Reuters/Ipsos data: Confederate monuments. www.ipsos.com/en-us/news-polls/reuters-ipsos-confederate-monuments-2017-08-22

  May 16, 2019. Peaceful handover of power, respecting elections cornerstones of American democracy. www.ipsos.com/sites/default/files/ct/news/documents/2019-05/ipsos-uva_democracy_poll_topline_051419_0.pdf

Iqbal, Zaryab, and Christopher Zorn. 2006. Sic semper tyrannis? Power, repression, and assassination since the Second World War. *Journal of Politics*, 68(3), 489–501.

Iyengar, Shanto, and Adam Simon. 1993. News coverage of the gulf crisis and public opinion: a study of agenda-setting, priming, and framing. *Communication Research*, 20(3), 365–383.

Iyengar, Shanto, and Sean J. Westwood. 2015. Fear and Loathing across party lines: new evidence on group polarization. *American Journal of Political Science* 59(3), 690–707.

Iyengar, Shanto, Yphtach Lelkes, Matthew Levendusky, Neil Malhotra, and Sean Westwood. 2019. The origins and consequences of affective polarization in the United States. *Annual Review of Political Science*, 22, 7.1–7.18.

Jardina, Ashley. 2019. *White Identity Politics*. New York: Cambridge University Press.

Jefferson, Hakeem. 2019. Policing norms: punishment and the politics of respectability among black Americans. Ph.D. dissertation, University of Michigan.

Jennings, M. Kent, Laura Stoker, and Jake Bowers. 2009. Politics across generations: family transmission reexamined. *Journal of Politics*, 71(3), 782–799.

Jimerson, Randall C. 1988. *The Private Civil War*. Baton Rouge: Louisiana State University Press.

Jones, Philip Edward. 2019. Partisanship, political awareness, and retrospective evaluations, 1956–2016. *Political Behavior*, Online First.

Kallina, Edmund F. 1985. Was the 1960 presidential election stolen? The case of Illinois. *Presidential Studies Quarterly*, 15(1), 113–118.

Kalmoe, Nathan P. 2014. Fueling the fire: violent metaphors, trait aggression, and support for political violence. *Political Communication*, 31, 545–563.

2015. Trait aggression in two representative U.S. surveys: testing the generalizability of college samples. *Aggressive Behavior*, 41, 171–188. doi:10.1002/ab.21547

2017. Legitimizing partisan violence. Midwest Political Science Association conference paper. www.dropbox.com/s/olwz6jso16rgoip/Kalmoe%20-%20Legitimizing%20Partisan%20Violence.pdf?dl=0

Kalmoe, Nathan P., and Lilliana Mason. 2018. Lethal mass partisanship. APSA conference paper. www.dropbox.com/s/bs618kn939gqode/Kalmoe%20%26%20Mason%20APSA%202018%20-%20Lethal%20Mass%20Partisanship.pdf?dl=0

Kalmoe, Nathan P., and Spencer Piston 2013. Is implicit racial prejudice against blacks politically consequential? *Public Opinion Quarterly*, 77(1), 305–322.

Kalyvas, Stathis. 2001. "New" and "old" civil wars: a valid distinction? *World Politics*, 54(1), 99–118.

2006. *The Logic of Violence in Civil Wars*. New York: Cambridge University Press.

Kam, Cindy D. 2005. Who toes the line? Cues, values, and individual differences. *Political Behavior*, 27(2), 163–182.

Karol, David, and Edward Miguel. 2007. The electoral cost of war: Iraq casualties and the 2004 U.S. presidential election. *Journal of Politics*, 69(3), 633–648.

Karpowitz, Christopher F., and Tali Mendelberg. 2014. *The Silent Sex: Gender, Deliberation, and Institutions*. Princeton, NJ: Princeton University Press.

Karpowitz, Christopher F., J. Quin Monson, and Jessica Preece. 2017. How to elect more women: gender and candidate success in a field experiment. *American Journal of Political Science*, 61(4), 927–943.

Keith, Bruce E., David B. Magleby, Candice J. Nelson, Elizabeth Orr, Mark C. Westyle, and Raymond E. Wolfinger. 1986. The partisan affinities of Independent "leaners." *British Journal of Political Science*, 16(2), 155–185.

Key, Vladimir O. 1949. *Southern Politics in State and Nation*. Knoxville: University of Tennessee Press.

Kinder, Donald R. 2003. Belief systems after Converse. In *Electoral Democracy*, ed. Michael B. MacKuen and George Rabinowitz. Ann Arbor: University of Michigan Press.

Kinder, Donald R., and Cindy D. Kam. 2010. *Us against Them*. Chicago: University of Chicago Press.

Kinder, Donald R., and Lynn M. Sanders. 1996. *Divided by Color*. Chicago: University of Chicago Press.

Kinder, Donald R., and Nathan P. Kalmoe. 2017. *Neither Liberal nor Conservative: Ideological Innocence in the American Public*. Chicago: University of Chicago Press.

Kinder, Donald R., and D. Roderick Kiewiet 1981. Sociotropic politics: the American case. *British Journal of Political Science*, 11, 129–161.

Klar, Samara. 2013. The influence of competing identity primes on political preferences. *Journal of Politics*, 75(4), 1108–1124.

2014. Partisanship in a social setting. *American Journal of Political Science*, 58(3), 687-704.

Klar, Samara, and Yanna Krupnikov. 2016. *Independent Politics*. New York: Cambridge University Press.

Kleppner, Paul. 1979. *The Third Electoral System, 1853–1892*. Chapel Hill: University of North Carolina Press.

Klinghard, Daniel. 2010. *The Nationalization of American Political Parties, 1880–1896*. New York: Cambridge University Press.

Kreidberg, Marvin A., and Merton G. Henry. 1955. *History of Military Mobilization in the United States Army, 1775–1945*. Washington, DC: Department of the Army.

Kriner, Douglas L., and Francis X. Shen. 2007. Iraq casualties and the 2006 Senate elections. *Legislative Studies Quarterly*, 32(4), 507–530.

2012. How citizens respond to combat casualties: the differential impact of local casualties on support for the war in Afghanistan. *Public Opinion Quarterly*, 76(4), 761–770.

2014. Responding to war on Capitol Hill: battlefield casualties, congressional response, and public support for the war in Iraq. *American Journal of Political Science*, 58(1), 157–174.

Krupnikov, Yanna. 2011. When does negativity demobilize? Tracing the conditional effect of negative campaigning on voter turnout. *American Journal of Political Science*, 55(4), 797–813.

Krupnikov, Yanna, and Beth C. Easter. 2013. Negative campaigns: are they good for American democracy? In *New Directions in Media and Politics*, ed. Travis Ridout. London: Routledge.

Kunda, Ziva. 1990. The case for motivated reasoning. *Psychological Bulletin*, 108(3), 480–498.

Kuo, Alexander, Neil Malhotra, and Cecilia Hyungjung Mo. 2017. Social exclusion and political identity: the case of Asian American partisanship. *Journal of Politics*, 79(1), 17–32.

Kuziemko, Ilyana, and Ebona Washington. 2018. Why did the Democrats lose the South? Bringing new data to an old debate. *American Economic Review*, 108(10), 2830–2867.

Lasswell, Harold. 1936. *Politics: Who Gets What, When, How*. New York: Whittlesey House.

Lawson, Melinda. 2002. *Patriot Fires*. New York: Oxford University Press.

Lazarsfeld, Paul, Bernard Berelson, and Hazel Gaudet. 1944. *The People's Choice*. New York: Duell, Sloan, and Pearce.

LeBas, Adrienne. 2006. Polarization as craft: party formation and state violence in Zimbabwe. *Comparative Politics*, 38(4), 419–438.

Lee, Taeku. 2002. *Mobilizing Public Opinion*. Chicago: University of Chicago Press.

Lelkes, Yphtach, Gaurav Sood, and Shanto Iyengar. 2017. The hostile audience: the effect of access to broadband internet on partisan affect. *American Journal of Political Science*, 61(1), 5–20.

Lenz, Gabe. 2012. *Follow the Leader? How Voters Respond to Politicians' Policies and Performance*. Chicago: University of Chicago Press.

Lerman, Amye E., Meredith L. Sadin, and Samuel Trachtman. 2017. *American Political Science Review*, 111(4), 755–740.

Levendusky, Matthew. 2009. *The Partisan Sort*. Chicago: University of Chicago Press.

   2013. *How Partisan Media Polarize America*. Chicago: University of Chicago Press.

Levitsky, Steven, and Daniel Ziblatt. 2018. *How Democracies Die*. New York: Crown.

Lewis-Beck, Michael S., William G. Jacoby, Helmut Norpoth, and Herbert F. Weisberg. 2008. *The American Voter Revisited*. Ann Arbor: University of Michigan Press.

Lodge, Milton, and Charles S. Taber. 2013. *The Rationalizing Voter*. New York: Cambridge University Press.

Loewen, Peter J., and Daniel Rubenson. 2012. Canadian War Deaths in Afghanistan: costly Policies and Support for Incumbents. Working Paper. http://individual.utoronto.ca/loewen/Research_files/war_deaths_vfinal%20.pdf

Lyall, Jason, Graeme Blair, and Kosuke Imai. 2013. Explaining support for combatants during wartime: a survey experiment in Afghanistan. *American Political Science Review*, 107(4), 679–705.

Mackie, Diane M., Thierry Devos, and Eliot R. Smith. 2000. Intergroup emotions: Explaining offensive action tendencies in an intergroup context. *Journal of Personality & Social Psychology*, 79(4), 602–616.

MacKuen, Michael, Jennifer Wolak, Luke Keele, and George E. Marcus. 2010. Civic engagements: resolute partisanship or reflective deliberation. *American Journal of Political Science*, 54, 440–458.

Malka, Ariel, and Yphtach Lelkes. 2017. In a new poll, half of Republicans say they would support postponing the 2020 election if Trump proposed it. *Washington Post*. www.washingtonpost.com/news/monkey-cage/wp/2017/08/10/in-a-new-poll-half-of-republicans-say-they-would-support-postponing-the-2020-election-if-trump-proposed-it/

Manning, Chandra. 2007. *What This Cruel War Was Over*. New York: Vintage Civil War Library.

Margolis, Michele. 2018. How politics affects religion: partisanship, socialization, and religiosity in America. *Journal of Politics*, 80(1), 30–43.

Mason, Lilliana. 2018. *Uncivil Agreement*. Chicago: University of Chicago Press.

Matsui, John H. 2016. *The First Republican Army*. Charlottesville: University of Virginia Press.

Mayhew, David R. 2002. *Electoral Realignments*. New Haven, CT: Yale University Press.

Mazumder, Soumyajit. 2018. The persistent effect of the U.S. civil rights movement on political attitudes. *American Journal of Political Science*, 62(4), 922–935.

McConnaughy, Corrine M. 2013. *The Woman Suffrage Movement in America*. New York: Cambridge University Press.

McConnell, Stuart. 1992. *Glorious Contentment: The Grand Army of the Republic, 1865–1900*. Chapel Hill: University of North Carolina Press.

McCormick, Richard P. 1966. *The Second American Party System*. Chapel Hill: University of North Carolina Press

McPherson, James. 1988. *Battle Cry of Freedom*. New York: Oxford University Press.

1997. *For Cause and Comrades*. New York: Oxford University Press.

2002. *Crossroads of Freedom*. New York: Oxford University Press.

2008. *Tried by War*. New York: Penguin.

2015. *The War That Forged a Nation*. New York: Oxford University Press.

McRae, Elizabeth G. 2018. *Mothers of Massive Resistance: White Women and the Politics of White Supremacy*. New York: Oxford University Press.

Mendelberg, Tali. 2001. *The Race Card*. Princeton, NJ: Princeton University Press.

Mickey, Robert. 2015. *Paths Out of Dixie: The Democratization of Authoritarian Enclaves in America's Deep South, 1944–1972*. Princeton, NJ: Princeton University Press.

Milgram, Stanley. 1965. Some conditions of obedience and disobedience to authority. *Human Relations*, 18(1), 57–76.

Miller, DeAnne, and Cook, Lauren. 2003. *They Fought Like Demons*. New York: Vintage.

Miller, Patrick R., and Pamela J. Conover. 2015. Red and blue states of mind: partisan hostility and voting in the United States. *Political Research Quarterly*, 68(2), 225–239.

Miller, Gary, and Norman Schofield. 2003. Activists and partisan realignment in the United States. *American Political Science Review*, 97(2), 245–260.

Mirer, Michael L., and Leticia Bode. 2015. Tweeting in defeat: how candidates concede and claim victory in 140 characters. *New Media & Society*, 17(3), 453–469.

Mueller, John. 1973. *War, Presidents and Public Opinion*. Lanham, MD: University Press of America.

Mummolo, Jonathan, and Clayton Nall. 2017. Why partisans do not sort: constraints on political segregation. *Journal of Politics*, 79(1), 45–59.

Mutz, Diana. 1998. *Impersonal Influence*. New York: Cambridge University Press.

2006. *Hearing the Other Side*. New York: Cambridge University Press.

Neely, Mark E. 2002. *The Union Divided*. Cambridge, MA: Harvard University press.

2017. *Lincoln and the Democrats*. New York: Cambridge University Press.

Newell, Clayton R. 2014. *The Regular Army before the Civil War, 1845–1860*. Washington, DC: Center of Military History.

Nickerson, David W. 2008. Is voting contagious? Evidence from two field experiments. *American Political Science Review*, 102(1), 49–57.

Nisbett, Richard E., and Timothy D. Wilson. 1977. Telling more than we can know: verbal reports on mental processes. *Psychological Review*, 84(3), 231–259.

Noelle-Neuman, Elisabeth. 1974. The spiral of silence a theory of public opinion. *Journal of Communication*, 24(2), 43–51.

Norrander, Barbara. 1999. The evolution of the gender gap. *Public Opinion Quarterly*, 63(4), 566–576.

North, Douglas, John Joseph Wallis, and Barry Weingast. 2009. *Violence and Social Orders*. New York: Cambridge University Press.

Nyhan, Brendan, Ethan Porter, Jason Reifler, and Thomas Wood. 2019. Taking fact-checks literally but not seriously? The effects of journalistic fact-checking on factual beliefs and candidate favorability. *Political Behavior*.

Nyhan, Brendan, and Jason Reifler. 2010. When corrections fail: the persistence of political misperceptions. 2010. *Political Behavior*, 32(2), 303–330.

Orr, Timothy J. 2006. "A viler enemy in our rear": Pennsylvania soldiers confront the North's antiwar movement. In *The View from the Ground: The Experiences of Civil War Soldiers*. Jackson: University Press of Kentucky.

Ostfeld, Mara C. 2018. The new white flight? The effects of political appeals to Latinos on white Democrats. *Political Behavior*.

Pacilli, Maria Giuseppina, Michel Roccato, Stefano Pagliaro, and Silvia Russo. 2016. From political opponents to enemies? The role of perceived moral distance in the animalistic dehumanization of the political outgroup. *Group Processes & Intergroup Relations*, 19(3), 360–373.

Parker, Christopher S. 2010. *Fighting for Democracy: Black Veterans and the Struggle against White Supremacy in the Postwar South*. Princeton, NJ: Princeton University Press.

Payne, Ed, Matt Smith, and Carol Cratty. April 19, 2013. FBI confirms letters to Obama, others contained ricin. *CNN*. www.cnn.com/2013/04/18/politics/tainted-letter-intercepted/index.html

Pew Research Center. March 10, 1998. Deconstructing distrust: how Americans view government. Report.

October 21, 2014. Political polarization & media habits. www.journalism.org/2014/10/21/political-polarization-media-habits/

March 20, 2018. Wide gender gap, growing educational divide in voters' party identification. www.people-press.org/2018/03/20/wide-gender-gap-growing-educational-divide-in-voters-party-identification/

Philpot, Tasha S. 2017. *Conservative but Not Republican: The Paradox of Party Identification and Ideology among African Americans*. New York: Cambridge University Press.

Poole, Keith. 2015. VoteView website.

Poole, Keith, and Howard Rosenthal. 1997. *Congress*. New York: Oxford University Press.

Posner, Daniel N. 2004. The political salience of cultural difference: Why Chewas and Tumbukas are allies in Zambia and adversaries in Malawi. *American Political Science Review*, 98(4), 529–545.

Potter, David M. 1977. *The Impending Crisis: America before the Civil War, 1848–1861.* New York: HarperCollins.

Powell, G. Bingham. 1981. Party systems and political system performance: Voting participation, government stability and mass violence in contemporary democracies. *American Political Science Review*, 75(4), 861–879.

Przeworski, Adam. 1991. *Democracy and the Market.* New York: Cambridge University Press.

Rahn, Wendy M. 1993. The role of partisan stereotypes in information processing about political candidates. *American Journal of Political Science*, 472-496.

Rappoport, David C., and Leonard Weinberg. 2000. Elections and violence. *Terrorism and Political Violence*, 12(3–4), 15–50.

Redlawsk, David, Andrew J. W. Civettini, and Karen M. Emmerson. 2010. The affective tipping point: Do motivated reasoners ever "get it"? *Political Psychology*, 31(4), 563–593.

Renda, Lex. 1997. *Running on the Record.* Charlottesville: University of Virginia Press.

Ritter, Kurt, and Buddy Howell. 2001. Ending the 2000 presidential election: Gore's concession speech and Bush's victory speech. *American Behavioral Scientist*, 44(12), 2314–2330.

Rosenstone, Steven J., and John Mark Hansen. 1993. *Mobilization, Participation, and Democracy in America.* New York: Macmillan.

Ryan, Timothy J. 2017. No compromise: political consequences of moralized attitudes. *American Journal of Political Science*, 61(2), 409–423.

Sandow, Robert M. 2009. *Deserter Country.* New York: Oxford University Press.

Schattschneider, Elmer E. 1942. *Party Government.* New York: Holt, Rinehart and Winston.

Schickler, Eric. 2016. *Racial Realignment.* Princeton, NJ: Princeton University Press.

Schudson, Michael, and Susan E. Tifft. 2005. American journalism in historical perspective. In *The Press*, ed. Geneva Overholser and Kathleen Hall Jamieson. New York: Oxford University Press, pp. 17–47.

Schultz, Jane E. 2004. *Women at the Front.* Chapel Hill: University of North Carolina Press.

Schwert, G. William. 1989. Why does stock market volatility change over time? *Journal of Finance*, 44(5), 1115–1153.

Searles, Kathleen, Glen Smith, and Mingxiao Sui. 2018. The effects of partisan media on electoral predictions. *Public Opinion Quarterly, Psychology of Elections*, 82(S1), 302–324.

Sheehan-Dean, Aaron. 2018. *The Calculus of Violence.* Cambridge, MA: Harvard University Press.

Sherif, Muzafer, O. J. Harvey, B. Jack White, William R. Hood, and Carolyn W. Sherif. 1988. *The Robbers Cave Experiment.* Middletown, CT: Wesleyan University Press.

Sides, John, and Lynn Vavreck. 2013. *The Gamble*. Princeton, NJ: Princeton University Press.

Sides, John, Michael Tesler, and Lynn Vavreck. 2018. *Identity Crisis*. Princeton, NJ: Princeton University Press.

Silbey, Joel H. 1977. *A Respectable Minority*. New York: Oxford University Press.

  1985. *The Partisan Imperative*. New York: Oxford University Press.

Sinclair, Betsy. 2012. *The Social Citizen*. Chicago: University of Chicago Press.

Skocpol, Theda. 1979. *States & Social Revolutions*. New York: Cambridge University Press.

  1992. *Protecting Widows and Mothers*. Cambridge, MA: Harvard University Press.

Skocpol, Theda, Marshall Ganz, and Ziad Munson. 2000. A nation of organizers: the institutional origins of civic voluntarism in the United States. *American Political Science Review*, 94(3), 527–546.

Smith, Adam I. P. 2006. *No Party Now*. New York: Oxford University Press.

  2014. Northern politics. In *A Companion to the Civil War*, ed. Aaron Sheehan-Dean. New York: John Wiley & Sons.

  2019. Northern Democrats. In *The Cambridge History of the American Civil War*, ed. Aaron Sheehan-Dean. Cambridge: Cambridge University Press.

Smith, Glen, and Kathleen Searles. 2014. Who let the attack dogs out? New evidence for partisan media effects. *Public Opinion Quarterly*, 78(1), 71–99.

Smith, Timothy B. 2008. *The Golden Age of Battlefield Preservation*. Knoxville: University of Tennessee Press.

Snyder, Jack L. 2000. *From Voting to Violence*. New York: Norton.

Sood, Guarav, and Shanto Iyengar. 2016. Coming to dislike your opponents: the polarizing impact of political campaigns. Working Paper. https://papers.ssrn.com/sol3/papers.cfm?abstract_id=2840225

Spahn, Bradley. 2019. Before the American voter. PhD. thesis, Stanford University.

Stoker, Laura. 1995. Life-cycle transitions and political participation: the case of marriage. *American Political Science Review*, 89(2), 421–433.

Stroud, Natalie. 2011. *Niche News*. New York: Oxford University Press.

Tajfel, Henri, and John Turner. 1979. An integrative theory of intergroup conflict. In *The Social Psychology of Intergroup Relations*, ed. W. G. Austin and S. Worchel. Monterey, CA: Brooks/Cole.

Tajfel, Henri, Michael G. Billig, Robert P. Bundy, and Claude Flament. 1971. Social categorization and intergroup behaviour. *European Journal of Social Psychology* 1(2), 149–178.

Tesler, Michael. 2016. *Post-Racial or Most-Racial?* Chicago: University of Chicago Press.

Tilly, Charles. 2003. *The Politics of Collective Violence*. New York: Cambridge University Press.

Tooby, John, and Leda Cosmides. 2010. Groups in mind: the coalitional roots of war and morality. In *Human Morality and Sociality: Evolutionary and Comparative Perspectives*, ed. Henrik Høgh-Olesen. London: Palgrave-Macmillan, pp. 91–234.

Towne, Stephen E. 2005. Works of indiscretion: violence against the Democratic press in Indiana during the Civil War. *Journalism History*, *31*(3), 138–149.

Treisman, Daniel. June 19, 2018. Is democracy really in danger? The picture is not as dire as you think. *Washington Post*.

Urdal, Henrik. 2008. Population, resources, and political violence: a subnational study of India, 1956–2002. *Journal of Conflict Resolution*, *52*(4), 590–617.

Valentino, Nicholas A., and David O. Sears. 2005. Old times there are not forgotten. *American Journal of Political Science*, *49*(3), 672–688.

Valentino, Nicholas A., Ted Brader, Eric W. Groenendyk, Krysha Gregorowicz, and Vincent Hutchings. 2011. Election night's alright for fighting: the role of emotions in political participation. *Journal of Politics*, *73*(1), 156–170.

Varshney, Ashutosh. 2003. *Ethnic Conflict and Civic Life: Hindus and Muslims in India*. New Haven, CT: Yale University Press.

Valentino, Nicholas A., Vincent L. Hutchings, and Ismail K. White. 2002. Cues that matter: how political ads prime racial attitudes during campaigns. *American Political Science Review*, *96*(1), 75–90.

Walton, Hanes, Jr. 1985. *Invisible Politics: Black Political Behavior*. Albany, NY: SUNY Press.

Walsh, Katherine Cramer. 2004. *Talking about Politics*. Chicago: University of Chicago Press.

 2007. *Talking about Race*. Chicago: University of Chicago Press.

Weber, Jennifer. 2006. *Copperheads*. New York: Oxford University Press.

Wells, Chris, Katherine J. Cramer, Michael W. Wagner, German Alvarez, Lewis A. Friedland, Dhavan V. Shah, Leticia Bode, Stephanie Edgerly, Itay Gabay, and Charles Franklin. 2017. When we stop talking politics: the maintenance and closing of conversation in contentious times. *Journal of Communication*, *67*, 131–157.

Westwood, Sean J., Shanto Iyengar, Stefaan Walgrave, Rafael Leonisio, Luis Miller, and Oliver Strijbis. 2018. The tie that divides: cross-national evidence of the primacy of partyism. *European Journal of Political Research*, *57*, 333–354.

White, Jonathan W. 2014. *Emancipation, the Union Army, and the Reelection of Abraham Lincoln*. Baton Rouge: Louisiana State University Press.

White, Ismail K. 2007. When race matters and when it doesn't: racial group differences in response to racial cues. *American Political Science Review*, *101*(2), 339–354.

White, Ismail K., Chryl N. Laird, and Troy D. Allen. 2014. Selling out? The politics of navigating conflicts between racial group interest and self-interest. *American Political Science Review*, *108*(4), 783–800.

Wilentz, Sean. 2005. *The Rise of American Democracy*. New York: Norton.

Wilkinson, Stephen I. 2006. *Votes and Violence*. New York: Cambridge University Press.

Willard, Kristen, Timothy Guinnane, and Harvey Rosen. 1996. Turning points in the Civil War: views from the greenback market. *American Economic Review*, *86*, 1001–1018.

Williams, George Washington. 2012. *A History of the Negro Troops in the War of the Rebellion, 1861–1865*. New York: Fordham University Press. (originally 1887, Harper & Bros., New York)

Wills, Garry. 1992. *Lincoln at Gettysburg*. New York: Simon & Schuster.

Wilson, Edward O. 2004. *On Human Nature*, 2nd ed. Cambridge, MA: Harvard University Press.

Wilson, Timothy D., Douglas J. Lisle, and Jonathan W. Schooler. 1993. Introspecting about reasons can reduce post-choice satisfaction. *Personality and Social Psychology Bulletin*, 19(3), 331–339.

Winter, Nicholas J. G. 2010. Masculine Republicans and feminine Democrats: gender and Americans' explicit and implicit images of the political parties. *Political Behavior*, 32(4), 587–618.

Wright, Carroll D. 1896. *Labor Laws of the United States*. Washington, DC: Government Printing Office.

Zaller, John. 1992. *The Nature and Origins of Mass Opinion*. New York: Cambridge University Press.

Index

power, partisan, 6–11
Presidential Ballots, 1836-1892 (Burnham), 81
psychology, partisan, 31–32
    endurance in, 30, 32–34
    resistant, 30, 34–35, 49–50
    violence and, 30, 35–37, 49–50

quantitative analysis, 232

race, 217
    Democrats on, 114–116, 133, 213
    in modern politics, 218–219, 222–223, 233
    partisan news on, 68, 113–116, 120, 129, 241
    racial violence, post-war, 188
    Republicans on, 114–116
    white supremacy, 114–116, 133, 198, 213, 218–219, 222–223, 240
Reconstruction, 5–6, 178, 187–190, 209
religion, 19, 238
    in anti-slavery movement, 22
    as identity, 31–33, 39–40, 84
representative evidence, 11–13
Republicans, 10–11, 35, 39–40, 245. *See also* elections, 1864; elections, wartime down-ballot; Lincoln, Abraham
    abolitionism of, 28, 114, 240
    black mobilization and, 95–99
    casualties and post-war, 186, 191–197, 207
    congressional, 1861-1862, 164–165
    Democrats, Northern, on, 110–111, 114–115, 210–211
    on Democrats, Northern, 36, 107, 110–112, 115–116, 191, 210–211
    desertion rates for, 86–88, 102
    in 1856 elections, 22–23, 44–45, 48, 83, 85, 87, 97, 234, 244
    in 1860 elections, 23–25, 30, 32, 44–45, 48, 50, 53, 81, 83, 85, 87, 89, 97, 141–142, 145–147, 180–181, 192, 209, 219–220, 233, 235
    1862 elections and, 110, 113, 115, 117, 121–122, 137–138, 142–143, 157, 164–174, 177, 180
    in 1868 elections, 45–49, 205–207, 212
    emergence of, 22–23, 28, 41–45, 50, 235
    Free Soil Party and, 22–23, 42, 44–46, 50, 209, 234–235

GAR and, 18, 186, 202–207
    memorialization and support for, 199–201, 207, 212
    modern, 5–6, 48–49, 189, 218–222, 225, 234–236, 243, 247
    partisan identity and opposition to, 42
    in partisan news, war views of, 62
    partisan news of, 53–54, 59–70, 72–74, 79, 107, 110–112, 116–118, 130–131, 245
    on Peace Democrats, 112–113
    post-war, 186–189, 202–207
    on race, 114–116
    secession and, 25–28, 30, 49, 162–163
    slavery and, 25, 28, 44–45, 114, 119–120, 165, 240
    soldiers supporting, voting by, 16–17, 78–80, 237–238, 240
    voting patterns for, 43–46
    war participation of, 77–80, 83–86, 102–103, 238
    wartime campaigns of, 108
    Whigs and, 20, 22, 42, 50, 234
Roosevelt, Teddy, 192
Rowell, George P., 13, 56, 111, 236
Rutland Herald, 65, 69, 72, 116–117, 122
    on black troops, 68
    moral disengagement in, 71–72
    on partisan violence, 133

Schultz, Jane, 100
secession, 24–28, 71, 161, 218–220, 233
    Democrats and, 10–11, 25–28, 49, 163–164, 208, 233
    Republicans and, 25–28, 30, 49, 162–163
Second Party System, 43
    slavery and, 21–23, 41–42, 44–45
    Third Party System and, 22–23, 41–48, 50, 182, 209, 246
Sen, Maya, 189, 214–215
Seymour, Horatio, 130–131
Sherman, William T., 158–159, 175–178, 245
Shiloh, Battle of, 165, 234
shirking, short-term, 88–89
Silbey, Joel, 182
Skocpol, Theda, 136
slavery, 22, 41, 49, 219, 231. *See also* abolitionists
    before Civil War, violence over, 28–30, 231

CPSIA information can be obtained
at www.ICGtesting.com
Printed in the USA
LVHW051636210820
663842LV00013B/275